Java 7 for Absolute Beginners

Jay Bryant

ISBN-13 (pbk): 978-1-4302-3686-3

ISBN-13 (electronic): 978-1-4302-3687-0

President and Publisher: Paul Manning
Lead Editor: Steve Anglin
Technical Reviewer: Massimo Nardone
Editorial Board: Steve Anglin, Mark Beckner, Ewan Buckingham, Gary Cornell, Morgan Ertel, Jonathan Gennick, Jonathan Hassell, Robert Hutchinson, Michelle Lowman, James Markham, Matthew Moodie, Jeff Olson, Jeffrey Pepper, Douglas Pundick, Ben Renow-Clarke, Dominic Shakeshaft, Gwenan Spearing, Matt Wade, Tom Welsh
Coordinating Editor: Adam Heath
Copy Editor: Chandra Clarke
Production Support: Patrick Cunningham
Indexer: SPi Global
Artist: SPi Global
Cover Designer: Anna Ishchenko

Distributed to the book trade worldwide by Springer Science+Business Media New York, 233 Spring Street, 6th Floor, New York, NY 10013. Phone 1-800-SPRINGER, fax (201) 348-4505, e-mail orders-ny@springer-sbm.com, or visit www.springeronline.com.

For information on translations, please e-mail rights@apress.com, or visit www.apress.com.

For Clancey, Kylie, and Philip
–Jay Bryant

Contents at a Glance

Contents

Foreword

This book happened because the daughter (hi, Kylie) of a friend (hi, Ross) asked me what I do. As it happened, I had my laptop with me at the time, so I showed her. Kylie was 15 at the time, so she promptly lost interest. I was working as a web developer (writing middleware and database code rather than front-end code), so I explained that Facebook worked in a similar way. That got her attention. It pays to know one's audience.

That experience gave me the idea of writing a book to get young people started on programming. Later that year, when Apress asked me to write a book, I managed to talk them into writing one for beginners.

So, if you want to try writing software, this book is for you. It's by no means an exhaustive explanation of either topic (how it works and how it's written are really two topics), but it's a start. I hope it's enough of a start that you can have a new hobby: writing software. If you then learn more, you might even make a career of it someday. I hope some of the people who read this book end up in the profession, as we need more sharp minds writing software.

If that happens to be you, welcome to the quirky, frustrating, fascinating, and sometimes lucrative world of software development.

Jay Bryant

About the Author

I started as a poet. I discovered that I had no "spark," though I was good enough at the mechanics. So I became a teacher. Having gotten two degrees in English literature while trying to be a poet, I naturally taught English. Starting in 1986, I also worked part-time writing software manuals.

As it happened, I had taken all the linguistics courses the university offered, purely because I enjoy concepts such as transformational grammar and morphology. When I was looking at code over a developer's shoulder, I said, "I see structure and syntax here. Tell me how it works." Phil Schlump was smart enough to not try to explain how C works while I looked over his shoulder. Instead, he told me to buy *The C Programming Language*, by Brian Kernighan and Dennis Ritchie. I read the book and did all the exercises, with a little coaching from Phil.

That got me started on my journey toward software development. From there, I read many more books and learned (and have forgotten some) more languages. When the university let me go in 1991, I continued on as a technical writer who programmed as a hobby until 1998, when I started writing code as part of my job. I was annoyed with the documentation tools I had, so I started writing some of my own. After a few years of doing even more programming to make documentation tools, I gave up writing as part of my job and became a full-time software developer in late 2004. I worked full-time as a Java and XSLT developer for three years and then full time as a Java Web Application Developer for three years.

By the end of those experiences, I knew enough to write a book about Java. Writing this book has taught me some more and helped to formalize the knowledge I already had. As ever, the act of teaching (and writing this kind of book is an exercise in teaching) also teaches the teacher.

Writing this book also reminded me that I really like writing. So I've taken a job that lets me both write and code. I'm writing API documentation. That is, I explain how software works to software developers, so that they can get more done in less time. The job title I like best for this sort of work is Programming Writer, so that's what I call myself these days.

When I'm not writing software and writing about software, I play games of all sorts (not just computer games), read fantasy and science fiction, and go out with friends. I live with an orange tabby cat named Oscar who alternates between feline terrorist and snugglemonster.

Jay Bryant

About the Technical Reviewer

Massimo Nardone was born under Mount Vesuvius and holds a Master of Science Degree in Computing Science from the University of Salerno, Italy. He currently works as a Senior IT Security, Cloud and Infrastructure Architect, and is the Finnish Invention Development Team Leader (FIDTL) for IBM Finland. With more then 16 years of experience in Mobile, Security, and WWW technology areas for both national and international projects, he has worked as a Project Manager, Software Engineer, Research Engineer, Chief Security Architect, and Software Specialist. Massimo is also a visiting lecturer and supervisor for exercises at the Networking Laboratory of the Helsinki University of Technology (TKK) for the course "Security of Communication Protocols".

Acknowledgments

I couldn't have written this book without some early influences in both writing and programming. So I have to thank to Dick Holland, Keith Hull, Janet Constantanides, Phil Schlump, and Pat LaFollett for my education (only three of those were my teachers – Phil and Pat are former co-workers who are natural mentors). More recently, I have to thank John Sederberg, Terry Dexter, and Daniel Padilla for taking a chance on a guy whose degrees were not in computer science. Finally, I have to thank Mary Jackson (good friend and fabulous software developer) for putting me in touch with Steve Anglin at Apress.

Ewan Buckingham and Adam Heath have put up with a lot from me, as I went from working on the book full-time to writing all day at work and having to write part-time at home, too. That made my response time slower than anyone liked at times. Also, Ewan and my technical reviewer, Massimo Nadone, have had a number of good ideas that have made the book better than I could have done on my own. They are intelligent and conscientious professionals, and I thank them for their efforts.

Jay Bryant

Introduction

Who This Book Is For

The title says "for Absolute Beginners." By that, I mean absolute beginners at programming. My original audience was teenagers whom I hope will go to college, get degrees in Mathematics, Computer Science, or Electrical Engineering (or perhaps Technical Communication or Graphic Design), and then enter the software industry. However, I quickly realized that adults might also wish to learn to program, as part of changing careers, as a hobby, or simply out of curiosity. As a result, I've written the book for anyone who wants to learn to program but doesn't have any programming knowledge, regardless of other characteristics such as age or future career paths.

How This Book Is Structured

The first chapter gets you started by showing you how to install a development environment and by getting you through writing your first program. The next few chapters cover the basics of how Java works, including operators, data types, branching and looping, and how object-oriented languages define and solve problems. The middle chapters detail some of the "bread and butter" tasks that software developers must continually do, such as working with files and their contents and creating a user interface for a program. Once the book gets through all that, it turns to some topics that are more fun (I think), such as creating animations and video games. The book closes with a chapter that briefly introduces two topics that, although somewhat advanced, may let you do good things in your own programs once you finish the book.

All through the book, I include code samples that you can type into your development environment and run. You can also get the code from the Apress web site. I've also included lessons from my 25 years (twenty of them full-time) in software development. I hope those real-world experiences make the highly abstract field of software development more concrete for you. It pays to remember that, although the field is by nature theoretical, the problems we want to solve mostly exist in the real world.

Conventions

This book uses a number of formatting conventions that should make it easier to read. Formatting can't substitute for poor writing or poor coding, but it can help to make either more clear. To that end, the book incorporates the following conventions:

Code within other text, usually within a paragraph, appears as follows: `java.lang.System`
Code listings appear as follows:

Listing Intro-1. Sample Code Block

```java
public static void main(String[] args) {
  System.out.println("Hello, World!");
}
```

Within procedures, interface items (such as buttons and menu choices) that you should use appear as bold text in sentences, as follows: "From the **File** menu, choose **New**." The names of objects that appear within the file system (such as files and directories) appear in a monospace font, as follows: `C:\temp`

I should also mention that I've intentionally used an informal (almost "folksy") style and tone. When I'm sharing my experiences, I use the first-person singular ("I"). When I hope you're doing the same thing I did when I wrote the book (usually writing code or thinking about a problem in a particular way), I use the first-person plural ("We"). When I want you to do something, I use the second-person ("You"). Also, I've made liberal use of contractions, such as "I've." I hope you'll find the book to be more engaging for being informal in its presentation.

Prerequisites

Before reading this book, you need to know your way around at least one operating system, such as Windows or Mac OS X. In particular, you need to know how to create and delete files on your computer. If you've looked into how "command" or "batch" files work on your computer, that would be even better, as that is a kind of light-weight programming.

You don't need any other prerequisites to read this book. You don't need to know math or logic or computer science. The book covers bits and pieces of all those subjects at times, but in a pragmatic way that doesn't rely on the reader having any existing knowledge.

All you really need is a desire to learn to program.

CHAPTER 1

Writing Your First Java Program

To write a program in Java, you need the Java Development Kit (JDK). Strictly speaking, the JDK is all you need; however, other tools can make writing a Java application easier. Most software developers like to use an Integrated Development Environment (IDE). One of the most popular IDEs is Eclipse. Fortunately, both the JDK and Eclipse are free downloads. This chapter describes how to download and install both products and how to set up your first Java project in Eclipse. By the end of this chapter, you will have typed in and run your first Java program.

Installing the JDK

JDK is a collection of programs that enables you to write programs in Java. The two programs you'll use most are javac.exe and java.exe. The javac.exe program is the compiler, which means it's the program that turns code you can read (the code you write in Java) into code your computer can read (the collection of 0s and 1s that a computer needs when it runs a program). The java.exe program runs the programs that you write. After javac.exe compiles them, java.exe starts them and manages all the things a program needs (a connection to the operating system, handles for files, and a lot of other things). Because you'll use Eclipse (which we discuss shortly), you don't need to run javac.exe and java.exe. Eclipse does that for you. But it's handy to know what they do, so that you can run programs directly from a command window when you want to do so.

Before you can install it, you have to download it, of course. To get the latest version of the JDK, follow these steps:

1. Open `http://www.oracle.com/technetwork/java/javase/downloads/index.html` in a web browser.

2. Click the **Download JDK** button.

3. Follow the instructions provided by the web site.

4. Run the installer and accept any defaults.

■ **Note**   If you don't have administrator rights on your computer, clear (that is, uncheck) the checkbox that lets you install the program for all users. This enables you to still install the JDK.I would provide more details, but the web site changes from time to time, so more detailed instructions would probably be wrong (and confusing and irritating).

You can put the JDK anywhere you'd put any other program. The default location works just fine.

Installing Eclipse

Eclipse is an IDE. Basically, it provides a convenient tool for writing and testing your programs. Among other things, it identifies your errors as you make them, which makes correcting them much easier and faster than writing code in a text file and compiling it from the command line. Eclipse also colors parts of your code. After you get used to the color scheme (which happens very quickly), you'll be able to write code more quickly.

Again, before you can install Eclipse, you have to download it. To do so, follow these steps:

1. Open http://www.eclipse.org/downloads/ in a web browser.

2. Find the **Eclipse IDE for Java Developers** choice and select the 32-bit version.

■ **Note**   If you have a 64-bit operating system, choose the 32-bit version of Eclipse anyway. At the time of this writing, the 64-bit version of Eclipse has issues that make Java development more difficult than it needs to be.

---

3. Follow the instructions provided by the web site.

4. Run the installer and accept any defaults.

Again, I would try to provide more detail, but the web site changes from time to time, so more detailed instructions would probably be wrong (and so confusing and irritating).

You can put Eclipse anywhere you'd put any other program. Again, the default location works just fine.

Creating Your First Project

When you use Eclipse, you have to create a separate project for each program. That way, Eclipse can keep the details of one program separate from another. Each project consists of the source code files you write for your program and, potentially, a number of other resources that you might attach to a program. For example, you might include images and files that contain settings to load at run time and many other possible items.

After you've started Eclipse, you can make a new project as follows:

1. From the **File** menu, select **New,** and then select **Project**. The New Project window appears, as shown in Figure 1-1.

Figure 1-1. Eclipse's New Project window.

2. In the New Project window, double-click **Java Project**. The New Java Project window appears, as shown in Figure 1-2.

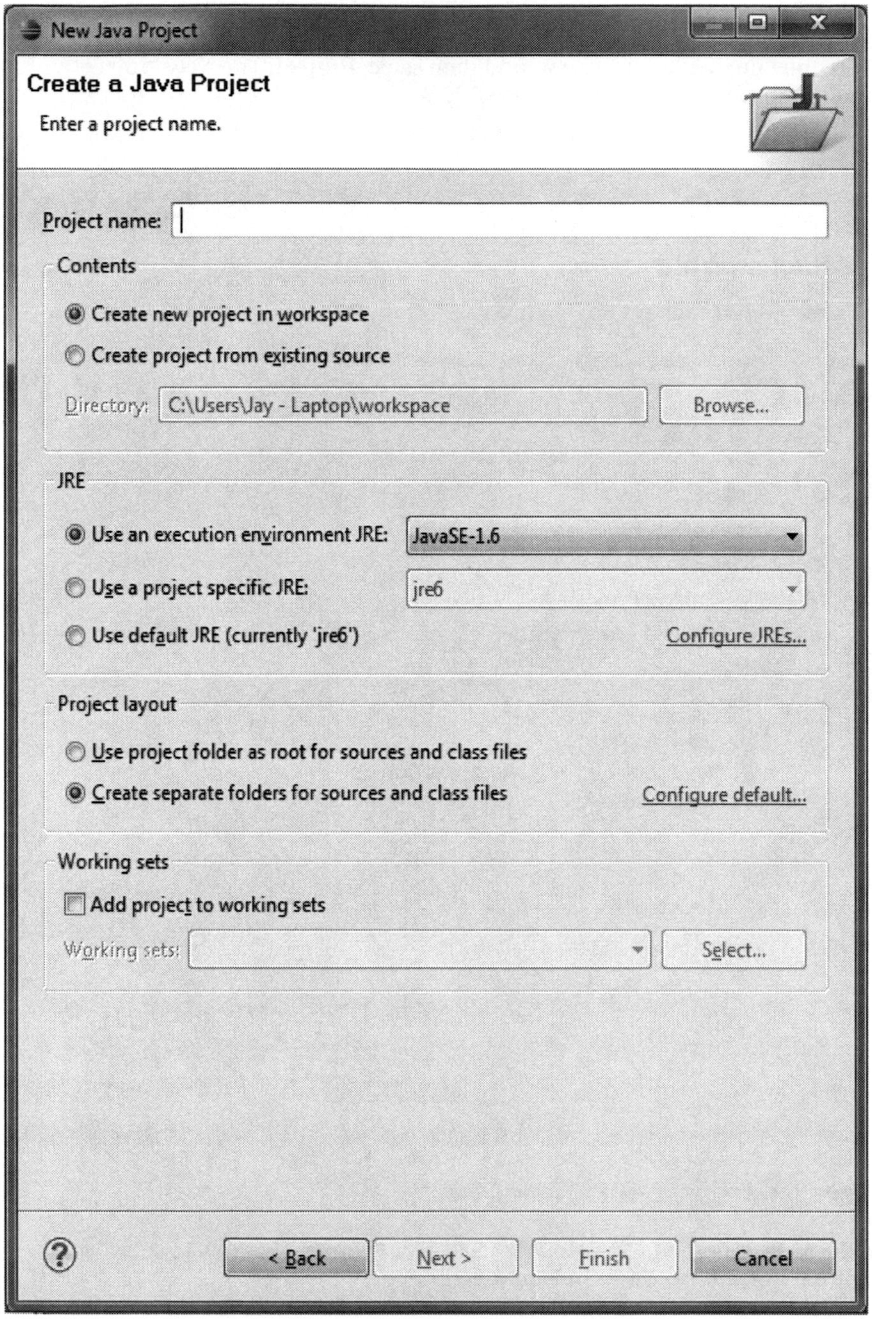

Figure 1-2. *Eclipse's New Java Project window.*

3. Type Hello in the **Project name** field.

▨ **Note** Be careful to pick meaningful names. I've chosen Hello for this example because the first program we're going to write is one that says Hello. One common mistake for new software developers is to choose names such as Project1 and Project2. It probably won't be long before you can't remember the details of any of them. Instead, if you're writing a minesweeper game, call your project Minesweeper. Then, when you're also working on an instant messaging program, you can distinguish Minesweeper from InstantMessenger much more readily than you can distinguish Project1 from Project2.

---

4. Click **OK**. You can change a number of other options here. However, for our purposes, the default settings work just fine. You should now have a window that looks something like the one in Figure 1-3.

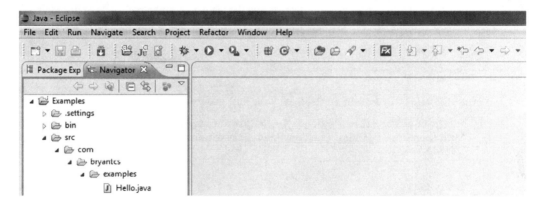

Figure 1-3. *The main area of the Eclipse IDE.*

Creating the Program

Every Java program has one class that is the program's starting point .(often called an entry point). A class is a bit of code that groups other bits of code together in a particular way. We'll get to classes in the next chapter. The thing that makes that class special is the existence of the main method. A method is a bit of code that does one particular thing – in this case, it starts the program. We'll cover methods in the next chapter, too. The main method accepts inputs and starts the program. Ever Java program has one and only one main method.

■ **Note** That said, some code bases actually have a number of `main` methods. They exist so that classes can be tested individually. Strictly speaking, each one starts a separate Java program, even though the people working on them might think of them as just parts of the larger program. For our purposes, just remember that a Java program must have a `main` method.

The class that contains the `main` method .determines the name of the program. The name of the program is the name of that class. For example, the program we write later in this chapter is called Hello because the class that holds its main method is named `Hello`. (Of course, the marketing department can call it anything, but it's the `Hello` program to Java and Java developers.) This naming arrangement happens because of the way Java programs are started: The Java runtime engine requires the name of a class that contains a `main` method.

■ **Note** The file that holds a Java class must have exactly the same name as the Java class. For example, the `Hello` class must be stored in a file named Hello.java. If the file were named hello.java, it wouldn't work. A lowercase h is not an uppercase H, and the Java compiler won't recognize that hello.java contains the `Hello` class.

To create a class with a main method for your first program, follow these steps:

1. Right-click the `Hello` project in the Eclipse Package Explorer, choose **New**, and then choose **Class**. The New Java Class window displays, as shown in Figure 1-4.

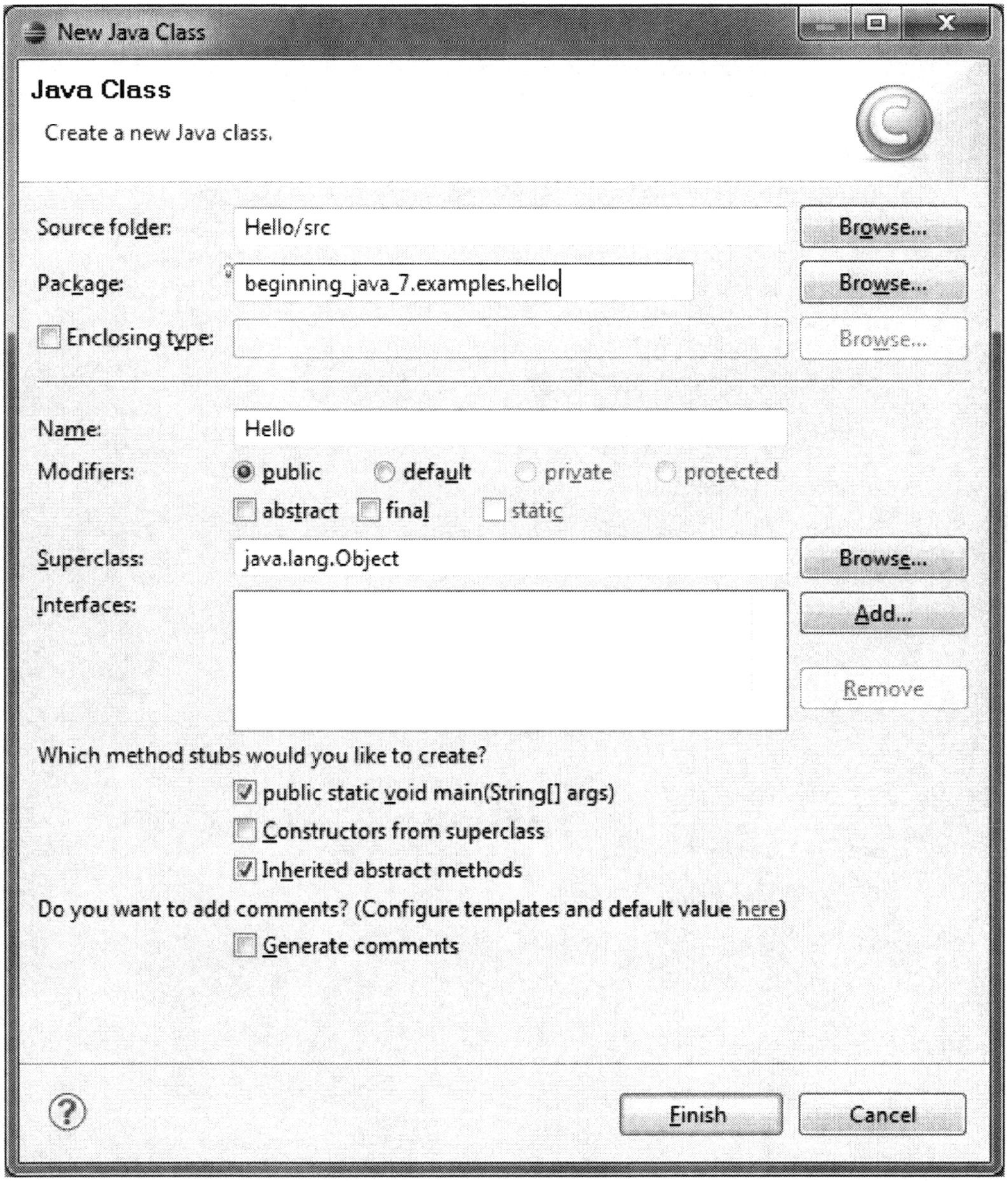

Figure 1-4. *Eclipse's New Java Class window.*

2. In the **Package** field, type whatever you like for the package, but remember to use a name you can remember and keep it separate from your other projects. A package is a way to group classes together. For small projects, you don't need them. Large projects would be impossible to manage without them, though. We'll cover classes in the next chapterIn the **Name** field, type Hello. This is the name of your class.

3. Check the checkbox that gives you a `main` method (`public static void main (String args[])`). When you're done, you should have a class similar to the one in Listing 1-1.

   Remember that Java is case-sensitive. "Hello" is not the same as "hello" to Java.

Listing 1-1*: Preliminary Hello class*

```
package com.bryantcs.examples.hello;

public class Hello {

  /**
   * @param args
   */
  public static void main(String[] args) {
    // TODO Auto-generated method stub

  }

}
```

4. Remove the comments. We don't need a comment (the lines that start with /* and end with /* and the line that starts with //), and we're about to fill in that autogenerated stub.

5. Within the `main` method, type:

   ```
   System.out.println("Hello, World!");
   ```

   Your class should now look similar to Listing 1-2.

Listing 1-2*: Basic Hello program*

```
package com.bryantcs.examples.hello;

public class Hello {

  public static void main(String[] args) {
    System.out.println("Hello, World!");
  }

}
```

That's a complete Java program. You can now run your program by clicking the Run button in the toolbar or by choosing **Run** from the **Run** menu. Figure 1.5 shows where to find the Run button.

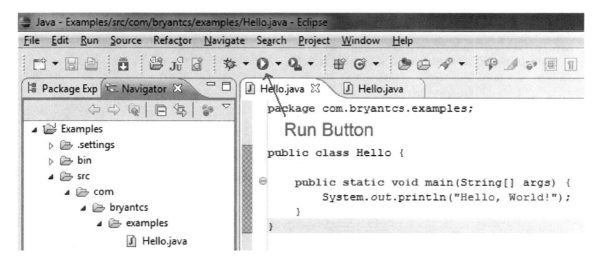

Figure 1-5. *Where to find the Run button.*

Eclipse then displays a console panel under the code area that shows the output of your program. In this case, it says, "Hello, World!" Writing a program that outputs "Hello, World!" is an old tradition, by the way. If you tell experienced developers that you're at the "Hello, World!" stage in learning how to program, they'll know that you've just taken your first steps on the road to being a software developer. Most software developers remember that day fondly.

The String[] args part is the mechanism that a Java program uses to read in options (more properly called arguments) that you can give to your program. The word String refers to a collection of characters that we can treat as a single object. A name is a classic example of a string. The [] indicates an array, which is a collection of values (strings in this case). The collection (that is, the array) of strings is called args. We add the capability to use an argument to our Hello program later in the chapter, we cover arrays in the next chapter, and we cover strings in Chapter 3, "Data Types."

Adding More Functionality

Now that you have a working program, let's make it do more. Specifically, let's make it read in your name and say hello to you rather than to the whole world.

Look at the declaration for the `main` method. The `args` array holds all the values that were provided to the Java runtime engine when someone started your program. Often, these are configuration settings of various types. One common practice is to pass in the path to a file that contains more information (such as difficulty settings for a game or the most recently opened files for a word processor)—that is, the path to a configuration file. We read files later in the book. For now, we get the arguments from Eclipse. First, though, we need to write the code to read the arguments and put the first argument into our message. Listing 1-3 shows how to do this.

Listing 1-3: *Reading arguments*

```java
package com.apress.java7forabsolutebeginners;

public class Hello {

  public static void main(String[] args) {
    System.out.println("Hello, " + args[0] + "!");
  }

}
```

■ **Note**   Computers start counting at 0 rather than 1. Consequently, the first member of an array can be found at 0. Typing `args[1]` here generates an out-of-bounds exception, by which Java means that it expects to find two strings, but you provided only one. You'll quickly get used to computers starting their counting at 0.

`System.out.println` accepts a single `String` object as its argument. In this case, we've got three `String` objects, but the plus signs concatenate them together to create a single string, satisfying the requirement (for just one string) of the `println` method. The plus sign is Java's string concatenation operator (in addition to being a plus sign when used for mathematical operations). We cover operators in Chapter 4, "Operators."

To provide a value for the argument in Eclipse, follow these steps:

1.   From the **Run** menu, choose **Run Configurations**. The Run Configurations window appears. Figure 1.6 shows the Run Configurations window.

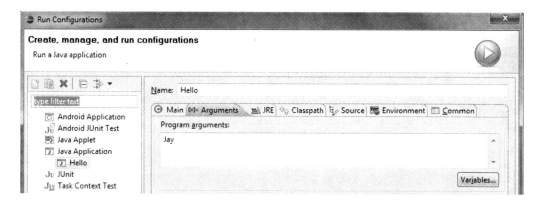

Figure 1-6. The Run Configurations window.

2.   In the **Arguments** tab, type your name.

3.   Click the **Run** button.

This time, your program says hello to you.

Congratulations. At this point, you've created a program that does the basic things all programs do: accepts input, modifies the input to accomplish something, and produces output. It might not seem like much, but it's the first step on a fun path. We do much more before we're done.

Further Development

Just for fun, let's tack on a bit more functionality. When programs generate console output, they often include the date and time. Formatting a date takes more code than most people would expect until they've had to do it. That's because the real world has so many different date formats. In the United States, month/day/year (MDY) format prevails. In Europe, day/month/year (DMY) prevails. In addition to the date formats used by people, computer systems also have various ways of representing dates, from simple variations such as year/month/day (YMD) to far more arcane arrangements. Java, having inherited from C, uses the same date storage technique as C and Unix (which was originally coded mostly in C) and Linux (which shares much with Unix). Consequently, Java stores dates as the number of seconds since January 1, 1970. In more detailed and technical terms, Java's "epoch" started at January 1, 1970, 00:00:00 GMT.

So, how do we turn the number of seconds since 1970 into a nicely formatted time stamp for our output? Listing 1-4 shows one way. (Part of both the joy and the pain of software development is that there's almost always more than one way to do something.) I explain more about the new pieces of code in the next section.

Listing 1-4*: Adding a timestamp to Hello*

```java
package com.apress.java7forabsolutebeginners;

import java.text.SimpleDateFormat;
import java.util.Date;

public class Hello {

  public static void main(String[] args) {
    // First, get the date as seconds since 1/1/1970
    // Note that a Date object also contains time information
    Date now = new Date();
    // Second, create a formatter object
    SimpleDateFormat formatter =
      new SimpleDateFormat("EEE, MMM dd, yyyy HH:mm:ss");
    // Third, apply the formatter to the date
    String formattedDate = formatter.format(now);
    // Finally, add our formatted date to our output
    System.out.println(formattedDate + "> Hello, " + args[0] + "!");
  }

}
```

When you run this program, you'll see a date and time stamp before your other output.

About Java Objects

Notice how we had to use two kinds of objects (`Date` and `SimpleDateFormat`) to create a nicely formatted date. `Date` and `SimpleDateFormat` are defined by class files, just as your Hello program is defined by a class file. We told our Java program where to find those classes with the import statement near the top of the file. Your program cannot run without them, so we have to tell Java where to find them.

For any class or other bit of code that's part of the Java standard libraries, you can learn all about it from the Javadoc that Oracle maintains for each version of Java. Javadoc is a special document format that lets Java programmers embed documentation directly into code. That way, you can look at the documentation for classes you want to use as you program your own classes. As you do more programming, you'll spend a lot of time reading this documentation. As a good learning exercise, look up the `SimpleDateFormat` class and look at all the options you can use when formatting a date.

For Java 7, you can find the API (short for Application Programming Interface) documentation at http://download.oracle.com/javase/7/docs/api/.

■ **Note** Eclipse provides the Javadoc information for items in the standard API. Hover your mouse over any method or object that you're using, and you'll see the Javadoc information for that item. When you see the Javadoc, press **F2** to open a separate window that lets you see more.

Summary

In this chapter, we did the following tasks:

- Downloaded and installed the Java Development Kit

- Downloaded and installed Eclipse, which we use to write Java programs

- Created the code for our first program within Eclipse

- Ran our first program ("Hello, world!")

- Modified the first program to do a bit more (say hello to you specifically)

- Modified the program still more (to include the date and time)

- Learned where to find more information about the other code used in future programs

Many of these tasks constitute the day-to-day work of full-time software developers. We spend a lot of time (more than we'd like, usually) setting up tools. We also spend most of our time either writing new classes or (far more often) rewriting existing classes, either to add new functionality or to correct a problem. We also certainly spend plenty of time reading documentation or wishing we had more documentation to read.

I guarantee that you'll find yourself returning to these tasks many, many times if you stick with software development, whether as a hobby or as a profession. You'll also do some of these tasks (especially writing and modifying code) as you work your way through this book. I hope you find it to be fun. I usually do.

CHAPTER 2

Java Syntax

The syntax of any language is the rules that any speaker of the language follows so that other speakers of that language can understand. In other words, syntax is a set of rules that all the speakers of a language agree to follow so that they can communicate. If you violate the rules, people listening to you are either going to ask, "Huh? What?" or think you're being silly (which might be appropriate in some settings but will often cause a problem).

Computer languages work in much the same way, except that they're never spoken (though I won't be surprised to see, or should I say hear, oral programming languages someday). If you decide to do your own thing, don't be surprised when your computer doesn't do what you had in mind. If you fail to code clearly and follow the rules of your programming language, all you'll get is confusion, though your computer will generate error messages rather than say, "Huh? What?"

Java gets most of its syntax from another language called C++. C++ in turn gets most of its syntax from C. And C was influenced by other languages. The people who created Java chose C++ as the basis for Java's syntax because C++ was one of the most widely used languages at the time, and that gave many developers some familiarity with Java syntax. Java's success (it's now widely used) depends on many factors, but adopting an already widely known syntax certainly didn't hurt.

An Example

I created two classes and an interface that together demonstrate almost all of Java's syntax. We learned in Chapter 1 that a class is a bit of code that contains other bits of code (which we get to later in this chapter). An interface is basically a contract; a class that uses an interface must do all the things specified by the interface. (In proper Java terms, a class that implements an interface must implement all the methods specified by the interface)I might have missed some obscure bits, but understanding this much syntax serves you well for a long time. We refer to these three listings throughout the rest of the chapter. If the listings seem long, don't let that bother you. For now, just read through them. As we work through this chapter, come back to these three listings and things should become clearer. Let's start with an interface, as shown in Listing 2-1.

Listing 2-1. *The Average interface*

```
package com.apress.java7forabsolutebeginners.syntaxExample;

public interface Average {

  public int[] getInts();
```

```
  public void setInts(int[] ints);
  public float getAverage();
}
```

Any class that uses our **Average** interface has to include (that is, implement) the `getInts`, `setInts`, and `getAverage` methods. Also, those methods within the implementing class must have the same arguments. So a class that includes the following method whose signature is `getInts(int numberOfIntsToGet)` does not satisfy the interface's contract unless it also includes a method whose signature is `getInts()`. Don't worry too much about this just now. We work through some examples as we go, and those should clear up your understanding nicely.

Listing 2-2*. The AverageImpl class*

```
package com.apress.java7forabsolutebeginners.syntaxExample;

public class AverageImpl extends Object implements Average {
  private long begin;
  private long end;
  private int[] ints;
  private static final String EXCEPTION_MESSAGE =
    "ints must contain at least one int";

  public AverageImpl(int[] ints) throws IllegalArgumentException {
    if (ints.length == 0){
      throw new IllegalArgumentException(EXCEPTION_MESSAGE);
    }
    this.ints = ints;
  }

  @Override
  public float getAverage() {
    begin = System.nanoTime();
    int result = 0;
    for (int i = 0; i < ints.length; i++) {
      result += ints[i];
    }
    end = System.nanoTime();
    return (float) result / ints.length;
  }

  public static float averageTwoNumbers(int a, int b) {
    return (float) (a + b) / 2;
  }

  // a classic getter method
  @Override
  public int[] getInts() {
    return ints;
  }

  // a classic setter method
  @Override
```

```
public void setInts(int[] ints) throws IllegalArgumentException {
  if (ints.length == 0){
    throw new IllegalArgumentException(EXCEPTION_MESSAGE);
  }
  this.ints = ints;
}

public long getRunTime() {
  return end - begin;
}
}
```

The **AverageImpl** implements the **Average** interface. ("Impl" is an abbreviation that is often used for a class that implements an interface.) In particular, it implements the three methods defined by the **Average** interface. As you can see, it does some other things, too, including defining a message to use when things go wrong (an exception is Java's way of saying it found something didn't work) and giving us the tools to keep track of how long it takes to average whatever numbers we provide as input.

Listing 2-3. *The AverageTest class*

```
package com.bryantcs.examples.syntaxExample;

import java.text.SimpleDateFormat;
import java.util.Date;

public class AverageTest {

  public static void main(String[] args) {
    // set up a test for AverageImpl
    int[] ints = {1, 2, 3, 4};
    AverageImpl averageImpl = new AverageImpl(ints);
    // do one test
    String testString = buildTestString(averageImpl.getInts(),
        averageImpl.getAverage(), averageImpl.getRunTime());
    System.out.println(testString);

    // set up a second test (using setInts)
    ints[0] = 2;
    ints[1] = 3;
    ints[2] = 4;
    ints[3] = 5;
    averageImpl.setInts(ints);

    // do the second test
    testString = buildTestString(averageImpl.getInts(),
        averageImpl.getAverage(), averageImpl.getRunTime());
    System.out.println(testString);

    // Test the exception
    int[] ints2 = {};
    try {
      averageImpl.setInts(ints2);
```

```java
      } catch(IllegalArgumentException iae) {
        System.out.println("Oops! can't use an empty array");
      }

      // add a test for the convenience method
      System.out.println("AverageImpl.averageTwoNumbers(1, 2) = "
          + AverageImpl.averageTwoNumbers(1, 2));
    }

    private static String buildTestString(int[] values, float average, long time) {
      // set up a timestamp for our tests
      Date now = new Date();
      SimpleDateFormat formatter = new SimpleDateFormat("HH:mm:ss");
      String timeStamp = formatter.format(now);

      StringBuffer sb = new StringBuffer(timeStamp);
      sb.append(">Averaged {");
      for (int i = 0; i < values.length; i++) {
        sb.append(values[i]);
        if (i < values.length - 1) {
          sb.append(", ");
        }
      }
      sb.append("} and got ");
      sb.append(average);
      sb.append(" in ");
      sb.append(time);
      sb.append(" nanoseconds");
      return sb.toString();
    }
}
```

Finally, the AverageTest class creates a program (you can tell because it has a main method, as we saw in Chapter 1) that lets us test our Average interface and AverageImpl class. It tests all the methods in the AverageImpl class and even creates an exception (that is, an error) so that we can see how that works. It also creates a String object that we use as the message to the user to display our results.

Lines

Java files (classes and interfaces) consist of lines of code. Although that might seem obvious, it's actually important. We measure code in lines (remember in the movie *Jurassic Park* where the programmer played by Samuel L. Jackson says that there are two million lines of code and we are supposed to think the program is complex?) and use lines to separate bits of code from other bits of code. Java has several kinds of lines, including statements (such as i = 2;), declarations, and just plain old empty lines (which are often handy for making a program easier to read). Java marks the end of statements with a particular character, the semicolon (;). That matters because a long statement can be broken across multiple lines in the file but can still be a single statement from Java's perspective. Sometimes, when you debug a bit of Java code, that can be important. The examples in Listings 2-2 and 2-3 both have statements that have to be split because of the width of the page.

To make your programming simpler and easier (and not drive other programmers crazy), keep your lines (both statements and declarations) as short as possible. For historical reasons, 80 characters is often used as a suggested limit for the length of a line. If you get to 80 characters, find a way to divide the line into two lines. (The 80-character value comes from punch cards having 80 characters.) You can certainly have longer lines (and there are times when it's acceptable), but hold down on really long lines, for sanity's sake.

Avoid Overly Complex Code

There's an old joke in which one person writes, "Simplify!" and someone else rewrites it as "Eschew Obfuscation." Coding is a lot like writing in some ways (in fact, we enjoy both because of the similarities). One such way is that you often have choices about how to do things. Although it might be a fun challenge to see how complex you can make a line, you should avoid coding that way. Your fellow developers will thank you, and you'll thank yourself when you come back to an old project, if your code is as readable as possible. Let's consider an example in Listing 2-4:

Listing 2-4. *Dense code*

```
someValue = someMethodToGetABooleanValue() != someOtherMethodToGetABooleanValue() ?
   someMethodToDoSomething() : someMethodToDoSomethingElse();
```

The issue here is density. The previous line has too much meaning in one place. So let's rewrite it into simpler code in Listing 2-5.

Listing 2-5. *Simplified code example*

```
boolean firstBooleanValue = someMethodToGetABooleanValue();
boolean secondBooleanValue = someOtherMethodToGetABooleanValue();

if (firstBooleanValue != secondBooleanValue) {
        someMethodToDoSomething();
} else {
        someMethodToDoSomethingElse();
}
```

Don't worry about the details. Just consider the structure. We get to the meaning of all these bits and pieces later in this chapter and the next chapter.

Notice that the simplified code is much longer. Rather than one line of code (on two lines of the file), the simplified code occupies eight lines of code. Simplification definitely has a cost (making you scroll more to read it). However, it's far more readable. You (and your fellow developers) can understand it quickly, where you (probably) have to stop and puzzle out the meaning of the single, dense line.

Some developers would say that we over-simplified the code. They'd point out that the two `boolean` variables don't really help (the methods that return those values could be in the `if`) and that the braces are unnecessary (you don't need braces for `if` and `else` if the block belonging to each is only one line long). Those things are true. The code would look something like Listing 2-6.

Listing 2-6. *Moderately simplified code*

```
if (someMethodToGetABooleanValue() != someOtherMethodToGetABooleanValue())
        someMethodToDoSomething();
else
        someMethodToDoSomethingElse();
```

The issue here is one of style. Individual developers have their own thresholds for when code is too complex (that is, when the information is too dense). Some folks like it really complex and see nothing wrong with the original line, whereas others like to have every little thing broken out. To the computer, it doesn't matter. So this is a purely human issue.

You find that developers get serious about coding style. In fact, some of the most serious disagreements we've seen in the software development community have been about coding style. As a beginner, your best bet is to keep things simple and avoid overly dense code. Eventually, you'll develop your own threshold for what's too complex.

Package Declaration

Let's start at the top, with the package declaration:

```
package com.bryantcs.examples.syntaxExample;
```

That line says this class belongs to a particular package. A package can contain any number of classes and interfaces. As you develop more complex programs, you'll want to divide your classes and interfaces into groups, so that you can more easily find any given class or interface. For example, in web applications, it's common to divide the classes that talk to the database (the data layer) from the classes that make web pages for the users (the presentation layer). (Those kinds of applications generally have a middle layer, too, where the data gets transformed into meaningful information for the user.)

Another good reason for multiple packages is so that separate packages can contain classes with the same name. For example, the standard Java libraries contain `java.util.Date` (which is in this example) and `java.sql.Date`. They each do slightly different things (for example, they have different ways of formatting dates). If they were in the same package, only one could be called `Date`.

■ **Note** Package declarations are optional; however, they are a good idea. Even if you develop only as a hobby, you want to keep your projects separate from one another.

By convention, the package declaration follows a particular format. Although not strictly Java syntax (a program can work without it), most Java developers think ill of you if you don't follow the format. It's easiest to unravel this format by working from right to left:

- `syntaxExample` indicates the local name of the package. `AverageTest` is a simple application and so had just the one package.

- `examples` indicates the parent package for the local package. We keep all of the examples for this book in the `examples` package.

- `com.bryantcs` is the identifier for all of the applications, to keep them separate from those of other people when they get out on the Internet. After all, many people are likely to have an `examples` package, and someone else might even have an `examples.syntaxExample` package. Package declarations often look like reverse URLS. You might expect to see something like `bryantcs.com/examples/syntaxExample` (but don't visit that site; it doesn't exist). As we see next, the domain portion (com.bryantcs) provides the final bit of insurance that our class is unique.

`com.bryantcs` prevents the troubles that arise from having two packages with the same name. By convention, this part of the package name is done in reverse, because the domain name is more specific than the domain category name, and package names should work from less specific on the left to more specific on the right. Thus, when reading from left to right, we get the domain category (`com`), the domain (`bryantcs`), the kind of application (`examples`), and finally the name of the innermost package (`syntaxExample`). The first two (`com.bryantcs`) are part of the standard Java naming convention. The last two (`examples.syntaxExample`) are just our own convention for keeping the programs from getting tangled up with one another.

Here's another example of a package declaration:

> `org.apache.fop`

That refers to the FOP (Formatting Objects Processor) project at apache.org. (Apache is a leading provider of open-source software and a great place to get involved as a Java developer or tester.)

Package names can be much longer, because they grow to indicate packages within packages (within packages, and so on). Here's a longer example from the FOP project:

> `org.apache.fop.fo.pagination.bookmarks`

That one refers to the `bookmarks` package, which is within the `pagination` package, which is within the `fo` package, which is within the `fop` package. Packages nested several levels deep is a common practice in commercial projects. Few useful applications can reasonably fit into just one package.

You can include code from other people's projects (and your own existing projects) by including the package in which the code you want used resides. This mechanism enables developers to share code and lets one company write (and charge money for) code that other companies use.

Imports

After the package declaration, we get the `import` section (shown in Listing 2-3, earlier in this chapter). Any number of `import` statements can be present.

An `import` statement says your class uses one or more classes or interfaces from another package. That way, you can write two entirely separate applications but share code between them. Also, someone else can write a library that you can then use by importing the parts of the library you want to use.

Let's examine our `import` statements in Listing 2-7:

Listing 2-7. Import statements

```
import java.text.SimpleDateFormat;
import java.util.Date;
```

After the `import` keyword, we get a class identifier. Again, it pays to read from right to left when making sense of a class identifier. `java.text.SimpleDateFormat` says the `SimpleDateFormat` is within the `util` package, which is within the `java` package.

That particular class is from the official Java library. This `import` statement tells experienced Java developers that `AverageTest` is going to format a date.

Now, suppose we want to use other classes within the same package. We can then use a wildcard character (*) to specify any class within the package, thus:

```
import java.text.*;
```

Every different development shop has a different standard for when to stop being specific and use the wildcard. We prefer to use the wildcard when we have three classes or interfaces from the same package. Other folks use a wildcard whenever they have just two members of the same package. Still other developers never use wildcards because wildcards prevent you from seeing which objects are actually used.

Classes

The class line identifies this particular class. Don't forget that the file that holds the class must have the same name as the class, including the same capitalization.

```
public class AverageImpl extends Object implements Average {
```

All classes extend some other class. However, when a class extends `Object` (which is Java's root object), you can omit `extends Object`. As we mentioned before, software developers are by nature minimalists; we don't write anything that doesn't help. Consequently, few Java developers include the `extends` keyword when the class being extended is `Object`.

Let's pick apart that class declaration and see what all the pieces mean. The first word, `public`, is the access modifier for this class. See "Access Modifiers" later in this chapter, for more detail.

The second word, `class`, indicates that we define a class. In other words, we define a kind of object that can be created in the system. In that case, we define a class that will never be an actual object. Abstract classes are used for other classes to extend and as references. If this class were abstract, its syntax would be as follows:

```
public abstract class AverageImpl extends Object implements Average {
```

Classes can also be static. On a class, the `static` keyword means that only one instance of that class exists. You can't create a new instance of a static class (but the runtime engine creates one for you). As an aside, you might find it interesting to know that a static class can still be cloned, so the static keyword by itself does not guarantee a singleton (a class that has exactly one instance).

■ **Note** The alternative to defining a class is defining an interface. We get to interfaces later in this chapter.

The third word, `AverageImpl`, is the name of the class. Java has only two rules about class (and other names). Each name must start with a letter. Each name must consist of only certain characters: a-z, A-Z, 0-9, and the underscore (_) and dollar sign ($) characters.

■ **Note** `Impl` is short for implementation, by the way. It's a fairly common practice to have an interface and a class that provides an implementation for that interface. In those cases, a common naming convention is to name the class with the name of the interface plus `Impl`. Don't worry, we get to what "implementation" means in the "Interfaces" section.

In addition to the actual rules, the Java community follows certain customary guidelines for naming classes.

- The first custom is that each class name should start with a capital letter.

- Second, each logical word within the name should start with a capital letter.

- Third, we rarely use underscores in class names. Dollar signs are used only in generated code (that is, code written by programs rather than by people).

You can't break the rules (your programs won't work if you do), but you can break the community's conventions. However, you should have a good reason for doing so. The conventions let us all communicate more easily with one another, so follow them unless you have a good reason to do otherwise and comment your reasons.

The fourth word, extends, lets us know the class's parent class. A class's parent (more properly, a super) class is the class from which the current class gets the bases of its definition. In particular, a class can use all public and protected methods in its parent class just as though they had been defined in the class at hand. In this case, we extend Java's root class: Object. The extends keyword tells us that this class is a variety of its parent class. In this case, AverageImpl is a variety of Object. If you look at the relationship between a class and its parent class and it doesn't make sense, you need to rethink what you're doing or, if it's not a class you wrote, more closely examine the library you're using.

The fifth word, Object, tells us the name of the base class that we're extending. Sometimes, the name is meaningful and tells us something about the parent. Sometimes, as here, the name of the parent class doesn't tell us much (because every class ultimately extends Object). Good software developers strive for meaningful names, but it's not always possible.

The sixth word, implements, tells us that this class uses one or more interfaces. We visit them later in this chapter.

The seventh (and last, in this example) word, Average, tells us the name of the interface this class implements. A class can implement any number of interfaces, though few implement more than two or three and many classes implement no interfaces at all.

Fields

A *field* is a member of a class or (rarely) an interface that holds a value. Fields let us store the bits of information that we care about when we use a particular class. For example, the height and width fields in a class that defines rectangles are important to the purpose of the class. In the AverageImpl class listed earlier in this chapter, the following line defines a field:

```
private long begin;
```

This particular field contains a value of type long (which is a really big number—we get to data types in the next chapter). In this case, the field contains null (a keyword meaning that something has no value assigned to it and, for object references, refers to no object) until some other bit of code defines it. You can also directly assign a field's value, as shown in Listing 2-8.

Listing 2-8. Field examples

```
int[] ints = {1, 2, 3, 4};
AverageImpl averageImpl = new AverageImpl(ints);
```

For primitives (such as int), you can use a value. In this case, we assign values to an array of ints. For objects, you have to use the new keyword and call the object's constructor. We cover both the differences between primitives and objects in the next chapter.

On a field, the `static` keyword has a similar effect as it does on a method: A static field has one instance that's used by all the objects defined by that class. Consequently, a static field is also known as a class field (because it applies only to the class, not to the objects created from the class). Static fields are mostly used to define constants (values that never change). We get to constants later in this chapter.

▨ **Warning** Static fields can cause problems. Suppose you have two parts of a program running at once, each of which is working with an object whose class definition has a static field. If both classes try to modify the field at the same time, bad things (including both race conditions—parts of the program waiting for one another—and the field's value not being correct) can happen. For this reason, all static fields other than constants (which are both static and final) should usually be private.

Constants

Many programming languages support the concept of a *constant*. A constant is a value that never changes. For example, Java includes a class called Math, and the `Math` class includes a constant called PI, which holds the value of Pi to a high level of precision.

In Java, a constant is a field with a particular set of modifiers: static and final. Most are also public, though it is possible (and sometimes useful) to have private, package, and protected constants. We use a private constant in the `AverageImpl` class to avoid typing the same string twice. By convention, the names of constants are all uppercase and have underscores between the units that are logically words as in Listing 2-9.

Listing 2-9. A constant

```
private static final String EXCEPTION_MESSAGE =
    "ints must contain at least one int";
```

Methods

A *method* is basically something that a class can do. One common metaphor for classes and objects is that classes are nouns and methods are verbs. As with all metaphors, it's sometimes true and sometimes false, but it's often a handy way to check whether your design makes sense. Methods often do something with the other members (fields and methods) of the class. However, some methods (usually static methods) do nothing with the other members of the class, effectively operating on their own.

Thanks to the capability of methods to do lots of different things, it's hard to make a meaningful generalization about methods beyond just saying, "Methods do things." Perhaps some examples will help (see Listing 2-10).

Listing 2-10. Methods

```java
// a classic getter method
@Override
public int[] getInts() {
  return ints;
}

// a classic setter method
@Override
public void setInts(int[] ints) throws IllegalArgumentException {
  if (ints.length == 0){
    throw new IllegalArgumentException(EXCEPTION_MESSAGE);
  }
  this.ints = ints;
}
```

Let's have a closer look at the "setter" method, starting with the first line (not counting the comment, which starts with //. We cover comments later in the chapter).

`public` is the method's access modifier. We cover access modifiers earlier in the chapter.

`void` is the return type. The return type tells any code that called this method what to expect. All methods must have a return type. `void` indicates that the method won't return anything. So, all methods must have a return type, but not all methods must return something. If we look at the other methods in the class, we can see that they often do return something.

`setInts` is the method's name. By convention, method names start with a lowercase letter and have capital letters wherever a logical word appears. This is sometimes called camel case.

The parentheses contain a list of arguments. In this example, the list is only one argument long. Each argument has a type and a name. In this case, the type is `int[]` (the brackets indicate an array), and the name is `ints`. The arguments are separated by commas when more than one is present, as in the following method declaration from the **AverageTest** class:

```java
private static String buildTestString(int[] values, float average, long time) {
```

The brace character opens the code block that is the method's body. We cover blocks later in this chapter.

Methods can also be static. On a method, the `static` keyword means that only one such method exists in the system, no matter how many objects of that class might exist. For that reason, a static method is also known as a class method. Also, the method cannot use any of the class's fields other than fields that have themselves been declared static (usually constants). Static methods can be a handy way to provide utility methods for use throughout your code. For example, a method that takes a date and returns a formatted string might be static, provided it doesn't need to use any of its containing class's non-static methods. Also, static methods can be slightly more efficient, because they don't access anything outside the method body.

▨ **Warning** Static methods can cause problems. Suppose you have two threads, each of which is working with an object whose class definition has a static method. If both classes try to access the method at the same time, bad things can happen. For one thing, any fields modified by the method can end up with the wrong value, because the threads might run in the wrong order. Also, a static method has just one instance (the class itself), so a class that takes a long time to do whatever it does can keep the second (and third, fourth, and so on) thread waiting.

Constructors

The `AverageImpl` class includes a constructor, as shown in Listing 2-11.

Listing 2-11. A constructor

```
public AverageImpl(int[] ints) throws IllegalArgumentException {
        if (ints.length == 0){
                throw new IllegalArgumentException(EXCEPTION_MESSAGE);
        }
        this.ints = ints;
}
```

Constructors look like methods but aren't. Notice the lack of a return type and the name being identical to the class name. They are called when we first create an object and enable us to set up the object before we do anything with it. Creating the object is called *instantiation.*

What needs to be done varies tremendously by class. Many constructors (such as the one shown in this example) set some values. Other classes might create other objects, open a database connection or a file, or start some other process (and the possibilities don't stop there).

If you don't define a constructor, Java still creates a default constructor, to enable the new keyword to work. Otherwise, no one would ever be able to create an instance of your class. Constructors can have all the usual access modifiers.

You can also create multiple constructors for a single class. For example, suppose we want to provide a handy way to average any other number with 2. We can do that with a constructor such as in Listing 2-12:

Listing 2-12. Another constructor

```
public AverageImpl(int otherNumber) {
        ints = new int[] {2, otherNumber};
}
```

Now we have two ways to create an instance of the `AverageImpl` class.

▨ **Note** The `this` keyword is a reference to the object the class defines. In this case, the `this` keyword is necessary to distinguish the `ints` field in the class from the `ints` argument in the constructor's argument list.

Access Modifiers

Classes, interfaces, fields, and methods all use various access modifiers to indicate which other classes and interfaces can see and (potentially) modify the item in question. Java has four access modifiers: `private`, `package-private`, `protected`, and `public`.

- `private` means that only the other members (that is, fields and methods) within a class can see and (for fields) modify the method or field at hand. Private classes and interfaces appear only within classes, never as stand-alone constructs.

- `package-private` (often just called package) means that other members of the same package have access to the item. `package-private` is the default access modifier and does not have a keyword, because `package` is used to specify the package for a class or interface. To declare package access for something, use no access modifier.

- `protected` indicates that only descendants of the class can access the item. Classes can be protected, but protected classes generally appear only within other classes (an idiom called an inner class). Similarly, interfaces can be protected (provided they are within a class), but it's rare (I've never seen one). `protected` is most often used on fields and methods within classes.

- `public` indicates that any object has access to the item. `public` is often used (and probably overused quite a bit). It pays to get into the habit of asking whether anything should be public.

One other thing to know is that the access modifiers are hierarchical. `private` includes package-private (that is, if something can see a private object, it can see a package-private object, too), package-private includes `protected`, and `protected` includes `public`. Hard-to-find problems can arise when people forget that the access modifiers are hierarchical. Imagine a package with multiple classes and within that package, some class has a method visible to the package and another class has a protected method of the same name. Potentially, code can end up calling the wrong method. It doesn't happen often, but it's tough to figure out when it does.

▓ **Note** Access modifiers can be tricky. In the course of writing this brief description of them, I tripped over all kinds of uses I hadn't previously considered (it's been a learning experience). For example, I thought that interfaces could not be protected. However, they can be protected (or private) when they appear within classes. `private` and `public` are easy to understand and use. For `package` and `protected`, think carefully before deciding to use that modifier.

Interfaces

Interfaces define behaviors that classes must implement if they implement the interface. Interfaces are always abstract, and all the methods they contain are also always abstract. *Abstract* (which Java supports with `abstract` keyword) means that the class or method or field or whatever cannot be instantiated (that is, created) where it is defined. Some other object must instantiate the item in question. In the case of interfaces, that means a class that implements the interface must implement the methods defined in the interface (as we already learned, but now you know why that's the case). Consequently, interfaces never implement anything. Also, interfaces, and the methods they contain, are always static. Consequently, each interface (and its methods) exists exactly once in the system.

Interfaces generally contain only method definitions. They can also contain fields, but those fields are always constants.

Consider the getAverage() method from the Average interface listed earlier in the chapter. As you can see, the method has no body, not even braces. That's a method definition (also called a method signature), as opposed to a method. Any class that implements the interface must implement that method, including its modifiers and arguments. In this example, a class that implements Average must contain a method with the same modifiers. That is, the class must contain a public float getAverage() method with a body that does whatever needs to be done and returns a float value. (We cover data types in the next chapter.)

Interfaces offer a handy way to ensure that similar classes implement similar (but not necessarily the same) behavior. Consider a set of classes that model the animal kingdom. Such a model might have a Predator interface with a hunt() method. Both cats and dogs hunt, but they do it differently (cats tend to pounce, and dogs tend to chase). By leaving the details to the classes, the Predator interface lets us know that predators hunt but leaves room for each kind of predator to hunt in their own way.

Exceptions

When something bad happens, Java raises an error through a process known as "throwing an exception." Exception is a class with many (and many levels of) descendants. The AverageImpl class throws an IllegalArgumentException if someone tries to use an empty array, because the getAverage method divides by the length of the array and it's illegal to divide by 0. (In fact, trying to divide by zero creates an ArithmeticException, but AverageImpl doesn't let things get that far.)

When you can anticipate that someone might try something that will cause a problem, you should test for that problem and throw an appropriate exception. Let's look at one of the places where AverageImpl throws an exception in more detail in Listing 2-13:

Listing 2-13. Throwing an exception

```java
public AverageImpl(int[] ints) throws IllegalArgumentException {
        if (ints.length == 0){
                throw new IllegalArgumentException(EXCEPTION_MESSAGE);
        }
        this.ints = ints;
}
```

As you can see, the method declaration includes the throws keyword and then the name of the exception that the method throws. A method can throw any number of exceptions (and many do). When a method can throw more than one kind of exception, use a comma to separate them.

Within the method, you can see the test for a problem we want to catch, namely an empty array as the value of ints. Once we detect the problem, we use the throw keyword to throw a new instance of the appropriate exception.

When a method throws an exception, any object that uses that method must handle that exception. You can see that happen in the AverageTest class, in Listing 2-14:

Listing 2-14. Handling an exception

```
try {
  averageImpl.setInts(ints2);
} catch(IllegalArgumentException iae) {
  System.out.println("Oops! can't use an empty array");
}
```

That structure is called a **try-catch** block. As you can see, it's really two blocks—one within the **try** statement and one within the **catch** statement. If the code in the **try** block throws an exception, the code in the **catch** statement gets run. You can have multiple **catch** statements, each catching a different kind of exception, within a single **try-catch** block. That way, you can take different actions for different kinds of exceptions. You can also add a **finally** block to a **try-catch** block. Listing 2-15 shows a more elaborate example based on the existing example:

Listing 2-15. Try-catch-finally

```
try {
        averageImpl.setInts(ints2);
} catch(IllegalArgumentException iae) {
        System.out.println("Oops! can't use an empty array");
} catch(ArithmeticException ae) {
        throw ae;
} finally {
        System.out.println("Made it past the exception!");
}
```

Notice that the second **catch** block re-throws that particular kind of exception. In this case, you probably wouldn't do that, but the example illustrates a common practice. Exceptions often get re-thrown, so that they can get handled by the method that makes the most sense for handling that particular exception. Often, a developer writes a method and has no idea to handle the exception while writing that method, so the developer re-throws and figures the next method (or the one after that and so on) will know what to do with it. Of course, if the exception never gets handled, you have a problem that might crash the program, stick embarrassing exception messages in your output, or otherwise leave you wiping egg off your face and trying to placate angry users. When you re-throw an exception, the method containing your **try-catch** block needs to throw the exception, too. In that fashion, methods can pass an exception through many methods to get it to a method that knows how to handle it.

The **finally** keyword lets you create a block of code that gets run no matter what. Even if an exception happens, the code in the **finally** block gets run. In the example shown here, it doesn't do much. **finally** often isn't included precisely because nothing needs to be done. However, it's sometimes critically important that a **finally** block exist to do something. The classic use for a **finally** block is to close a database connection. If you open a database connection to do some work but then hit an exception, the database connection still needs to get closed. Too many open connections slow database performance and can ultimately crash a database (a disaster for most commercial software).

One last thing to know about exceptions is that Java has two categories of exceptions: checked exceptions and runtime exceptions. Checked exceptions are called that because the compiler (which is the program that turns your code into machine code that your computer can understand) checks for them when you try to compile your code. One big reason to use Eclipse is that it checks for problems as you write your code. If you use a method that throws checked exceptions, you must handle those exceptions in your code (though re-throwing them counts as handling them). The compiler does not check for runtime exceptions. Eclipse runs a compiler for us and checks our code as we type it, so we know immediately when we need to catch checked exceptions. Runtime exceptions (as the name implies) can only be caught at run time, so Eclipse can't warn us about those as we write our code.

Checked exceptions represent things beyond the program's control, such as bad user input or a file not existing. Runtime exceptions represent things that can be fixed with more or better code. One school of thought says that checked exceptions represent things the program should recover from. For example, if the program encounters a missing file (that is, some method gets an `IOException` when it expects a file handle), the program should ask the user where the file is or let the user cancel the operation. Runtime exceptions represent errors (usually oversights) in the code that developers should fix. If you get a `NullPointerException`, you don't ask the user to do anything (though you might tell the user to call customer support and report the problem). Instead, you fix the point in the code where something is passing null when it shouldn't. One concept that nearly all experienced programmers embrace is *defensive programming*, which means we try to not let things get to a point where exceptions can happen. Instead, we do things like checking to see whether something is null before we try to use it.

As it happens, `IllegalArgumentException` is a runtime exception. If you remove the `try-catch` blocks from `AverageTest`, you get no error. However, because I can anticipate the problem, I elect to specifically throw that error, so that I can attach a meaningful error message.

Blocks

Blocks are units of code that (usually) consist of more than one line and are defined by brace characters ({}). (Brace characters have several names, which can be pretty far-fetched. Throughout the book, I call them braces, for the sake of consistency.)

Braces define blocks of code for methods, classes, and various statements (such as `if` and `for`). Let's look at a simple block from the AverageImpl class in Listing 2-16:

Listing 2-16. *A simple block*

```
for (int i = 0; i < ints.length; i++) {
  result += ints[i];
}
```

Static BlocksStatic blocks are handy bits of code that let you define one block of code and have it be included in every constructor. Let's consider an example (in the form of a different class) in Listing 2-17.

Listing 2-17. *Static block example*

```
package com.bryantcs.examples;

public class StaticBlockClass {

        private static String name;
        private String whichOne;

        static {
                name = "StaticBlockClass";
        }
```

```
        public StaticBlockClass(int identifier) {
                whichOne = Integer.toString(identifier);
        }

        public StaticBlockClass(String identifier) {
                whichOne = identifier;
        }
}
```

As you can see, the field we set also has to be static. However, because we don't want to change it, that's just fine. In this case, we don't gain much by having a static block. However, imagine if we have ten values to set and four constructors.

Aside from saving space (though not in this example), the real value of static blocks makes sure that everything the class needs gets into each constructor. You can get bugs from having things set in some constructors but not others, and static blocks can help you manage that problem.

Comments

Comments are lines of code that are (usually) meant purely for humans to read. The compiler utterly ignores comments. Java supports two styles of comments, end-of-line comments and block comments. The code examples I provide have many end-of-line comments. *End-of-line comments* begin with two slash characters (//), thus:

```
// end-of-line comment that happens to be the only thing on the line
```

End-of-line comments can also start after other code on the line, thus:

```
int counter = 0; // Initialize the counter
```

Code cannot follow an end-of-line comment on the same line. It would become part of the comment.

Block comments begin with a slash and an asterisk (/*) and end with an asterisk and a slash (*/). Block comments can be on one line, but they can also consist of multiple lines. Block comments can start on the same line as other code. In fact, block comments can occur between code elements on the same line (possibly making the line of code consist of multiple lines in the file). As ever, examples help. Here's a block comment by itself on a single line:

```
/* comment */
```

And here's a line of code with a comment in the middle of it:

```
int counter /* comment */ = 0;
```

Please don't do that. It's legal, but it's poor coding practice, because it makes the code harder to read.

Now let's look at multi-line block comments in Listing 2-18.

Listing 2-18. *Multi-line block comment*

```
/* Now is the time for all good coders to write meaningful comments,
so that the rest of us can understand what the code is doing. */
```

Listing 2-19 shows another multi-line block comment, mingled with code.

Listing 2-19. Bad style in a multi-line block comment

```
int counter /*
Please don't
do this */ = 0;
```

By convention (which I break to provide you with examples that you shouldn't emulate), multi-line comments have the beginning of the comment (/*) on its own line, have the end of the comment (*/) on its own line, and have each of the middle lines start with an asterisk, as shown in Listing 2-20.

Listing 2-20. Properly formatted multi-line block comment

```
/*
 * Now is the time for all good coders to write meaningful comments,
 * so that the rest of us can understand what the code is doing.
 * And now this comment is properly formatted, too.
 */
```

This is easier to read, isn't it?

JAVADOC

Java includes a mechanism to generate documentation from within classes and interfaces. That mechanism is called Javadoc, and it uses of a special kind of block comment (and here's a comment meant for both humans and systems to read). A Javadoc comment starts with a slash and two asterisks (/**) and ends with an asterisk and a slash (*/), much like a block comment but with an additional asterisk in the starting syntax. The content of the comment then ends up in a document that the Javadoc tool creates. By convention, any class meant for public consumption should have Javadoc comments on the class and all methods that someone might use or extend (usually public and protected methods).

When the Javadoc tool runs, it examines all the classes and interfaces and creates a set of HTML pages (or sometimes other output, depending on various settings) with headings and subheading corresponding to the classes, interfaces, and methods in the program. Various markers help the Javadoc tool indicate descriptions for arguments and return values, who wrote the Javadoc comment, and other special content.

When coding a program for yourself, you don't need to insert Javadoc comments. If you start coding for an open-source project or for a company, you might be asked to add Javadoc comments to your code.

Listing 2-21 shows an example of a Javadoc comment and the method declaration it describes.

Listing 2-21. A Javadoc comment for a method

```
/**
 * This method makes a Cat object chase the given Mouse object.
 * @param mouse an instance of the Mouse class for our cat to chase
 */
void chase(Mouse mouse) {
```

Because you probably won't need to create Javadoc for a while, let's stop there. When you do need to know more about it, you can find the Javadoc tool home page at `http://www.oracle.com/technetwork/java/javase/documentation/index-jsp-135444.html`.

Summary

So, what did we learn in this chapter?
   We considered:

- The structure of a Java file, looking at statements and declarations

- The components that comprise a Java program (classes and interfaces)

- The components that comprise classes and interfaces (methods, fields, constructors, blocks, and comments)

- The basics of Javadoc

Whole books have been written about the content we covered in a single chapter, but those are awfully dry books for a beginner. I thought it would be more fun to learn the basics and then work with files, create animations, and create your own video games. We do all those things later in the book.I recommend reading the chapter again, thinking about what you learned from later in the chapter as you go. I also recommend stopping to do a little programming of your own. Try some simple things, such as a program to print a small multiplication table (say up to 4 x 4) and a program that accepts multiple Strings as arguments and combines them in interesting ways. There's no substitute for learning by doing it yourself.

CHAPTER 3

Data Types

Most programming languages have data types. Java has several data types. The first characteristic of a data type is whether it's a primitive or an object. Anything that's not a primitive is an object of some sort.

Primitive Data Types

Primitive means that no class exists to define a variable of that type. Java supports a number of primitive data types. In the code samples in previous chapters, you saw several variables whose data types were primitive. Anywhere you saw `int` or `boolean`, those were primitive data types (usually called "primitives"). Primitives fall into several broad categories. From the language's point of view, the categories don't exist, but they do help people keep the primitives straight from one another.

Integer Primitives

An *integer primitive* is one whose value can be only an integer. It cannot be a real number (that is, one with a fractional value). The numbers 0, 1, 16, and 37 are all integers. The number 12.34 is not an integer. The distinguishing feature between the various integer primitives is how many bits make up each one. Because a type made of more bits can hold a bigger number, the practical effect of the different number of bits is to increase the maximum value of that type. The possible detrimental effect of increasing the number of bits is to consume more memory. Often, it doesn't matter, but it's good practice to use data elements no larger than you need.

Integer primitives are signed (unless you use the `unsigned` keyword, which we discuss more in a moment), so their values range from a negative number to a positive number.

Table 3-1 shows the details of the various integer primitives.

Table 3-1. Integer primitives

Type	Bits	Minimum Value	Maximum Value
byte	8	-128	127
short	16	-32768	32767
int	32	-2,147,483,648	2,147,483,647
long	64	-9,223,372,036,854,775,808	9,223,372,036,854,775,807

Do you need even bigger numbers? Real-world applications sometimes need numbers even bigger than the maximum value of long. In those cases, Java provides a class called BigInteger. A number represented by a BigInteger object can be of any size, because the BigInteger class allocates enough bytes to store a representation of any number. It's a little tricky to use and operations on BigInteger objects are slow, but it's sometimes the only way. BigInteger is not a primitive.

Real Primitives

Real numbers have decimal points and values after the decimal point. Even if that value is 0, and even if you didn't type a decimal point and anything after it, the decimal point and the zeros after it are there behind the scenes. They must exist so that operations on the value can compare to the full value, so the JVM (the Java Virtual Machine, which is the program that runs your programs) fills them in even if you don't.

■ **Note**   0 and 0.00 are different values in Java. To the average person, they both mean zero. To a scientist or mathematician, the one indicates greater precision than the other, but they still both mean zero. But to a compiler, they are different data types and have nothing to do with one another.

Java supports two real primitives, float and double. float gets its name from the idea of a floating point number. The decimal point can move, so it's said to "float." double gets its name because it takes twice the storage space of a float. Table 3-2 shows the details of float and double.

Table 3-2. Real primitives

Type	Bytes	Minimum Value	Maximum Value
float	4	1.40129846432481707e-45	3.40282346638528860e+38

Again, sometimes even that isn't enough. For those cases, Java provides a class called BigDecimal. As with BigInteger, it can be tricky to use, and operations on it are slow. But when you absolutely have to have a number bigger than a double, use BigDecimal. As with BigInteger, BigDecimal is not a primitive.

boolean

The `boolean` data type indicates whether something is true or false. In fact, those two words (`true` and `false`) are the only two values `boolean` data types can have.

▨ **Note**   `true` and `false` are reserved words in Java. You can't use them for anything other than the value of a boolean variable. For example, trying to create an `int` called `true` throws an error.

---

char

The `char` data type holds two 8-bit bytes and is meant to represent characters. It's stored as an unsigned 16-bit integer with a minimum value of 0 and a maximum value of 65,535. However, you should never use a `char` to store a number, because that can lead to confusion. Use `char` variables to hold individual characters, and you'll avoid trouble.

So why is the maximum so big when relatively few characters exist? Well, when you look at all the character sets in use all around the world, 65,535 isn't so unreasonable. In fact, it's not enough when dealing with traditional Chinese.

▨ **Tip**   If you're curious about how to handle characters from other languages, look up Unicode, which is a standard that defines all the world's characters. For more on handling multi-byte characters, look up variable-width encoding.

The Special Type: String

`String` is a type that has some of the characteristics of both a primitive and an object. Strictly speaking, it is an object; that is, a `String` class defines it. A `String` object is a sequence of characters (and Java provides utilities for turning a `String` object into a collection of `char` primitives and for making a `String` object from such a collection). It's often handy to work on the collection (the string) rather than on each character, so Java (and nearly all other programming languages) provides a `String` object.

Java offers special support for the `String` class that lets `String` objects act a little like primitives. In particular, you can create a `String` object by using the equals sign (=), and you can concatenate `String` objects with the plus sign (+), as shown in Listing 3-1. Concatenation applies only to strings, by the way. If you use a plus symbol with the other data types, you either get an error (try adding two `boolean` values and you'll see it) or you get the mathematical plus operation that you usually associate with the plus symbol.

Listing 3-1. *String examples*

```
String myString = "my string";
String yourString = "your string";
String ourString = myString + " " + yourString;
System.out.println(myString);
System.out.println(yourString);
System.out.println(ourString);
```

The output is in Listing 3-2.

Listing 3-2. *String example output*

```
my string
your string
my string your string
```

Notice that the value of ourString consists of the concatenation of three values: myString, " ", and yourString. " " is a String literal. That's another way String differs from other objects; no other object (remember, primitives aren't objects) can have a literal.

Literals

All the primitives and the String class can have literal values. A *literal* is a constant value that corresponds to a particular data type. Table 3-2 provides examples for each of the primitive data types and the String class.

Table 3-2. *Literal examples*

Type	Literal
byte	int a = -100;
short	int b = 1000;
int	int c = -10000;
long	int d = 100000000000;
float	float e = 12.34f;
double	double f = -56.78;
boolean	boolean iLoveJava = true;
char	char aChar = 'a';
String	String greeting = "Hi, there!";

■ **Note** Declaring a float literal requires appending f to the end of the literal. Otherwise, the compiler tries to make it into a double value and then complains that it can't cast from double to float. Similarly, you can put d at the end of a double literal's declaration. However, that is redundant because double is the default floating-point type.

Literals pop up all over the place, often without anyone stopping to think about it (after all, we're usually trying to get the computer to do something). Every time we write a loop that starts at 0 and counts to some value, we use a literal (in that case, an integer literal). A number of other literals are common in nearly all programming languages and tasks. In set theory (which informs a lot of programming and especially database programming), the only three values that matter are 0, 1, and many. Consequently, 0 and 1 appear over and over again throughout all kinds of software. The empty string (""—sometimes handy for comparing String objects) and the single space (" "—handy for linking String objects without inventing a new and large word in the process) also appear often.

Escaping Characters

Variables of type char can have several special values. First, singe quotation marks ('), double quotation marks ("), and backslashes (\) all have to be marked as special (that's called escaping a character), so that the JVM knows you want one of those characters. Otherwise, it would process all your single quotations as the beginning or end of a char and all your double quotations as the beginning or end of a String object. The backslash character has to be escaped because it is the escape character. If it couldn't itself be escaped, then every backslash would indicate an escaped character, which would be a real problem. *Escaped characters* (often called escape sequences because they consist of at least two characters—the escape character and at least one other character) are also used for non-graphical characters (often called control characters). There's even a character called Bell. It never appears, but it can (if your computer enables it) make your computer beep. The Bell (or Alert) character's escape sequence is \a. All of that might not make sense, so let's consider some examples in Listing 3-3 to make things clearer.

Listing 3-3. Examples of escaping characters

```
// Let's start with double quotation marks
// The following line throws an error because meow isn't defined
System.out.println("My cat says, "meow."");
// so the line has to be
System.out.println("My cat says, \"meow.\"");
// which will produce this output: My cat says, "meow."

// And now single quotation marks
// The following line throws an error because ' never has a matching '
System.out.println("' is my favorite character");
// so the line has to be
System.out.println("\' is my favorite character");
```

```
// which will produce this: ' is my favorite character
// (my actual favorite character is ;)

// And now the backslash itself
// The following line throws an error because it's missing a closing "
// (The compiler takes \" as a literal " and then can't find an end to the string.)
System.out.println("I want a \");
// so the line has to be
System.out.println("I want a \\");
// which will produce this: I want a \
```

Java also supports several special escape sequences (all beginning with a backslash). Table 3-3 shows each escape sequence and describes its effect. It begins with the three we already covered.

Table 3-3. *Escape sequences*

Escape Sequence	Effect
\'	Create a single quotation mark
\"	Create a double quotation mark
\\	Create a backslash character
\n	Create a new line (often called the newline character)
\t	Create a tab
\b	Create a backspace character (which might delete the preceding character, depending on the output device)
\r	Return to the start of the line (but do not make a new line)
\f	Form feed (move to the top of the next page for printers)
\a	The alert (or bell) character

The newline character (\n) sees a lot of use for things like creating readable error messages, separating lines in files, and other output. Tabs are less common but still sometimes used (to line up pieces of output to make things easier to read). The others are much more rarely used, because software developers hardly ever create unstructured output these days. When programmers used punch cards for input and line printers for output, programmers made extensive use of the form feed and start-of-line characters. We still produce plenty of output, of course, but it's usually HTML, XML, or some other structured format.

In addition to being possible values for variables of type char, **String** objects can also contain escape sequences. Many **String** objects contain a newline sequence or two. Listing 3-4 shows a short example.

Listing 3-4. String with escape sequence

```
String errorMessage = "The whatsit didn't work!\nCheck the doohickey.";
System.out.println(errorMessage);
```

That code snippet produces the output in Listing 3-5.

Listing 3-5. Newline output

```
The whatsit didn't work!
Check the doohickey.
```

Wrapper Classes

Each of the primitives (remember, `String` is an object rather than a primitive) has a corresponding class that provides several useful abilities that are otherwise unavailable to a primitive. You can think of the wrapper classes as each being a package of useful abilities wrapped around a primitive of the corresponding type. Table 3-4 shows the corresponding class for each primitive:

Table 3-4. Wrapper classes

Primitive	Class
byte	Byte
short	Short
int	Integer
long	Long
float	Float
double	Double
boolean	Boolean
char	Character

The most commonly used methods of those classes are the various `parse`, `Value`, and `valueOf` methods, because those methods let you turn a `String` into a primitive. Each class also supports `toString` methods to turn primitives into `String` objects. Listing 3-6 shows what you can do with an `int` primitive.

Listing 3-6. Integer example

```
// declare an int
int myInt = 1;

// and a String that contains a number
String myString = "1";

// turn myInt into a String
String myIntString = Integer.toString(myInt);

// turn myString into an int
int myStringInt = Integer.parseInt(myString);

// turn myString into an Integer
// be prepared for an exception if myString does not hold a number
Integer myStringInteger = new Integer(myString);

// and then turn myStringInteger into an int
int myOtherStringInt = myStringInteger.intValue();

// Now for more unusual things
// convert an int to a float (perhaps for further floating-point work)
float myFloat = new Integer(myInt).floatValue();

// convert an int to a byte
// be prepared for an exception if the value is out of byte's range
byte myByte = new Integer(myInt).byteValue();

// convert an int to a long
// no need to worry about an exception this time
long myLong = new Integer(myInt).longValue();

// just for fun, get the binary string representation of myInt
// creates a String object that holds "1"
String myIntBinary = Integer.toBinaryString(myInt);
```

The other numeric primitives (byte, short, long, float, and double) all work in a similar way. You can convert any of them to any other, though you might have to handle an exception if the conversion can't be done with the value you provide. For example, if you have an int variable that holds a value of 300, converting it to a byte gives an error, because a byte can't hold that value. We cover this concept in greater detail in the next chapter, when discussing casting values.

The Boolean and Character classes work a little differently. You can still convert strings to boolean or char values and vice-versa, but you can't convert boolean and char primitives into other primitives. Also, the Boolean class includes an equals method, and the Character class includes many methods for dealing with issues such as characters that are meant to be read from right to left (for example, characters from Arabic and Hebrew) and other special issues that relate only to characters. All of those operations are fairly unusual, though, so we don't cover them. If you want to learn more about them (and good for you if you do), look at the Javadoc for the Boolean and Character classes. As you might recall from Chapter 1, JavaDoc is a special kind of documentation that is built into the code itself. Oracle (the company that makes Java) provides extensive JavaDoc for all the standard Java libraries. You can find the JavaDoc for the Boolean class at http://download.oracle.com/javase/7/docs/api/java/

lang/Boolean.html and the JavaDoc for the Character class at http://download.oracle.com/javase/7/
docs/api/java/lang/Character.html. You can find all the JavaDoc for Java 7 at http://download.oracle.
com/javase/7/docs/api/ (as you can see, the other topics are branches of the overall API
documentation).

Arrays

An *array* is a data structure that holds a group of variables under a single identifier. Java supports arrays
for both primitives and objects. Square brackets after a variable's name indicate that it is an array.
Listing 3-7 shows several arrays and how to manipulate them.

***Listing 3-7.** Arrays of primitives*

```
int[] a; // array declaration without assignment
a = new int[2]; // specify the length of an existing array
int[] b = {1, 2, 3, 4}; // array declaration with assignment
int bLength = b.length; // how to get the length of an array

// arrays start at 0, not 1
b[0] = 2; // have to reassign each value in the array individually
```

Let's look at the code one line at a time. The first line creates an array of int primitives but doesn't
assign anything to it (a is null at that point). The second line shows how to set an array to be a particular
length. If a had values, its values would be replaced by the default values of the new type (0 in this case).
The third line shows how to create an array with a set of starting values. You can use that block
assignment syntax only when creating an array, not when assigning new values to an existing array. The
fourth line shows how to get the length of an array. The last line shows how to reassign one of the values
in an array and shows that array addresses start at 0. (Most programming languages start counting at 0.)

Now let's consider an array of objects in Listing 3-8, which reveals some interesting things.

***Listing 3-8.** Arrays of objects*

```
Integer[] myIntegers = new Integer[4];
for (int i = 0; i < myIntegers.length; i++) {
        myIntegers[i] = new Integer(i);
}
```

Again, let's go line by line. As you can see, the syntax for creating an array of objects differs a bit
from that for primitives. The part to the left of the equal sign looks the same (the kind of object, the array
indicator, and the name of the variable), but the part to the right of the equal sign differs by having the
new keyword before the type of the item going into the array. To create a new instance of an object, we
usually use the new keyword (though other ways exist), which calls a constructor for the object. However,
all of the Integer class's constructors require an object (either an int or a String object that holds an
integer value), so this array ends up holding four null references. (We dive into what null means in a
moment.)

This listing also shows how to loop through an array and, in this case, create an object for each of
the null objects. Notice that we have to use the new keyword again, even though we used it when we
created the array. Because we got four null references rather than actual objects from the original
assignment, we have to create new ones here. In this case, we end up with four Integer objects having
values of 0, 1, 2, and 3.

Java provides a convenience class for arrays. The **Arrays** class consists of many static methods to do handy things such as copy and sort arrays. For example, Listing 3-9 shows one way to sort an array of ints.

Listing 3-9. *Using the Arrays convenience class*

```
int[] a = {5, 4, 3, 2};
// at the top of the program, we had to import
// java.util.Arrays for this to work correctly
Arrays.sort(a);
for (int i = 0; i < a.length; i++) {
  System.out.println(a[i]);
}
```

The result is 2, 3, 4, 5 (each on its own line) in the console.

The Non-Existent Type: null

Java includes a value that isn't anything: null. It refers to a memory address that has not been assigned. In Java terms, that means it refers to an object or primitive that has not been created. As I mentioned in the "Arrays" section, when you create an array without specifying its values, you are creating a collection of null values. They have no memory address, no corresponding primitive or object exists for them, and so they are null. That might sound like a problem, and the whole concept of null often causes novice programmers some trouble. You can keep it straight by remembering that a null is a non-existent reference.

The oft-maligned null has its uses (otherwise, it wouldn't exist—programmers are pragmatic people, most of the time). For example, we often compare an object to null to be sure that something exists before we try to use it. If the graphics library is supposed to give us an object of type Color and we get null instead, we have a problem. So we might compare that Color value to null to ensure that we are getting a Color object and do something useful (such as trying another way or at least logging an error) if not.

Also, it's common practice to create a variable in one place and assign it in another place. In between the creation and assignment, the value of that variable might be null (it also might not be null because some primitives, such as int, have default values). This technique is handy because we might want to assign different values to the variable based on some logic. For example, a series of if-else statements or a switch statement might contain code to assign the value of a variable. Let's consider a small example (from a minesweeper game), shown in Listing 3-10.

Listing 3-10. *Using a null value*

```
public getMineIcon(int x, int y) {

// x and y are the position within the game grid
  int numberOfAdjacentMines = getNumberOfAdjacentMines(x, y);

  MineIcon mineIcon = null; // here's our null
```

```
  if (numberOfAdjacentMines == 1) {
    mineIcon = new MineIcon(1);
  } else if (numberOfAdjacentMines == 2) {
    mineIcon = new MineIcon(2);
  }
  // and so on up to 8

  return mineIcon;
}
```

In this case, we can assume a MineIcon class exists and that its constructor will take two integer values and return an icon (a type of image) that shows the value of that integer argument. Because a square in a minesweeper game can have no more than eight neighboring mines, we stop at eight. We also let the method return null, to represent the case where a square has no neighboring mines. Consequently, the code that calls this method then has to know what to do with a null value. As it happens, the setIcon method that we need to use accepts a null argument as a way of saying that no icon needs to be set.

We create a full-blown minesweeper program in Chapter 7, "Creating a User Interface." When we do, you see a different way to use set the mine icon, but it still uses a null reference. For now, just remember that null is just another value (though a special one that indicates a non-existent reference) and that it can be used for purposes other than just checking for missing objects.

Enumerations

An *enumeration* (often written as "enum") is a data type that consists of a fixed number of constants. For example, if you are writing a game that involves navigation, you might have an enumeration to define the four cardinal directions, similar to the one shown in Listing 3-11.

Listing 3-11. Enum for directions

```
public enum Direction {
    NORTH, EAST, SOUTH, WEST;
}
```

As Listing 3-11 shows, the declaration of an enumeration consists of the enum keyword, a name for the enumeration, and the values that comprise the enumeration. The values are just names and have no type of their own. That works because we need unique identifiers but don't need a type for each one.

The value of enumerations is that they are type-safe (meaning that it can't be confused with another type—enums used to be created with integers, so confusing an enum with an integer was a real problem). Without enumerations, we'd have to set up constants in a different way—usually with integers, as shown in Listing 3-12.

Listing 3-12. Constants to define directions

```
public static final int NORTH = 0;
public static final int EAST = 1;
public static final int SOUTH = 2;
public static final int WEST = 3;
```

▪ **Caution** Do not write collections of constants this way. They can be compared to int values, and that's almost certain to be the wrong thing to do. That's why Java has enumerations.The enumeration value, `Direction.NORTH`, can't be treated as an integer (not even by accident), whereas the constant, `NORTH`, can be. Also, constants are static and final (and often public). Enumerations remove the need for those modifiers, which gives us greater flexibility when using enumerations.

Each `enum` is actually a class. (You might have noticed that its declaration syntax is similar to a class.) All `enum` objects implicitly extend `java.lang.Enum`. That lets us make more meaningful enums than just lists of constants. To continue with our example, we can set the degrees for each direction, as shown in Listing 3-13.

Listing 3-13. Enum with more information

```
public enum Direction {
  NORTH (0),
  EAST (90),
  SOUTH (180),
  WEST (270);

  private final int degrees;
  Direction(int degrees) {
    this.degrees = degrees;
  }

  public int getDegrees() {
    return degrees;
  }
}
```

From there, we can write code to get the additional information associated with each value in the enumeration, as shown in Listing 3-14.

Listing 3-14. Getting details from an enum

```
for (Direction d : Direction.values()) {
  System.out.println(d + " is " + d.degrees + "degrees.");
}
```

We can also write methods that work with the enumeration's values. For example, we can write a method that, given a direction in degrees, tells you which cardinal direction is closest. Listing 3-15 shows one way to write such a method.

Listing 3-15. *findCardinalDirection method*

```
public static Direction findCardinalDirection (int degrees) {
  if (degrees < 45) {
    return NORTH;
  } else if (degrees < 135) {
    return EAST;
  } else if (degrees < 225) {
    return SOUTH;
  } else if (degrees < 315) {
    return WEST;
  } else {
    return NORTH;
  }
}
```

You might also notice the different syntax for iterating through a for loop. That syntax is not unique to enumerations, but it is especially handy for them. We cover these alternate ways of using a for loop when we get to looping in a later chapter.

As you can see, an enumeration is far more powerful than a simple list of constants. It's also safer, because no one can confuse Direction.North with 0.

Listing 3-16 shows the full code for the Direction enumeration.

Listing 3-16. *Complete enumeration example*

```
package com.bryantcs.examples.enumExample;

public enum Direction {
  NORTH (0),
  EAST (90),
  SOUTH (180),
  WEST (270);

  private final int degrees;
  Direction(int degrees) {
    this.degrees = degrees;
  }

  public int getDegrees() {
    return degrees;
  }

  // static because it doesn't rely on a particular direction
  public static Direction findCardinalDirection (int degrees) {
    if (degrees < 45) {
      return NORTH;
    } else if (degrees < 135) {
      return EAST;
    } else if (degrees < 225) {
      return SOUTH;
    } else if (degrees < 315) {
      return WEST;
```

```
    } else {
      return NORTH;
    }
  }
}
```

Now that we have our completed enumeration, we need a test program to see how it works. Listing 3-17 shows a program class that does the job.

Listing 3-17. *A test class for our enumeration*

```
package com.bryantcs.examples.enumExample;

public class EnumExample {

  public static void main(String[] args) {
    int[] compassPoints = {22, 77, 144, 288};
    for (int i = 0; i < compassPoints.length; i++) {
      System.out.println(compassPoints[i] + " degrees is (very roughly) "
        + Direction.findCardinalDirection(compassPoints[i]));
    }
    for (Direction d : Direction.values()) {
      System.out.println(d + " is " + d.getDegrees() + " degrees.");
    }
  }
}
```

EnumExample produces the output in the console shown in Listing 3-18.

Listing 3-18. *EnumExample output*

```
22 degrees is (very roughly) NORTH
77 degrees is (very roughly) EAST
144 degrees is (very roughly) SOUTH
288 degrees is (very roughly) WEST
NORTH is 0 degrees.
EAST is 90 degrees.
SOUTH is 180 degrees.
WEST is 270 degrees.
```

Summary

In this chapter, we learned the basics about the various data types that are available in Java. We found out:

- The size restrictions of the various numeric data types
- How the boolean data type works
- How char variables and String objects work and a bit about how they can interact

- How arrays work

- What a null is and how to use one to good effect

- How to create and use enumerations

We make repeated use of all these concepts and techniques throughout the rest of the book. As we work more with Java, you'll do a lot with primitives, the `String` object, primitive and `String` literals, and arrays. Enumerations appear less often in most code, but they offer important advantages (most notably type safety) when we need them.

CHAPTER 4

Operators

Java includes many operators, from ordinary mathematical operators such as a minus sign (-) to operators that only make sense for object-oriented programming, such as `instanceof`. To start with, let's look at the list of operators in Table 4-1.

Table 4-1. Java Operators

Category	Operators
postfix	expr++ expr--
unary	++expr --expr +expr -expr ~ !
casting	(*type*)
multiplicative	* / %
additive	+ -
shift	<< >> >>>
relational	< > <= >= instanceof
equality	== !=
bitwise AND	&
bitwise exclusive OR	^
bitwise inclusive OR	|
logical AND	&&

Continued

Category	Operators
logical OR	‖
ternary	? :
assignment	= += -= *= /= %= &= ^= |= <<= >>= >>>=

Operator Precedence

The first thing to know about operators is that they have precedence. I can't forget Mr. Smith in junior high algebra class teaching us to memorize Please Excuse My Dear Aunt Sally. That odd phrase is an effective mnemonic for the order of operations (another name for operator precedence) in algebra. It shortens to PEMDAS, which gives us Parentheses, Exponent, Multiplication,Division, Addition, and Subtraction. Thanks to operator precedence (and, in my case, Mr. Smith), when we work with algebra equations, we know to resolve parentheses before we resolve exponents, exponents before multiplication, and so on.

The same kind of thing holds true in Java (and many other programming languages). However, as shown previously, Java has a lot more than six operators. Also, Java has some operators that have the same level of precedence. In those cases, precedence proceeds from left to right for binary operators (except assignment operators) and right to left for assignment operators. That's probably as clear as mud, but we get to some examples shortly that clarify the order of operations and identify some of the problem spots where people often trip.

The Missing Operator: Parentheses

Parentheses aren't in the list of Java operators, but they act as an operator with the highest precedence. Anything in parentheses is resolved first. When a line has several sets of parentheses, they are resolved from innermost to outermost and from left to right. Let's consider some examples in Listing 4-1.

Listing 4-1. *Parentheses as an operator*

```
System.out.println(2 + 4 / 2); // division processed first, so prints 4
System.out.println((2 + 4) / 2); // addition processed first, so prints 3
System.out.println((2 + 4) / 3 * 2); // prints 4, not 1 - see below for why
System.out.println((2 + 4) / (3 * 2)); // prints 1
System.out.println((2 + 4) / (2 * 2)); // prints 1 - note the truncation
System.out.println((2.0 + 4.0) / (2.0 * 2.0)); // prints 1.5
```

The bolded line prints 4 because the division operator gets processed before the multiplication operator. That happens because operators of equal precedence get processed from left to right. In algebra, multiplication comes before division. However, Java is not algebra, and that sometimes trips up new Java developers who remember their algebra. (I've tripped over that difference at least once.)

The fifth line prints 1 because we use integer literals (as we covered in the previous chapter). Consequently, we get back an integer literal. Java truncates (that is, throws away) any remainder when dealing with integers, so 1.5 becomes 1. The last line uses floating-point literals, so it returns 1.5. A value of 1.9 would also be truncated to 1. Truncation is not a kind of rounding; a truncated value has any value to the right of the decimal place removed.

As a rule, remember to use parentheses to clarify your code and to ensure the proper order for your operations. I mention clarity first for a reason: Clarity helps a lot. If you can gain clarity by splitting a line onto multiple lines to make your operations clear for other developers (and for yourself when you return to the code at a later date), then do so. Your fellow developers will thank you if they can understand your code without a struggle.

Postfix Operators

The term *postfix* has a number of meanings in mathematics, linguistics, and other fields. In computer science, it means an operator that follows an expression. Java's two postfix operators increment (increase by one) and decrement (decrease by one) values. Listing 4-2 shows some examples:

Listing 4-2. *Postfix operators*

```
private int getC() {
  int c = 0;
  c++; // c = 1 now
  c--; // c = 0 now
  return c++; //returns 0;
}
```

So why does that return 0? Because the postfix operators first return the original value and then assign the new value to the variable. That particular language detail bites a lot of new Java programmers. To fix it, use the unary ++ operator (next on our list) before the expression rather than the postfix operator after the expression or move your return statement to its own line. Parentheses around the expression (c++) do not make this method return 1, by the way, because c would have been set to 0 within the parentheses.

Unary Operators

Strictly speaking, a *unary operator* is an operator that takes just one operand. By that definition, the postfix operators are also unary operators. However, Java distinguishes between the postfix operators and the other unary operators. As we learned previously, the postfix operators return the value before the postfix operation has been applied. The unary operators return their values after the operator has been applied. Table 4-2 briefly describes the unary operators (other than the postfix operators):

Table 4-2. Unary operators

Operator	Name	Description
++expr	Prefix increment	Adds 1 to the value of the expression that follows
--expr	Prefix decrement	Subtracts 1 from the value of the expression that follows
+expr	Unary plus	Indicates a positive number (usually redundant)
-expr	Unary minus	Negates an expression (including literals)
~	Bitwise complement	Performs a bit-by-bit reversal of an integer value
!	Logical complement	Reverses true and false

Let's consider a code example that exercises each of the unary operators (see Listing 4-3):

Listing 4-3. Unary operators

```
byte a = 0;
++a; // unary prefix increment operator - now a has a value of 1
--a; // unary prefix decrement operator - back to 0
byte b = +1; // unary plus operator (unnecessary)
byte c = -1; // unary minus operator to create a negative number
System.out.println(~b); // bitwise complement operator - prints -2
System.out.println(~c); // bitwise complement operator - prints 0
boolean myCatScratchesTheCouch = false;
System.out.println(!myCatScratchesTheCouch); // logical complement operator - prints true
```

Understanding the Bitwise Complement Operator

Java (and all programming languages) store values in one or more bytes, and each byte consists of 32 bits. When we talk about bytes in this context, we mean the units computers use for memory. That's not the same as Java's data type called "Byte" (which has a minimum value of -128 and a maximum value of of 127). The JVM stores a value of one as the following binary string: 00000000000000000000000000000001 (a 32-bit binary value that consists of 31 zeroes and a single one). When you use the bitwise complement operator on it, the JVM turns all the zeroes into ones and all the ones into zeroes, resulting in 11111111111111111111111111111110, which evaluates to -2. Similarly, -1 in binary is 11111111111111111111111111111111. Because that's all ones, the bitwise complement operator turns it to all zeroes, so its value is 0.

I won't blame you if you think that's all meaningless trivia, but the bitwise complement operator does have real-world uses. For example, in graphics programming, the color white is generally represented by all the bits being 1. Applying the bitwise complement operator sets all the bits to 0, which generally indicates the color black. The same principle applies to other colors (which have various bits set to 0 or 1). In this fashion, a graphics program can quickly create a negative of an image without any mathematical processing.

The bitwise complement operator promotes the values of byte, short, and char variables to 32 bits before applying the ~ operator. The result of the operator is an int in those cases. That's why the binary strings have 32 characters. This process is called *unary numeric promotion*. Consider the following code in Listing 4-4:

Listing 4-4. *Unary numeric promotion*

```
byte a = 0;
Byte b = new Byte(a); // no problem
Byte c = new Byte(~a); // won't compile because the Byte constructor cannot accept an int
int d = ~a; // no problem
```

Casting

Software developers often find that they need a variable of one type to be a variable of another type. In Java (and most programming languages), you can't change the type of a variable. Instead, you should create a new variable and convert the existing variable into the new variable's type. That process is called *casting*, and Java provides an operator of sorts for doing it. I say, "of sorts," because the casting operator differs according to the data type to which you're casting. In particular, you wrap parentheses around the name of the type to which you're casting and put that operator before the value you want to cast. Casting is often necessary to prevent the compiler from throwing errors when we convert one data type to another. As ever, examples go a long way toward clarifying things (see Listing 4-5).

Listing 4-5. *Casting*

```
// Cast a byte to an int
byte b = 123;
int bInt = b; // no casting necessary

// Cast an int to a short
int i = 123;
short s = (short) i; //(short) is the casting operator - beware of values that are too large

// Cast a float to an int
float f = 12.34f;
int floatInt = (int) f; // floatInt = 12 - the original value is truncated

// Cast a char to a String - oops
char c = 'c'; // can't directly cast a char to a string
Character cChar = new Character(c); // so get a Character wrapper object for our char
String s = cChar.toString(); // and get a String object from the wrapper
```

In the first example shown previously, casting a **byte** to an **int** does not require a cast operator. Because there's no possibility of data loss (an int can hold any value that a **byte** can hold), the JVM does what's sometimes called "an implicit upcast"—implicit because you don't have to add any syntax to make it happen and upcast because you've gone from smaller to larger in terms of both value range and number of bits. It's also called a *widening cast*.

In the second example, casting an int to a short, we must have a cast operator, to tell the compiler that we really mean to do that. That's necessary because data loss can occur when casting from a type with more bits (32 in this case) to a type with fewer bits (16 in this case). Suppose i equals 65537. s would then equal 1. That's because the maximum value of a short is 65536. The JVM divides the original value by the maximum value of the variable you're casting into and returns the remainder. As you can imagine, that can produce havoc and be hard to track down. As a rule, don't use narrowing casts (which place the value of a data type with more available bits into a data type with fewer available bits). Widening casts (which place the value of a data type with fewer available bits into a data type with more available bits) aren't a problem (though don't do it unless you have a reason for it), but narrowing casts are dangerous.

The third example shows another hazard involved in casting: loss of precision. If you cast a float or a double to an integral type (any of the numeric types with no floating point component), the JVM truncates (that is, removes) the mantissa. So 12.34 becomes 12. Even if it was originally 12.999, it would get truncated to 12. In other words, it doesn't round; it removes. Similarly, casting from a double to a float can lose precision, because a double has more bits than a float and can therefore have greater precision. Again, narrowing casts are risky. Hard-to-find errors can arise from narrowing casts. Don't do it unless you must, and it's a good idea to add some defensive code (which we get to shortly).

■ **Caution** Widening casts are fine; however, narrowing casts are dangerous. Take steps to ensure that your narrowing casts can't receive values that cause trouble.

The fourth example isn't a cast, but it shows how to get from a primitive (a char in this case) to a String. The same pattern applies for all the primitives: First get a wrapper for the primitive and then use the wrapper's toString method.

I mentioned defensive coding for narrowing casts. Defensive coding is a good idea any time you can't be sure the provided value won't cause a problem. In fact, in some kinds of applications (distributed applications are a prime example), it's standard practice to validate (that is, ensure workable values for) all the arguments to a method. Listing 4-6 is an example of defensive coding for a narrowing cast from an int to a byte:

Listing 4-6. *Defensive coding for a narrowing cast*

```
private static byte intToByte(int i) {
  if (i > Byte.MAX_VALUE || i < Byte.MIN_VALUE) {
    throw new IllegalArgumentException("integer argument " +
        "is too large or too small to cast to a byte");
  }
  return (byte) i;
}
```

Then the code that calls intToByte can decide what to do about the problem. Moving the validation to its own method can be a good idea, both to encapsulate each bit of validation and to permit multiple methods to make use of the same bit of validation. Many systems have validation classes (and sometimes packages) that offer a number of such methods, so that the methods in other classes can make use of consistent validation. You get used to that kind of design as you learn to use object-oriented languages, including Java.

Multiplicative Operators

Java has three multiplicative operators: multiplication (*), division (/), and modulus (%). (The modulus operator is often called mod or modulo; in Java shops, you hear expressions such as "a mod b" when someone reads code aloud.)

As I mentioned earlier when discussing parentheses, there's no implicit order of operations between these three operators. To the JVM, they all have the same precedence. Because that's the case, the JVM processes them from left to right. Again, Java isn't algebra, though some of the operators and concepts exist in both.

Multiplication and division are obvious enough, but let's look at the modulus operator. As ever, examples help a lot (see Listing 4-7).

Listing 4-7. Modulus operator examples

```
int a = 9;
int b = 2;
int c = a % b; // c equals 1
float f = 1.9f;
float g = 0.4f;
float h = f % g; // h equals 0.3 - but beware of rounding
```

As this brief listing shows, the modulus operator divides the first operand by the second operand and returns the remainder.

▓ **Caution** Beware of rounding when using the modulus operator on floats and doubles. I rounded this to 0.3, but my JVM actually assigned 0.29999995 to h when I ran this bit of code in Eclipse. That might not matter if you're plotting the location of an avatar in a video game (because the screen has a fairly low number of pixels, so the error isn't large enough to put the avatar in the wrong spot). However, imagine the same error in code that controls a rocket going to Mars. Then it's a large enough error to ensure that your rocket doesn't end up in the right spot to go into orbit, and that's an expensive error indeed. Rounding tends to be problematic in many applications.

Additive Operators

You might not think I'd have much to say about plus (+) and minus (-). However, even they have subtleties worth noting when used in a Java application. As with the multiplicative operators, the order of precedence for the additive operators is the same, so they get processed from left to right, even when the minus precedes the plus operator on a line. That usually doesn't matter. However, when it does matter, it can be a difficult problem to spot.

Also, the plus sign is the string concatenation operator. As we see in various examples, `someString + someOtherString = aThirdString`. Strictly speaking, the addition operator and the string concatenation operator are different operators. However, they use the same character. The JVM figures whether to use a plus sign as the addition operator or as the string concatenation operator by context. If the JVM determines that the context is numeric, it performs addition operations. If the JVM determines that the context is textual, it performs concatenation operations. Listing 4-8 demonstrates what happens when the JVM encounters different contexts:

Listing 4-8. *The ShiftDemo context switching example*

```
int a = 1;
int b = 2;
int c = 3;
System.out.println(a + b + c);
System.out.println("a + b + c = " + a + b + c);
System.out.println("a + b + c = " + (a + b + c));
```

When run in a program, that code produces the following output (see Listing 4-9):

Listing 4-9. *Contect switching example output*

```
6
a + b + c = 123
a + b + c = 6
```

The context for the first line is numeric, because the first value processed by the `println` method is numeric. The context for the second line is textual because the first value processed by the `println` method is a String literal. The third line gets the right value because the parentheses force the addition to happen first, even though the context is textual.

Shift Operators

The shift operators take us back to working with bits. The shift operators require two operands: The integral (no floating-point values allowed) value to shift and the number of places to shift the bits that comprise the value. The signed left shift operator (<<) shifts bits to the left. The signed right shift operator (>>) shifts bits to the right. The signed right shift operator (>>>) shifts bits to the right and fills the left bits with zeroes.

■ **Note** The shift operators work only on integer values.

Listing 4-10 demonstrates what the shift operators do to the value of an int variable.

Listing 4-10. *ShiftDemo*

```
package com.apress.javaforabsolutebeginners .examples.shiftDemo;

public class ShiftDemo {

  public static void main(String[] args) throws Exception {
    int b = 127;
    System.out.println("b: " + b);
```

```
    System.out.println("b as binary: " + Integer.toBinaryString(b));
    String leftShiftString = Integer.toBinaryString(b<<3);
    System.out.println("binary after signed left shifting 3 places: " +
      leftShiftString);
    System.out.println("value of b after signed shifting left 3 places: " +
      Integer.parseInt(leftShiftString, 2));
    String rightShiftString = Integer.toBinaryString(b>>3);
    System.out.println("binary after signed shifting right 3 places: " +
      rightShiftString);
    System.out.println("value of b after signed shifting right 3 places: " +
      Integer.parseInt(rightShiftString, 2));
    String unsignedRightShiftString = Integer.toBinaryString(b>>>3);
    System.out.println("binary after unsigned shifting right 3 places: " +
      unsignedRightShiftString);
    System.out.println("value of b after unsigned shifting right 3 places: " +
      Integer.parseInt(unsignedRightShiftString, 2));
    b = -128;
    System.out.println("Resetting b to " + b);
    System.out.println("b as binary: " + Integer.toBinaryString(b));
    unsignedRightShiftString = Integer.toBinaryString(b>>>3);
    System.out.println("binary after unsigned shifting right 3 places: " +
unsignedRightShiftString);
    System.out.println("value of b after unsigned shifting right 3 places: " +
      Integer.parseInt(unsignedRightShiftString, 2));
  }
}
```

Running ShiftDemo produces the following output (see Listing 4-11):

Listing 4-11. ShiftDemo output

```
b: 127
b as binary: 1111111
binary after signed left shifting 3 places: 1111111000
value of b after signed shifting left 3 places: 1016
binary after signed shifting right 3 places: 1111
value of b after signed shifting right 3 places: 15
binary after unsigned shifting right 3 places: 1111
value of b after unsigned shifting right 3 places: 15
Resetting b to -128
b as binary: 11111111111111111111111110000000
binary after unsigned shifting right 3 places: 11111111111111111111111110000
value of b after unsigned shifting right 3 places: 536870896
```

ShiftDemo and its output reveal a number of things worth knowing about the shift operators:

- The left-hand operator represents the value to be shifted, and the right-hand operator indicates the number of bits by which to shift (known as the shift distance).

- Using a shift operator on byte, char, or short values promotes those values to `int` values. Unary numeric promotion strikes again. It's unary because both operands are separately promoted before the operation is performed. So, a byte value shifted by another byte value leads to two separate unary promotions before the shift operation happens. Sometimes, that doesn't matter. Other times, you might need to account for the promotion when assigning the result of the shift to another variable.

- Signed shifting causes trouble with negative values. In the ShiftDemo example, I didn't use the signed shift operators (<< and >>) because doing so on that value produces an exception. That happens because of the way Java stores negative numbers; shifting the bits that comprise a negative number results in a binary string that Java can't recognize as any number.

- `Integer.toBinaryString` shows the minimum possible number of digits. In many of the values shown by the `ShiftDemo` results, the internal representation is 32 bits long, with all the bits to the left of the value shown being 0 (that is, those values are 0-padded). That's why the binary strings for the unsigned right shift operator are 32 bits long.

- When used on a relatively small negative number, the unsigned shift operator can create a large positive number. That happens because the result of the operation is a string of binary digits that the JVM can recognize as a number. However, that large number might not be what you have in mind. And that takes us to our last point:

- Shifting is tricky. Test very carefully when you use the shift operators.

So why use the shift operators? Because they are the fastest possible operators. The simplest and fastest operation a computer can do is to shift a binary value. If you can be sure that shifting produces the values you want or if you happen to be working with values that aren't really values but rather collections of switches (such as graphics settings), the shift operators can provide efficient ways to manipulate those values or switches. We cover the idea of using a value as a series of switches when we get to the bitwise operators, later in this chapter.

Relational Operators

The relational operators compare things to one another. In particular, they determine whether one value is greater than, less than, equal to, or not equal to another value. For the relational operators to work, the items being compared have to be comparable. That sounds obvious, but it has a particular meaning in Java. The language specification defines what it means to be comparable for the primitives. Thus, you can compare an `int` to a `float` and get a meaningful result (the JVM promotes the `int` to a `float` and then does the comparison). So long as one or the other can be cast to the other value, Java can meaningfully compare primitives, and Eclipse tells you when they can't be.

> (greater than), < (less than), >= (greater than or equal to), and <= (less than or equal to) all work on primitives, but they don't work on objects. Conversely, `instanceof` works on objects but not on primitives. Java does provide ways to compare objects to one another, but not through any operators. We get to comparing objects later in this chapter.

Listing 4-12 illustrates the comparison of primitives

Listing 4-12. *Comparing primitives*

```
int a = 0;
float b = 1.0f;
System.out.println(a > b);
```

That bit of code prints "false" in the console.

The instanceof operator can be a bit tricky, because a class that extends another class is also an instance of the parent class. Consider the following small program, implemented in three classes (see Listing 4-13).

Listing 4-13. *instanceof test*

```
package com.apress.javaforabsolutebeginners .examples.instanceofTest;

public class Person {
  String firstName;
  String lastName;

  public Person (String firstName, String lastName) {
    this.firstName = firstName;
    this.lastName = lastName;
  }
}

package com.apress.javaforabsolutebeginners .examples.instanceofTest;

public class Student extends Person {
  String schoolName;

  public Student (String firstName, String lastName, String schoolName) {
    super(firstName, lastName);
    this.schoolName = schoolName;
  }
}


package com.apress.javaforabsolutebeginners .examples.instanceofTest;

public class InstanceofTest {

  public static void main(String[] args) {
    Student student = new Student("Sam", "Spade", "Noir U");
    System.out.println(student instanceof Student);
    System.out.println(student instanceof Person);
  }

}
```

61

Both print statements print "true" in the console. After all, a student is a person. The nature of object-oriented programming, where one class always extends another, demands that the `instanceof` operator works this way.

The `instanceof` operator can cause subtle problems. In particular, the `instanceof` operator won't throw an error if its right-hand operand is `null`. Instead, it always returns `false` in those cases. If you use something like `myClass instanceof myBaseClass` and have inadvertently set `myBaseClass` to `null`, the result is `false`. You might then think that `myClass` isn't an instance of `myBaseClass`, but you can't actually know that if you're comparing to `null`. This is another great place to practice defensive programming and make sure you're not getting `null` there.

If you're careful to make sure you know the relationships between the classes you use (which is part of being a good object-oriented programmer) and to ensure that you're not comparing to `null`, you shouldn't get into too much trouble with the `instanceof` operator.

Equality Operators

Java has two equality operators: `==` (equals) and `!=` (not equals). (The exclamation point, both in this context and in others, is sometimes called a "bang" by software developers.) The equality operator (`==`) and the inequality operator (`!=`)work the same way (each is the negative of the other), so I'll confine this discussion to the equality operator.

Java uses a single equal sign as the base assignment operator (we get to the assignment operators later in this chapter), so it can't use a single equal sign for comparisons. Consequently, Java (and the other languages that share Java's basic syntax) uses two equal signs.

A common mistake among folks new to Java (and not-so-new folks who aren't careful with their typing) is to use a single equal sign (the assignment operator) when they should use two equal signs (the equality operator) and accidentally assign a value to a variable rather than compare the variable's value to something else. Consider the following example in Listing 4-14:

Listing 4-14*. Accidental assignment*

```
for (int counter = 0; counter < 10; counter++) {
  if (counter = 0) { // should be == rather than =
    // do something
  }
}
```

That bit of code, if not corrected, causes an infinite loop. In every iteration, `counter` gets set to 0, so its value is always less than 10. Fortunately, Eclipse and other modern development tools warn you when you do this. You can still do it, but at least you do it intentionally (though you really should re-structure your code if you need to reset a value). I have to admit that I have gotten into exactly that situation more than once (because of poor typing), though never since I started using Eclipse, thanks to its warnings. That's one of the reasons I had you install Eclipse at the start of this journey.

For primitives, the equality operators work exactly as you probably think they would. However, for objects, the equality operators indicate whether two references refer to the same instance. As ever, examples help (see Listing 4-15).

Listing 4-15. *Equality operator examples*

```
int a = 0;
int b = 1;
String s = "s";
String sToo = "s";
System.out.println(a == b);
System.out.println(s == sToo);
```

That bit of code prints "true" for a == b and "false" for s == sToo. That's because s and sToo are references to different instances of the **String** object. So, even though they have the same value, they are not equal in the eyes of the equality operators. Also, s == **"s"** prints false, because the string literal produces yet another instance of the **String** class.

To compare objects (including instances of the **String** class), Java programmers use the **equals** method. Any object whose instances can be compared to each other should implement the **equals** method (which is defined in the **Object** class). Because it makes sense for **String** objects to be compared to one another, the **String** class implements the **equals** method. That way, we can use code similar to Listing 4-16 to compare instances of **String**.

Listing 4-16. *Testing equality for objects*

```
String s = "s";
String sToo = "s";
System.out.println(s.equals(sToo));
System.out.println(s.equals("s"));
```

Both of these print statements produce "true" in the console. We cover comparing objects in more depth later in this chapter.

Bitwise AND Operator (&)

The bitwise AND operator (&) compares two binary values and sets each bit to 1 where each bit in the two values being compared is 1. As usual, an example helps (see Listing 4-17).

Listing 4-17. *Bitwise AND operator (&)*

```
Byte byte1 = Byte.parseByte("01010101", 2); // byte1 = 85
Byte byte2 = Byte.parseByte("00111111", 2); // byte2 = 63
int result = byte1 & byte2; // result = 21
```

The value of result is 21 because taking the bits where both bits in the compared value is 1 gives a binary result of 00010101, which happens to be the binary representation of 21.

Bitwise Exclusive OR Operator (^)

The bitwise Exclusive OR (often shortened to XOR) operator (^) compares two binary values and sets each bit to 1 if the bits differ. Again, examples make the best explanations for this kind of thing (see Listing 4-18).

Listing 4-18. Bitwise Exclusive OR operator (^)

```
Byte byte1 = Byte.parseByte("01010101", 2); // byte1 = 85
Byte byte2 = Byte.parseByte("00111111", 2); // byte2 = 63
int result = byte1 ^ byte2; // result = 106
```

The value of result is 106 because taking the bits where either bit in the compared values is 1 gives a binary result of 01101010, which happens to be the binary representation of 106.

Bitwise Inclusive OR Operator (|)

The bitwise Inclusive OR operator (|) compares two binary values and sets each bit to 1 if either bit is 1. Again, examples make the best explanations for this kind of thing (see Listing 4-19).

Listing 4-19. Bitwise Inclusive OR operator (|)

```
Byte byte1 = Byte.parseByte("01010101", 2); // byte1 = 85
Byte byte2 = Byte.parseByte("00111111", 2); // byte2 = 63
int result = byte1 | byte2; // result = 127
```

The value of result is 127 because taking the bits where either bit is 1 in the compared values is 1 gives a binary result of 01101010, which happens to be the binary representation of 127.

You might ask when anyone would ever use these bitwise operators. They have a number of useful applications, actually. Game developers often use bitwise operations for high-speed graphics processing. Again, imagine a game in which two objects merge somehow (maybe shooting a blue object with a red bullet makes the object turn purple). The bitwise and operator (&) provides a high-speed way to determine the new color. The bitwise operators are also often used to see which combination of mouse buttons have been pressed or to see whether a mouse button has been held down while the mouse was moved (creating a drag operation). So they might seem like oddball operators, but they definitely have their uses.

Logical AND Operator (&&)

The logical AND operator (&&) returns true if both arguments are true and false if either one is false. It's most often used within if statements but is handy anywhere you need to be sure that two boolean values are true. Also, the logical AND operator is one of the most-often used operators. If we had a nickel for every time we typed &&....

Listing 4-20 is an example.

Listing 4-20. Logical AND operator (&&)

```
if (2 > 1 && 1 > 0) {
  System.out.println("Numbers work as expected");
}
```

In that code snippet, we have three operators. Thanks to operator precedence, the two comparison operators (>) get evaluated before the logical AND operator (&&), so we don't need parentheses to make things work correctly (though you might want parentheses for clarity, depending on your coding style).

Also, you can chain multiple logical AND operators (and most other operators), as shown in Listing 4-21.

Listing 4-21. Chaining logical AND operators

```
if (3 > 2 && 2 > 1 && 1 > 0) {
  System.out.println("Numbers work as expected");
}
```

The result of the middle comparison (2 > 1) serves as an operator to both of the logical AND operators. That kind of chaining is common in all programming problems, regardless of language. We're fortunate that Java makes it easy to do.

Logical OR Operator (||)

The logical AND operator (||) returns true if either of its arguments are true and false only if both arguments are false. Otherwise, it works just like the logical AND operator.

Listing 4-22 is an example.

Listing 4-22. Logical AND operator (&&)

```
if (2 > 1 || 1 < 0) {
  System.out.println("Numbers work as expected");
}
```

As with logical AND operators, you can chain multiple logical AND operators, as shown in Listing 4-23.

Listing 4-23. Chaining logical AND operators

```
if (3 > 2 || 2 < 1 || 1 < 0) {
  System.out.println("Numbers work as expected");
}
```

■ **Note** Eclipse warns us that we have dead code within the comparisons when we run this code. Because 2 is always greater than 1, the JVM won't try to compare 1 to 0, so Eclipse tells us that we can remove that comparison. Of course, real-world examples check to make sure that a data stream isn't null and has at least some content. Listing 4-24 contains that code.

Listing 4-24. A more realistic use for the logical OR operator

```
if (dataStream == null || dataStream.length == 0) {
  log.error("No data available!");
}
```

Again, the equality operators have higher precedence, so we don't need additional parentheses.

Assignment Operators

The assignment operators set values and assign object references. The basic assignment operator (=) is by far the most often used operator. Every time we put something like `int = 0` (assigning a value to a primitive) or `Date now = new Date()` (assigning an object reference to a variable) into an example, we use the basic assignment operator.

Java provides a number of compound assignment operators (often called shortcut operators). Listing 4-25 is an example of one of the compound assignment operators.

Listing 4-25*. Compound assignment operator*

```
int myInt = 2;
myInt *= 2; // equivalent to myInt = myInt * 2;
System.out.println(myInt); // prints 4;
```

Each of the compound operators applies the first operator within the compound operator and the value after the compound operator and then applies the assignment operator. In the previous example, the multiplication operator is applied to `myInt` with the value after the compound operator (in this case, doubling the value of `myInt`) and then sets `myInt` to the result.

The compound assignment operators can lead to unexpected results. Consider the following code snippet in Listing 4-26. Before reading past the snippet, ask yourself "What is the value of `myInt` at the end?"

Listing 4-26*. Compound assignment problem*

```
int myInt = 2;
myInt *= (myInt = 4);
System.out.println(myInt);
```

The last assignment before the print statement is `myInt = 4`, so you might think the answer must be 4. But we set `myInt` to 4 and then multiply it by itself, so you might think the answer must be 16. In fact, neither is correct. The code snippet prints 8. It might seem odd at first, but it makes sense once you understand how the JVM deals with a compound operator. When the JVM encounters the compound operator, it knows myInt equals 2. Until the entire operator is resolved, the value of `myInt` can't be changed. (This is the only case we know of where parentheses aren't processed first, by the way.) Consequently, the assignment within the line is ignored, but the value within the assignment is used. After all that, the result is 2 times 4, or 8.

■ **Note** This issue is pretty much an academic curiosity. It's an issue the developers of the Java language had to account for, but smart programmers don't write code like this. Smart programmers break up their operations so that the effect of each line is clear with minimal interpretation. Remember, if you program for a living, other programmers have to read your code and understand it, and very few development shops will tolerate this kind of confused and confusing code.

Table 4.3 shows all the assignment operators, including the compound operators.

Table 4-3. *The assignment operators*

Operator	Description
=	This is the basic assignment operator.
+=	Add the right-hand operand to the left-hand operand and assign the result to the left-hand operand. x += 2 is the same as x = x + 2.
-=	Subtract the right-hand operand from the left-hand operand and assign the result to the left-hand operand. x -= 2 is the same as x = x – 2.
*=	Multiply the right-hand operand by the left-hand operand and assign the result to the left-hand operand. x *= 2 is the same as x = x * 2.
/=	Divide the right-hand operand by the left-hand operand and assign the result to the left-hand operand. x /= 2 is the same as x = x / 2.
%=	Use the right-hand operand to determine the modulus of the left-hand operator and assign the result to the left-hand operator. x %= 2 is the same as x = x % 2.
&=	Perform a bitwise and operation and assign the result to the left-hand operator. x &= y is the same as x = x & y.
l=	Perform a bitwise inclusive operation and assign the result to the left-hand operator. x l= y is the same as x = x l y.
^=	Perform a bitwise exxclusive or operation and assign the result to the left-hand operator. x ^= y is the same as x = x ^ y.
<<=	Perform a bitwise left-shift operation and assign the result to the left-hand operator. x <<= y is the same as x = x << y.
>>=	Perform a bitwise right-shift operation and assign the result to the left-hand operator. x &= y is the same as x = x & y.
>>>=	Perform a bitwise signed right-shift operation and assign the result to the left-hand operator. x &= y is the same as x = x & y.

Comparing and Sorting Objects

As I indicated previously, comparing objects differs from comparing primitives. The comparison operators work for primitives, but they do not work for objects. Instead, Java requires the use of a number of different interfaces and methods to compare objects.

Implementing the `equals` Method

The first comparison is to see whether one object is equal to another. As we saw previously, the equality and inequality operators determine only whether two objects use the same object reference (that is, the same place in memory). Consequently, two different objects, each with its own memory address, are never equal. The following class might help illustrate the issue (see Listing 4-27).

Listing 4-27. Using the equality operator with objects

```
package com.apress.javaforabsolutebeginners .examples.comparing;

public class CompareTest {

  public static void main(String[] args) {
    Object a = new Object();
    Object b = new Object();
    Object c = b;
    System.out.println(a == b);
    System.out.println(b == c);
  }

}
```

That code prints "false" for the first comparison and "true" for the second. In essence, we create a single object with two names (b and c), so the second comparison yields a value of "true." The new keyword offers a big hint here. For c, we don't create a new object, just another reference to an existing one. To see whether two objects are equal, we have to compare objects that implement the equals method. Let's return to our Person class and expand it to have an equals method (see Listing 4-28).

Listing 4-28. Person class with equals method

```
package com.apress.javaforabsolutebeginners .examples.comparing;

public class Person {
  String firstName;
  String lastName;

  public Person (String firstName, String lastName) {
    this.firstName = firstName;
    this.lastName = lastName;
  }

  public boolean equals(Person p) {
    if (p == null) {
      return false;
    }
    if (p == this) {
      return true;
    }
```

```
      if (!(p instanceof Person)) {
        return false;
      }
      if (p.lastName.equals(this.lastName)
          && p.firstName.equals(this.firstName)) {
        return true;
      } else {
        return false;
      }
    }

    public int hashCode() {
      int result = 17;
      result *= firstName.hashCode() * 37;
      result *= lastName.hashCode() * 37;
      return result;
    }
}
```

Let's examine that `equals` method. I followed a standard recipe for implementing it. (The Java community has best practices for many things, and we show them to you whenever they come up, as here.) First, I check for null, just to make sure we have an object. Then I check to see whether it's the same object, in which case they are certainly equal. Then we check to make sure that, if we do have an object, it's a `Person` object. If not, the comparison is always false. But remember that other classes might extend our `Person` class, so a `Student` object might be equal to our `Person` object. Because `Student` extends `Person`, this `equals` method works for both. However, `Student` might implement its own `equals` method to account for the school each student attends. Finally, I check all the relevant fields within the class. If they are all equal, it must be the same person. Naturally, a real-world `Person` class probably includes middle name, address fields, social security number, and possibly even ancestors and descendants. Two fields will do for the sake of a demonstration, though. Now, let's rewrite `CompareTest` to use our new `Person` object (see Listing 4-29).

Listing 4-29. Checking people objects for equality

```
package com.apress.javaforabsolutebeginners .examples.comparing;

public class CompareTest {

  public static void main(String[] args) {
    Person samSpade = new Person("Sam", "Spade");
    Person greatNoirDetective = new Person("Sam", "Spade");
    System.out.println(samSpade == greatNoirDetective);
    System.out.println(samSpade.equals(greatNoirDetective));
  }

}
```

`CompareTest` now prints "false" and then "true," even though `samSpade` and `greatNoirDetective` are different references to different `Person` objects. That's because our `equals` method isn't comparing references but rather the relevant fields of the two objects.

The hashCode and equals methods are closely related because they rely on the same premise. They add together a set of values to create a value that can be used for comparison (an equals-to comparison in the case of the equals method and equals-to, greater-than, and less-than comparisons in the case of the hashCode method).

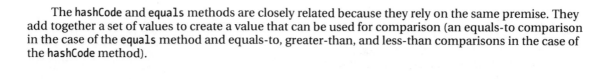

■ **Note**   When you implement the equals method, you must also implement the hashCode method. The hashCode method determines where an object reference goes when put into a collection that uses a hashing algorithm (such as the HashMap and HashTable classes). We address those two collections (and others) when we get to data structures, later in the book. The goal of the hashCode method is to return a unique (or at least nearly unique) identifier; that's why it starts with a prime number and multiplies by another prime number. Again, we get to that in much greater detail.

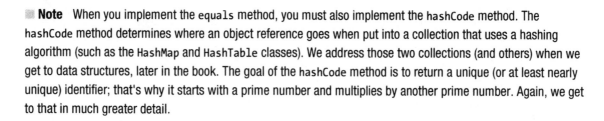

■ **Caution**   When you implement both equals and hashCode (and you should implement both if you implement one), you must make sure that they use the same fields. For example, if you use firstName and lastName in the equals method, you must use firstName and LastName in the hashCode method. Otherwise, your comparisons fail. Worse yet, you don't get exceptions; you get the wrong behavior and a hard-to-find bug.

■ **Caution**   The hashCode method must generate equal values for equal objects. Otherwise, comparisons that should succeed fail, and you have another hard-to-find bug.

Comparisons for Sorting

I include sorting in this topic because it's impossible to sort things without comparing them. Suppose you want to sort a bunch of colorful rocks into the spectrum. To do so, you pick up each rock, compare it to the other rocks, and use that information to decide where in the row of rocks each rock belongs. Sorting comes to most people pretty readily, with little training. However, a computer has to be told exactly how to do it. To that end, Java offers two mechanisms for creating comparisons that can be used for sorting: implementing the compareTo method from java.util.Comparable and creating a class that extends java.util.Comparator. We do both for our Person class. Classes don't have to implement both, but many do. The String class offers a fine example of a class that implements both comparison interfaces (and equals and hashCode), by the way.

To be able to compare objects with the goal of sorting them, we have to know more than whether one object equals another. We also have to know whether one object is greater than or less than another object. For our color-sorting example, we can assign an integer value to each color and then sort our rocks by putting each one to the left of all the rocks its color value is greater than and to the right of all the rocks its color value is less than. Rocks with the same color value make piles of rocks whenever that happens (and that's comparable to what happens in Java when hash code values are identical).

Implementing java.lang.Comparable

Another best practice acknowledged by the Java community is to use `java.lang.Comparable` for comparisons that are "natural" to the object. People naturally sort themselves by name (just look at a phone book), so it makes sense to implement `java.lang.Comparable` and have its `compareTo` method tell us whether a name is less than, equal to, or greater than another person's name. Listing 4-30 shows our `Person` class again, with the addition of implementing `java.lang.Comparable`. For our `Person` example, we get the numeric value of each `String` field, add them together, and use that as the numeric value of our `Person` object.

Listing 4-30. *Person class implementing java.lang.Comparable*

```
package com.apress.javaforabsolutebeginners .examples.comparing;

public class Person implements Comparable<Person> {
  String firstName;
  String lastName;
    public Person (String firstName, String lastName) {
    this.firstName = firstName;
    this.lastName = lastName;
  }

  public boolean equals(Person p) {
    if (p == null) {
      return false;
    }
    if (p == this) {
      return true;
    }
    if (!(p instanceof Person)) {
      return false;
    }
    if (p.lastName.equals(this.lastName)
        && p.firstName.equals(this.firstName)) {
      return true;
    } else {
      return false;
    }
  }

  public int hashCode() {
    int result = 17;
    result *= firstName.hashCode() * 37;
    result *= lastName.hashCode() * 37;
    return result;
  }

  public int compareTo(Person p) {
    int thisTotal = firstName.hashCode() + lastName.hashCode();
    int pTotal = p.firstName.hashCode() + p.lastName.hashCode();
    if (thisTotal > pTotal) {
```

```
      return 1;
    }
    if (thisTotal < pTotal) {
      return -1;
    }
    // must be equal
    return 0;
  }
}
```

The contract that the compareTo method guarantees (as described in its documentation) is that it will return a positive number if the local object is greater than the object in the argument, a negative number if the local object is less than the object in the argument, and 0 if the two are equal. It's also important that, given the same object as an argument, the equals method returns true and the compareTo method returns 0. To do that, just use the same fields in both methods. If you need to break the rule, be sure to document it in the Javadoc for the compareTo method.

■ **Tip**   A common problem is to try to cast a class that implements java.lang.Comparable to a class of your own. Because they are in different packages (your class is in your own package and the other class is in the java.lang.Comparable package), you can't cast your class to the other class. Integer is probably the class that most often causes this problem, but any class that extends java.lang.Comparable has the same issue. So, if you see a ClassCastException, remember this particular problem, because it is a likely cause of the exception.

Remember that to compare Person objects, you need to create another class with a main method, set up a few Person objects, and then compare them. I include a class to do just that at the end of the chapter, but why not give it a try now? As with so many other things, you can't learn to program unless you program.

Implementing java.util.ComparatorAlthough the Java community uses java.lang.Comparable for natural comparisons, we implement a Comparator when we want to compare objects in some arbitrary way. Also, because Comparator objects are themselves classes, it's possible to implement many different Comparator objects for the same class. Let's expand our Person object to have a field by which we probably wouldn't usually want to sort and then create a Comparator class to sort by it. That kind of thing happens pretty often, really, because it allows for grouping by not-so-obvious characteristics. Listing 4-31 shows the modified Person class.

Listing 4-31. Person class with a favorite book field

```
package com.apress.javaforabsolutebeginners .examples.comparing;

public class Person implements Comparable<Person> {
  String firstName;
  String lastName;
  String favoriteBook;
    public Person (String firstName, String lastName, String favoriteBook) {
    this.firstName = firstName;
```

```java
    this.lastName = lastName;
    this.favoriteBook = favoriteBook;
  }

  public boolean equals(Person p) {
    if (p == null) {
      return false;
    }
    if (p == this) {
      return true;
    }
    if (!(p instanceof Person)) {
      return false;
    }
    if (p.lastName.equals(this.lastName)
        && p.firstName.equals(this.firstName)) {
      return true;
    } else {
      return false;
    }
  }

  public int hashCode() {
    int result = 17;
    result *= firstName.hashCode() * 37;
    result *= lastName.hashCode() * 37;
    return result;
  }

  public int compareTo(Person p) {
    // sort by last name first
    if (lastName.compareTo(p.lastName) > 0) {
      return 1;
    }
    if (lastName.compareTo(p.lastName) < 0) {
      return -1;
    }
    // last names must be equal
    // so compare first names
    if (firstName.compareTo(p.firstName) > 0) {
      return 1;
    }
    if (firstName.compareTo(p.firstName) < 0) {
      return -1;
    }
    // both names must be equal
    return 0;
  }
}
```

And Listing 4-32 shows the book comparator class.

Listing 4-32. Book comparator class

```java
package com.apress.javaforabsolutebeginners .examples.comparing;

import java.util.Comparator;

public class BookComparator implements Comparator<Person> {

  public int compare(Person p1, Person p2) {
    return p1.favoriteBook.compareTo(p2.favoriteBook);
  }
}
```

In this case, all we have to do is use the `String` class's `compareTo` method. Note that we must tell the comparator what kind of thing to compare (with `Comparator<Person>`). Otherwise, we have to accept arguments of type `Object` and cast to objects of type `Person`.

■ **Note** You don't need comparators for arrays of primitives or for collections of any objects that implement `java.lang.Comparable` (such as `String` and `Integer`). Those objects are already comparable.

Finally, Listing 4-33 shows `CompareTest`, expanded to use both kinds of comparison.

Listing 4-33. CompareTest using both comparisons

```java
package com.apress.javaforabsolutebeginners .examples.comparing;

import java.util.ArrayList;
import java.util.Collections;

public class CompareTest {

  public static void main(String[] args) {
    Person samSpade = new Person("Sam", "Spade", "The Maltese Falcon");
    Person sherlockHolmes =
      new Person("Sherlock", "Holmes", "The Sign of the Four");
    Person johnWatson = new Person("John", "Watson", "A Study in Scarlet");
    Person drWatson = new Person("John", "Watson", "A Study in Scarlet");
    // compare the two that are really equal
    System.out.println(johnWatson == drWatson);
    System.out.println(johnWatson.equals(drWatson));
    System.out.println();
    System.out.println("Sorting by name");
    // Make a collection from our characters and sort them
    ArrayList<Person> characters = new ArrayList<Person>();
    characters.add(samSpade);
    characters.add(sherlockHolmes);
    characters.add(johnWatson);
```

```
      characters.add(drWatson);
      // sort by the natural values (uses compareTo())
      Collections.sort(characters);
      for (int i = 0; i < characters.size(); i++) {
        Person person = characters.get(i);
        System.out.println(person.firstName + " "
          + person.lastName + " likes " + person.favoriteBook);
      }
      System.out.println();
      System.out.println("Sorting by favorite book");
      // sort by book (uses the Comparator)
      Collections.sort(characters, new BookComparator());
      for (int i = 0; i < characters.size(); i++) {
        Person person = characters.get(i);
        System.out.println(person.firstName + " "
          + person.lastName + " likes " + person.favoriteBook);
      }
    }
  }
}
```

And Listing 4-34 shows the output from our test class.

Listing 4-34. CompareTest output

```
false
true

Sorting by name
Sherlock Holmes likes The Sign of the Four
Sam Spade likes The Maltese Falcon
John Watson likes A Study in Scarlet
John Watson likes A Study in Scarlet

Sorting by favorite book
John Watson likes A Study in Scarlet
John Watson likes A Study in Scarlet
Sam Spade likes The Maltese Falcon
Sherlock Holmes likes The Sign of the Four
```

Summary

In this chapter, we learned:

- Java has a large number of operators.

- Java's operators have precedence (that is, some operators are processed before other operators).

- Java has some seemingly odd operators (such as the bitwise operators) but that they all have their uses.

- The details of each of the operators.

- When and how to use the `equals` and `hashCode` methods.

- How to compare objects with their natural values and how to compare objects with arbitrary values.

This chapter presents a lot of complex information in a fairly short space. I recommend reading it again. Also, as I mentioned before, there's no substitute for doing some programming. You should create a few classes that can be compared in various ways and do some fiddling with the less-obvious operators (such as the bitwise operators).

CHAPTER 5

Control Flow, Looping, and Branching

Control flow, looping, and branching are fundamental concepts in all programming. Control flow consists of running different code under different conditions. Looping consists of running the same code (though often with different values or different objects each time) until some condition has been met. Branching consists of doing something else when some condition has been detected. The thread that ties them all together is detecting conditions.

Control Flow

Java offers two constructs for controlling the flow of a program.

- if and if-else
- switch

Note try-catch blocks offer a form of control flow, because you can try something and then do something else if the first thing you tried throws an exception. However, because that mechanism relies on catching exceptions, it's not really a control flow mechanism. Because exceptions happen only when something goes wrong, they shouldn't be thought of (and certainly shouldn't be used for) branching.

---

if and if-else Statements

You've already seen some examples of if statements, but let's examine another. Let's start with a sample that's about as simple as it can be, as shown in Listing 5-1.

Listing 5-1. A simple if statement

```
if (a > 0) {
  b = 1;
}
```

Let's examine a little more complex example. It's more realistic, but programs often make simple comparisons, so both Listing 5-1 and Listing 5-2 are realistic. Here's part of a program that generates an appropriate greeting based on the current time of day.

Listing 5-2. A more complex if statement example

```
GregorianCalendar gregorianCalendar = new GregorianCalendar();
int hour = gregorianCalendar.get(Calendar.HOUR_OF_DAY);
String greeting = "Good ";
if (hour < 12) {
  greeting += "morning";
}
```

The condition is simply whether the hour of the day is before 12 (that is, noon). If the hour of the day is before noon, we add "morning" to our greeting. For conditions, the equality operators (== and !=) and the comparison operators (>, <, <=, >=) are often used. However, any condition that evaluates to true or false works for a condition.

So what should our program do when it's not morning? For that case, we can use the else keyword and have another block of code that gets run for afternoons. Listing 5-2 shows that code.

Listing 5-2. if-else statement example

```
GregorianCalendar gregorianCalendar = new GregorianCalendar();
int hour = gregorianCalendar.get(Calendar.HOUR_OF_DAY);
String greeting = "Good ";
if (hour < 12) {
  greeting += "morning";
} else {
  greeting += "afternoon";
}
```

This structure represents a common arrangement in all software. Often, we need consider only two alternatives. In this case, though, we have a problem. Late in the day, we say, "Good evening," rather than "Good afternoon." So let's address that problem with some more code. In this case, we create a structure called an else-if. It's possible, as we see later, to create long chains of branches with else-if structures. Let's start with a fairly simple one, though, as shown in Listing 5-3.

Listing 5-3. else-if example

```
GregorianCalendar gregorianCalendar = new GregorianCalendar();
int hour = gregorianCalendar.get(Calendar.HOUR_OF_DAY);
String greeting = "Good ";
if (hour < 12) {
  greeting += "morning";
} else if (hour < 18) {
  greeting += "afterooon";
```

```
} else {
  greeting += "evening";
}
System.out.println(greeting);
```

You probably knew what we were going to do with that `greeting` string.

Notice the `else if` structure. We can attach additional `if` statements to our `else` statements. In this fashion, it's possible to step through any number of alternatives, providing a different behavior for each one. If you step through the code with various values (try 10, 13, and 19), you can see how any possible value gets caught and sets the `greeting` string appropriately. The key to that capability is the final else, which does not check for any condition. In this case, that's just a convenience that lets us avoid writing `if (hour < 24)`.

Sometimes, though, you want to use a final else to catch problems. In many real-world programs, a set of if-else statements catches all the expected conditions, whereas the final condition-free else statement throws an exception (which means the program lets us know that it found a problem) because the program found an unexpected condition. That's another example of defensive coding to put in your programming toolkit.

Let's consider a larger example in Listing 5-4, to show the mechanism in greater detail.

Listing 5-4. *A larger else-if example*

```
GregorianCalendar gregorianCalendar = new GregorianCalendar();
int day = gregorianCalendar.get(Calendar.DAY_OF_WEEK);
String greeting = "Good ";
if (day == 1) {
  greeting += "Sunday";
} else if (day == 2) {
  greeting += "Monday";
} else if (day == 3) {
  greeting += "Tuesday";
} else if (day == 4) {
  greeting += "Wednesday";
} else if (day == 5) {
  greeting += "Thursday";
} else if (day == 6) {
  greeting += "Friday";
} else if (day == 7) {
  greeting += "Saturday";
}
greeting += " to you.";
System.out.println(greeting );
```

Notice that we don't put in a final `else` statement. In this case, we know that the `GregorianCalendar` class can't produce values we don't expect (it instead throws an exception before even getting to our `if` statements), so there's no need for it. Use that final `else` trick when you can't be sure you'll always get an expected condition or (as in the earlier example) when you can use it as a shortcut.

switch Statements

The `switch` keyword lets us set up a structure that does the same thing as a set of `if-else` statements but that uses a different syntax. Personally, I'm so accustomed to reading if-else blocks that we prefer them, but many developers prefer `switch` statements. Also, a `switch` statement can be easier to debug, if your debugger doesn't support conditional breakpoints. Fortunately for us, the debugger built into Eclipse does support conditional breakpoints, as we will see in Chapter 11, "Debugging."

One difference between `if` statements and `switch` blocks is that `if` statements evaluate only `boolean` conditions. That is, the evaluation expression in an `if` statement must always resolve to `true` or `false`. A `switch` block evaluates any value of the type used as its argument. Consequently, a `switch` block evaluating `int` values evaluate any `int` value. In this way, `switch` blocks support any number of execution paths versus the two paths (`true` and `false`) of an `if` statement.

Also, the switch statement evaluates only integers, String objects, and enumerations. If you have a class that produces a set of other possibilities (such as a class that produces a different type of object for each possible result), you need to use an `if-else` structure rather than a switch statement.

A `switch` statement requires a number of case labels, each of which forms a comparison with the value defined as the `switch` statement's single argument. Let's consider Listing 5-5: creating a greeting based on the time of day (same output as Listing 5-3, but with a `switch` statement).

Listing 5-5. *Example switch statement*

```
GregorianCalendar gregorianCalendar = new GregorianCalendar();
int hour = gregorianCalendar.get(Calendar.HOUR_OF_DAY);
String greeting = "Good ";
switch(hour) {
  case (1):
  case (2):
  case (3):
  case (4):
  case (5):
  case (6):
  case (7):
  case (8):
  case (9):
  case (10):
  case (11): {
    greeting += "morning";
    break;
  }
  case (12):
  case (13):
  case (14):
  case (15):
  case (16):
  case (17): {
    greeting += "afternoon";
    break;
  }
  default: {
    greeting += "evening";
    break;
  }
}
System.out.println(greeting );
```

Note the `default` case at the end. That's a `switch` block's way of letting you do something with input that doesn't match any of the cases. In this example, we use it to catch the values between 18 and 24 (inclusive). We can do that because we know we won't get any other values. If we aren't sure that we wouldn't get an unexpected value, we would probably throw an exception in the `default` case, to let whatever code uses the `switch` block know that we found a problem.

One issue with a `switch` statement is that it cannot group its possible values (other than through the `default` keyword). Consequently, we end up with a lot of `case` labels that appear to do nothing. In fact, each group of `case` statements shares the next block of code they encounter within the `switch` statement. In this case, that means values 1 through 11 share the code that adds "morning" to the greeting and values 12 through 17 share the code that adds "afternoon" to the greeting.

Another issue with `switch` statements is that each block of code generally requires a `break` statement. Each `break` statement makes the program jump from the break statement to the end of the `switch` statement. Consider what happens if we assume the input is 10. As written, the output is "Good morning." Without the `break` statements, the output is "Good morningafternoonevening." That is, each of the blocks is run. This happens because any `case` label without a `break` statement falls through to the next `case` statement. That's the mechanism that lets multiple `case` labels share one block of code. With no `break` statements, every block of code in the `switch` statement gets run. Although running more than one block of code might be useful in some cases, it's generally an error (and can be hard to find because the code probably looks right).

A final issue is the `default` keyword. A `switch` statement doesn't require a `default` section. However, `switch` statements often do include `default` sections. A `default` section performs the same function as a final `else` statement in a group of `if-else` statements. As with the final `else`, you can use a `default` section for any remaining values, provided you are sure you won't get an unexpected value for the `switch` statement's argument. When you can't be sure of your input, use the `default` block to trap unexpected values and take some appropriate action (often either doing nothing or throwing an exception). `default` sections don't require `break` statements (the code "falls through" to the end of the `switch` statement anyway), but it's customary (and it's custom because it's a good idea) to add one, for consistency and readability.

Let's consider another example in Listing 5-6 of a switch statement, this one being parallel in function to Listing 5-4.

Listing 5-6. *Using a switch statement without a default section*

```
GregorianCalendar gregorianCalendar = new GregorianCalendar();
int day = gregorianCalendar.get(Calendar.DAY_OF_WEEK);
String greeting = "Good ";
switch (day) {
  case 1: {
    greeting += "Sunday";
  }
  case 2: {
    greeting += "Monday";
  }
  case 3: {
    greeting += "Tuesday";
  }
  case 4: {
    greeting += "Wednesday";
  }
```

```
    case 5: {
      greeting += "Thursday";
    }
    case 6: {
      greeting += "Friday";
    }
    case 7: {
      greeting += "Saturday";
    }
}
greeting += " to you.";
System.out.println(greeting );
```

Listing 5-4 could use a final `else` statement with no comparison. The final `case` in Listing 5-6 could be a `default` section. Either one works. When I make a single `case` for every option, I prefer to fill it in, but that's just a matter of style. As with the final `else`, you can use a `default` section either as a shortcut for all the cases you didn't define or as a way to trap an unexpected value. Only use `default` as a shortcut if you're absolutely sure of the values (as we can be when using `GregorianCalendar`).

Looping

Java offers three constructs for looping:

- for
- while
- do-while

`for` loops are the most commonly used, but `while` and `do-while` loops certainly have their uses.

■ **Note** All loops have three operations: initialize a variable, test it to see whether we're done, and update the variable to be tested again. Everything else is just additional detail or alternate syntax, as we see shortly.

For Loops

As a rule, use a `for` loop when you have some value that you can count. For example, whenever you have an array or a list or an enumeration, you can use a `for` loop based on the number of items present.

Remember our cardinal direction example from Chapter 3? Let's examine that more closely in Listing 5-7.

Listing 5-7. *Loop that finds directions*

```
int[] compassPoints = {22, 77, 144, 288};
for (int i = 0; i < compassPoints.length; i++) {
  System.out.println(compassPoints[i] + " degrees is (very roughly) "
      + Direction.findCardinalDirection(compassPoints[i]));
}
```

The for loop consists of two parts: the information that controls the looping and the block of code that gets run each time through the loop. The control section (within the parentheses) consists of three parts: initialization, termination, and increment. Each of these three parts ends with a semicolon, though the semicolon after the increment is often dropped. The names give us a good indication of what they do. The initialization code sets up whatever variable we use for our counting, the termination code indicates how to know when to stop looping, and the increment code dictates how to change the initialization variable each time through the loop. In this simple case, we set an int named i to 0, running the code in the loop for each item in the compassPoints array, and incrementing the initialization variable (i) by one each time.

Java programmers can certainly do things differently than shown here. Consider the following for statements in Listing 5-8.

Listing 5-8. *Alternate for loops*

```
// Process just half the compassPoints array
for (int i = compassPoints.length / 2; i < compassPoints.length; i++) {

}
// Process every other member of the compassPoints array
for (int i = 0; i < compassPoints.length; i += 2) {

}
```

The first of the two loops process the high-value half (items 2 and 3—remember that arrays start at 0) of the compassPoints array. The second loop processes items 0 and 2. If we use int i = 1, the second loop processes items 1 and 3. As a rule, any variable that can be counted (including char variables, but that's bad practice unless you process individual characters—otherwise, groups of characters should be treated as String objects, both for simplicity and for performance) can serve as the initialization value, and it can start at any of the variable's possible values (including negative numbers). Also, any valid mathematical operation can be performed in the increment value. Of course, if you also use the initialization variable as an index into an array, using a negative number gets you an ArrayOutOfBounds exception, because array indices don't use negative numbers. When you do these kinds of things, though, test thoroughly to be sure you get the results you expect.

Speaking of using the initialization variable as an index, that's exactly what we do in Listing 5-7. You can also perform mathematical operations on the initialization variable in the body of the loop, as shown in Listing 5-9.

Listing 5-9. Modifying the initialization variable in the loop body

```
int[] compassPoints = {22, 77, 144, 288};
for (int i = 0; i < compassPoints.length; i++) {
  System.out.println(compassPoints[i++] + " degrees is (very roughly) " +
Direction.findCardinalDirection(compassPoints[i]));
}
```

Notice that we add a postfix operator to the initialization variable at one point where it's used as an index. Consequently, this loop now processes items 0 and 2 in the compassPoints array. As you can see, this offers another way to process every other item. If we make i++ be i += 2, the loop processes every third item and processes items 0 and 3. Although potentially useful, this kind of thing can lead to problems. Again, test thoroughly.

By the way, the best practice for processing alternating items differently is not to write two for loops or do math on the increment value but to test each item as it goes through the loop and do the appropriate thing in each case, as shown in Listing 5-10.

Listing 5-10. Processing every other item in a single loop

```
int[] compassPoints = {22, 77, 144, 288};
for (int i = 0; i < compassPoints.length; i++) {
  if (i % 2 == 1) {
    System.out.println("[" + i + " is odd] " + compassPoints[i] +
        " degrees is (very roughly) " +
        Direction.findCardinalDirection(compassPoints[i]));
  } else {
    System.out.println("[" + i + " is even] " + compassPoints[i] +
        " degrees is (very roughly) " +
        Direction.findCardinalDirection(compassPoints[i]));
  }
}
```

Listing 5-11 shows the output of that loop.

Listing 5-11. Output from processing alternate items differently

```
[0 is even] 22 degrees is (very roughly) NORTH
[1 is odd] 77 degrees is (very roughly) EAST
[2 is even] 144 degrees is (very roughly) SOUTH
[3 is odd] 288 degrees is (very roughly) WEST
```

This kind of code is often used to alternate the colors of rows in tables and similar applications. Using if (i % 3 == 1) processes every third item differently, and so on.

for loops support an alternate (and sometimes handy) syntax, called *enhanced for syntax*. The enhanced for syntax consists of an initialization variable and an object (an array in this case) to associate with the initialization variable. Every item in the object gets processed by the loop, with the initialization variable providing access to the current index value (which is nearly always needed). Provided you want to process every item (though you can skip items with if statements in the loop body), the enhanced for syntax provides a nice shortcut. The enhanced for syntax was created for collections and arrays, but it can also be used with enumerations (as we saw in Chapter 3, "Operators"). Let's consider an example in Listing 5-12, using the same array that we saw in the previous examples.

The enhanced for syntax is also called "for each". I dislike that, because other languages (such as Perl) have an actual **foreach** keyword. Java has the notion of "for each of these items, run the following code", but it does not have an actual **foreach** keyword. Consequently, I prefer to call it the "enhanced for." It got the name when it was introduced in Java 5. Before Java 5, only the basic **for** structure was available to Java developers.

Listing 5-12. *Enhanced for syntax example*

```
int[] compassPoints = {22, 77, 144, 288};
for (int i: compassPoints) {
  System.out.println(compassPoints[i] + " degrees is (very roughly) " +
      Direction.findCardinalDirection(compassPoints[i]));
}
```

Listing 5-12 does the same thing as Listing 5-9.

One last thing that every Java developer should know about a **for** loop is that it is just a shortcut for a **while** loop. That is, every **for** loop can be rewritten as a **while** loop. Let's turn the loop from Listing 5-9 into a **while** loop in Listing 5-13.

Listing 5-13. *Turning a for loop into a while loop*

```
int i = 0;
while (i < compassPoints.length) {
  System.out.println(compassPoints[i] + " degrees is (very roughly) " +
      Direction.findCardinalDirection(compassPoints[i]));
  i++;
}
```

Listing 5-13 does the same thing as Listing 5-9 and 5-12. (You can almost always find multiple ways to do the same thing in most programming languages, including Java.)

While loops

As we just learned, **for** loops deal with a specific case of the more general purpose served by **while** loops. **for** loops (usually) deal with things that can be counted. **while** loops continue to loop as long as something is **true**. A **while** loop has only one argument: an expression that can be evaluated as **true** or **false**.

Before we go any further, let's look at the simplest possible **while** loop, as shown in Listing 5-14.

Listing 5-14. *A simple while loop*

```
while (counter < 10) {
  System.out.println(counter);
}
```

A **while** loop does not have an explicit initialization variable or an increment statement; you must provide that functionality yourself. (One of the reasons for the invention of the **for** loop was to put all three parts of a loop – initialize, test, and increment – in a single spot.) Though both initialization and increment often appear near (for initialization) or within (for incrementing) **while** loops, they are not part of the **while** loop syntax, as they are in **for** loops. So let's look at a more complete example, which includes initialization and incrementing, in addition to the test (see Listing 5-15).

Listing 5-15. A more complete while loop

```java
int counter = 0;
while (counter < 10) {
  System.out.println(counter);
  counter++;
}
```

That (still simple) example shows the typical structure of a while loop: declare a variable, test the variable at the top of the while loop, do some work in the while loop, and increment the variable in the while loop. After the test fails, the while loop is done, and the code below the while loop runs.

You can create a while loop that runs forever (or, more likely, until some condition that gets checked by an if statement in the body of the loop triggers a break statement) by using while(true). That construct is useful in some cases, but it's not a safe thing to do. Savvy programmers try to ensure that loops can't run forever (that's called an infinite loop). What if, due to unexpected input data, your break condition in the body of the loop never gets hit? Then your program is stuck (and that can be loads of fun if it happens to be writing into a file—you can quickly cause problems for your operating system this way). If you feel that you must use while(true), test thoroughly.

Another use for a while loop is to try something for a set amount of time when you don't know how long each try will take. For example, suppose a mail client tries for one minute to connect to a mail server and then gives up (that is, it times out). Listing 5-14 shows one way to wait for a connection.

Listing 5-14. While loop that waits for an event

```java
boolean connected = false;
long now = System.currentTimeMillis();
long oneMinuteFromStart = System.currentTimeMillis() + 60000;
while (!connected && now < oneMinuteFromStart) {
  System.out.println("Trying to connect....");
  if (MailServer.connect()) {
    connected = true;
    break;
  }
  // pause for two seconds
  // to let other processes work, too
  try {
    System.out.println("(letting other processes run)");
    Thread.sleep(2000);
  } catch (Exception e) {
    e.printStackTrace();
  }
  // reset now for the next comparison
  now = System.currentTimeMillis();
}
if (connected) {
  System.out.println("Connected to the mail server");
} else {
  System.out.println("Timed out while trying to connect to the mail server");
}
```

Code to connect to a server in a real-world application also checks for a number of exceptions and does not print to the console but rather updates a status window (that includes a cancel button) for the user.

Notice the `break` statement. If we do connect, we don't want to wait for the rest of the code to run (especially because it contains a sleep instruction). Consequently, we jump out of the `while` loop after we connect. The handy thing is that, if we connect on the first try, we never wait and never loop. We shoot through the code as though it were linear (except for the overhead of the comparison in the `while`) and we're done. If we usually do connect on the first try, that's a nice little optimization. We cover break statements in detail later in this chapter.

Notice also the try-catch block and the call to `Thread.sleep(2000)` within it. The `Thread.sleep()` method tells the current thread to sleep for some number of milliseconds, letting other processes run. In other words, it lets other processes get some work done while your process takes a break. If it weren't present, the JVM wouldn't try to do anything else until your `while` loop exited. That's generally a bad practice, because it can bring an entire application to a halt while everything waits for your code. Exactly how long to let your thread sleep varies by a number of factors (how long what you're doing takes, how important what you're doing is, and so on).

░ **Tip**   You should almost always put the current thread to sleep for a bit to let other processes work when you do anything that has to be timed.

Do-while Loops

Do-while loops work much like `while` loops. The difference is that checking the condition comes after the block of code runs. Put differently, the test comes at the bottom of the loop rather than at the top. That means the code always runs at least once. Because we always want our mail server connector to try at least once, it's a great case for converting to a do-while loop (see Listing 5-15).

Listing 5-15. *Do-while loop*

```
boolean connected = false;
long now = System.currentTimeMillis();
long oneMinuteFromStart = System.currentTimeMillis() + 60000;
do {
  System.out.println("Trying to connect....");
  if (MailServer.connect()) {
    connected = true;
    break;
  }
  // pause for two seconds
  // to let other processes work, too
  try {
    System.out.println("(letting other processes run)");
    Thread.sleep(2000);
  } catch (Exception e) {
    e.printStackTrace();
  }
```

```
  // reset now for the next comparison
  now = System.currentTimeMillis();
} while (!connected && now < oneMinuteFromStart);
if (connected) {
  System.out.println("Connected to the mail server");
} else {
  System.out.println("Timed out while trying to connect to the mail server");
}
```

In a do-while loop with a break statement, we can skip the overhead of the comparison. If our code happens to work the first time, we're done. That's a tiny optimization, but it's good practice to take advantage of that kind of thing whenever you can, because those little bits of time add up after a while.

Branching

The if and switch constructs are not strictly branching structures (though developers often speak of them as such). Strictly speaking, *branching* means "jumping" from one place in a program to another place in the same program. Some languages (such as Assembler) make extensive use of this kind of branching. Java uses the concept much more sparingly. The Java community regards arbitrarily jumping to some other point in the code to be at odds with the principles of object-oriented development. It's generally thought that object-oriented code that has to rely on jumping around is bad object-oriented code. Consequently, Java has no goto statement, and the Java community is careful about using the break and continue keywords.

Java offers three branching statements:

- break

- continue

- return

The break Statement

Many programming languages offer some form of break statement, because the need to stop the current execution path when some condition is met is a common problem. The break statement without a label moves the execution point (the bit of code the program is currently running) to the next statement that is outside of whatever structure contains the break statement. The only structures that can contain break statements are for, while, and do-while loops and switch statements.

The break statement has two forms, one (the most commonly used form) without a label and one with a label. We see several examples of break statements throughout this chapter. A break statement with a label breaks an outer loop, meaning that it is useful only within nested loops. As an example, suppose we search a chessboard to find a particular piece (say the black king). We might implement the search as a loop going left to right with a loop going across the board. (By the way, if we search for the position of a chess piece this way, we have a badly designed program; each piece should be an object, and we find its location by examining its properties, but this idea will do for an example as in Listing 5-16.)

Listing 5-16. Labeled break statement

```
String[][] pieces = {
  {"Black Castle", "Black Knight", "Black Bishop", "Black Queen",
    "Black King", "", "", ""},
  {"Black Pawn", "Black Pawn", "Black Pawn", "", "", "", "", ""},
  {"", "", "", "", "", "", "", ""},
  {"", "", "", "", "", "", "", ""},
  {"", "", "", "", "", "", "", ""},
  {"", "", "", "", "", "", "", ""},
  {"White Pawn", "White Pawn", "White Pawn", "", "", "", "", ""},
  {"White Castle", "White Knight", "White Bishop", "White Queen",
    "White King", "", "", ""}
  };
int x = 0, y = 0;
king:
for (int i = 0; i < 8; i++) {
  for (int j = 0; j < 8; j++) {
    if (pieces[i][j].equals("Black King")) {
      x = i;
      y = j;
      break king;
    }
  }
}
System.out.println("x: " + x + ", y: " + y);
```

The `king:` label indicates which loop the `break king;` statement should terminate. Code execution then resumes with the print statement below the outer loop.

The continue Statement

The `continue` statement works within loops. It stops the current iteration of the loop and moves to the next one. The `break` statement, on the other hand, exits the entire loop. In other words, the `continue` statement continues the loop, whereas the `break` statement breaks out of the loop (which explains the origin of these two keywords). The general idiom for its use is that the code in the loop has determined that it does not need to go further and can jump to processing the next item. It's Java's way of letting you say, "No, not that one. How about the next one?" Returning to our chessboard, suppose we want to count the number of surviving pawns (see Listing 5-17).

Listing 5-17. continue statement

```
String[][] pieces = {
  {"Black Castle", "Black Knight", "Black Bishop", "Black Queen", "Black King", "", "", ""},
  {"Black Pawn", "Black Pawn", "Black Pawn", "", "", "", "", ""},
  {"", "", "", "", "", "", "", ""},
  {"", "", "", "", "", "", "", ""},
  {"", "", "", "", "", "", "", ""},
  {"", "", "", "", "", "", "", ""},
  {"White Pawn", "White Pawn", "White Pawn", "", "", "", "", ""},
  {"White Castle", "White Knight", "White Bishop", "White Queen", "White King", "", "", ""}
```

```
};
int pawns = 0;
for (int i = 0; i < 8; i++) {
  for (int j = 0; j < 8; j++) {
    if (!pieces[i][j].contains("Pawn")) {
      continue;
    }
    pawns++;
  }
}
System.out.println("Surviving pawns: " + pawns);
```

When we encounter the continue statement, we jump over any other code in the loop and process the next item.

Note that we can rewrite the body of the inner loop to not use a continue statement as in Listing 5-18:

Listing 5-18. *Doing without the continue statement*

```
if (pieces[i][j].contains("Pawn")) {
  pawns++;
}
```

It turns out that writing an example of the continue statement that can't be rewritten to be simpler without the continue statement is fairly hard to do, which is why continue statements don't appear in code that often.

Like the **break** statement, the continue statement can use a label. As it happens, adding a label to a continue statement in the chess example yields the same result, though with more processing. So let's consider an example that counts the number of characters that appear before the first space in each string within an array of strings (see Listing 5-19).

Listing 5-19. *A continue statement with a label*

```
String[] detectives = {"Sam Spade", "Sherlock Holmes", "Charlie Chan"};
int charactersBeforeSpaces = 0;
outer:
for (String str : detectives) {
    char[] strChars = str.toCharArray();
    for (char ch : strChars) {
        if (ch == ' ') {
            continue outer;
        }
        charactersBeforeSpaces++;
    }
}
System.out.println(charactersBeforeSpaces);
```

This bit of code prints 18.

> **Note** As mentioned earlier in this chapter, the Java community frowns on the use of labels, because they dislike the use of goto-like idioms, and jumping to a label comes close to being a goto instruction. The designers of Java intentionally did not include a goto instruction, and the community has embraced the no-goto idea to the extent of frowning on labels as well. The accepted view is that if your code has to jump around, you've done a poor job designing your code. I concur, because I've never yet found a use for break or continue statements with labels, other than in writing examples to show how they work.

Let's redo that bit of code to show how it works without a label and thus fits the best practices of the Java community (see Listing 5-20).

Listing 5-20. Removing a label

```java
String[] detectives = {"Sam Spade", "Sherlock Holmes", "Charlie Chan"};
int charactersBeforeSpaces = 0;
for (String str : detectives) {
    char[] strChars = str.toCharArray();
    for (char ch : strChars) {
        if (ch == ' ') {
            break;
        }
        charactersBeforeSpaces++;
    }
}
System.out.println(charactersBeforeSpaces);
```

As you can see, removing the label and replacing the continue statement with a **break** statement produces the same result and is simpler to follow. Labels are appropriate in some rare cases, but you'll probably write Java code for a long time before you find such a case. (I've been writing Java code since 1995, and we've yet to need a label.) In the meantime, try to structure your code to avoid jumping around beyond the use of label-free **break** and **continue** statements. Instead, structure your code so that your logic catches every possible case. That way, you won't need to jump anywhere.

The return Statement

The final branching instruction is the **return** statement, which has two forms. If a method returns nothing (that is, its return type is **void**), the **return** statement has no arguments. If a method returns a value or object (that is, the return type is not **void**), the **return** statement takes one argument (the value or object being returned). Return statements stop any further processing within the method and return processing to the code that called the method. Let's consider an example of a method that returns a string (see Listing 5-21).

Listing 5-21. Using return to stop processing

```java
public String getAuthorForDetective (String detective) {
  if(detective.equals("Sam Spade")) {
    return "Dashiell Hammett";
  }
  if (detective.equals("Sherlock Holmes")) {
    return "Sir Arthur Conan Doyle";
  }
  if (detective.equals("Charlie Chan")) {
    return "Earl Derr Biggers";
  }
  return "Unknown author";
}
```

As you can see in this example, as soon as we find the author that matches the fictional character, we stop looking and return the name of the author. If all else fails, we admit to not knowing the name of the author. We don't need else statements because each if statement has a return statement; at each if statement, we stop processing if we get a match and continue processing if we don't get a match, so else is needless syntax. This idiom is common in Java programs. It works especially well when you can order your matches by likelihood. That way, you can often do as little processing as possible, which makes for a handy bit of optimization. For example, if you happen to code on behalf of the Sherlock Holmes Memorial Library (if there is such a thing), you'd put the "Sherlock Holmes" match at the top.

Let's consider a similar example in Listing 5-22 for a method that returns void.

Listing 5-22. Using return with no values

```java
public void printAuthorForDetective (String detective) {
  if(detective.equals("Sam Spade")) {
    System.out.println("Dashiell Hammett");
    return;
  }
  if (detective.equals("Sherlock Holmes")) {
    System.out.println("Sir Arthur Conan Doyle");
    return;
  }
  if (detective.equals("Charlie Chan")) {
    System.out.println("Earl Derr Biggers");
    return;
  }
  System.out.println("Unknown author");
}
```

Again, the return statements stop further processing within the method and return processing to the code that called the method. If we don't have the return statements, the method prints whatever match it found (if any) and then prints, "Unknown author." So, in addition to causing needless processing, leaving out the return statements also creates a bug. We don't need a return statement after the last statement because the method implicitly returns after the last instruction.

Summary

This chapter covered what many programmers consider to be the main purpose of programming: identifying conditions and doing appropriate things for each one. If we have no ability to change what we do based on the inputs we receive, no program could achieve the complexity to do anything useful. To that end, every programming language offers at least a few ways to change paths within the code.

As we learned in this chapter, Java offers:

- `if` and `if-else` (and `else if`) statements, for simple comparisons

- `switch` blocks, for comparing lots of values

- `for` (and enhanced for or "for each") loops, for easy-to-read looping

- `while` loops, for when we want to do something until a condition is met

- `do-while` loops, for when we want to have the test come last

- `break` statements, for jumping out of the current block

- `continue` statements, for moving on to the next item

- `return` statements, for saying we're done with this method and returning a value

Thanks to all these possibilities for controlling the flow of our logic, we can write programs that can handle any number of inputs and outputs and intermediate processing steps correctly and still be easy-to-read.

CHAPTER 6

Object-oriented Programming

Java is an object-oriented language. That means that Java lets programmers develop software by developing objects and specifying the relationships between the objects. The relationships are defined within the objects, so the objects are the central focus of any software development effort in Java.

Objects

So what's an object? In technical terms, an *object* is an instance of a class (or the class itself if it's static or a singleton—that is, a class of which there can be only one instance). So what exactly is an instance? Think of it this way: A class definition is the definition for an instance, and a particular item defined by that class is an instance. Suppose we have a class that defines documents (title, author, and so on). Then an object that describes a particular document is an instance.

Usually, an object is a software object that represents some important part of the system. (Unimportant parts of the system should be eliminated —most software developers are by nature or quickly become minimalists.) Sometimes, these objects correspond to actual physical items. For example, shipping software might have a class that represents shipping containers, and each instance of that class corresponds to a real shipping container somewhere in the world.

Far more often, though, objects in software define abstract items—that is, things that don't really exist. For example, the Math class defines a constant for pi. You can't touch a mathematical constant, though it might seem real to you (take enough math classes and such things seem very real). But even a mathematical constant is less abstract than some of the things that come up in software development. That's because object-oriented languages such as Java let us define purely abstract objects, such as a Shape class. In many shape-related systems, Shape itself can never be instantiated; you must instead create an instance of some other class that extends Shape (such as a Circle class). And sometimes an abstract class extends another abstract class, making for layers of abstraction.

Let's consider some other examples. The following are all objects that I have developed for one system or another:

- A class that handles button clicks

- A class that contains information about a three-dimensional structure (such as a pyramid or sphere)

- A class that contains that describes a paragraph within a document (font style, font size, and so on)

- A class that defines a print job (such as gets created when you click Print in a word processor)

Notice that I always say "a class." All objects in Java are classes. Enumerations are a special kind of class, because each enumeration has an implicit class provided by the compiler. Java also has primitives and interfaces, but primitives and interfaces are not objects. As we saw in earlier chapters, primitives define values, but they aren't objects. We get to why neither primitives nor interfaces are objects shortly. For now, just remember that a Java object is an instance of a class, and a class is code that defines something useful. Even an abstract class defines something useful, though it relies on the classes that extend it to provide the remaining information.

Object-oriented languages support three important features:

- Encapsulation

- Inheritance

- Polymorphis

We look at these in turn.

Encapsulation

Encapsulation means that an object holds its contents in such a way that other objects can't see or change those contents (though we have a number of ways to provide access to the contents of a class). That way, one object's contents can't get tangled up with the contents of another object. Given that an application can have thousands of classes, keeping the bits and pieces of all those classes separate is a really good idea. Otherwise, we'd never be able to find anything.

One of the key concerns of a Java developer when creating a new class (or modifying an existing one) is figuring out which bits and pieces to make visible to other classes. Another, related, concern is which classes get to see (and possibly modify) the contents of the current class. As that implies, you can make part of a class visible to just selected other classes rather than all other classes. We cover the mechanics of access modifiers in Chapter 3, "Data Types". We cover when you should use the various access modifiers in the next chapter.

Inheritance

Inheritance defines relationships between the classes (and so between the objects) within an object-oriented system. All classes in Java have some other object as a parent. Java developers say that one object *extends* another. If you think about it for a minute, you shortly realize that there must be some object that starts it all. That special object (the only one that has no parent) is a class called `Object`. All other Java objects are descendants (sometimes through many levels) of `Object`.

Let's consider a simple example from the field of Biology (with apologies to biologists for vastly over-simplifying and thanks to Caroline Valentine at Valentine Human Resources for the idea). Suppose we want to represent certain animals (in particular, cats, dogs, and mice). They're all mammals, so we might start with a class called `Mammal`.

Then we have three more classes called `Cat`, `Dog`, and `Mouse`. Each of those classes extend the `Mammal` class.

■ **Note** You can always tell if you're right to make a new class by asking a simple question: Is this new class a member of the old class? That's called the "is-a" test or the "is-one-of" test. A cat is a mammal, so we can make our Cat class extend our Mammal class. The same is true for our Dog and Mouse classes. If we had a Snake class, it would not be wise to create it by extending the Mammal class. It's not always so obvious, but it's a good place to start when you need to figure out which class your new class should extend.

Of course, there are substantial differences among cats, dogs, and mice, and we cover how to model those differences when we get to Polymorphism, later in this chapter.

Multiple Inheritance

Java does not support *multiple inheritance* (though interfaces give us a way to get most of the benefits of multiple inheritance without the one big problem, which we discuss shortly, that comes with it). That is, an object cannot extend more than one parent object. Other languages (such as C++) do permit inheriting from more than one parent. The designers of Java determined that Java could be made without that level of complexity. The problem with multiple inheritance is that a single class can extend two other classes, and those two classes might in turn extend the same ancestor class. How would your code know which ancestor class provides the right information? That's sometimes called "the diamond problem," because it looks like a diamond when graphed (see Figure 6-1).

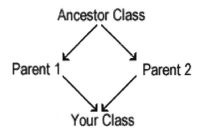

Figure 6-1. The diamond problem

You might think that the diamond problem is easy to avoid. However, remember that most software is created by multiple teams of people. At the time of this writing, I'm working with two development teams and a testing team in another country to create a software product that no fewer than 75 other software development teams in the same company will use as the basis for yet more software. In those circumstances, it's not hard to imagine how one team might implement a class that extends a class, the other team might extend the same class, and, if we had multiple inheritance, someone in the client teams might try to extend both and run right into the diamond problem. It's easy to get into a situation where a single method might extend methods from two other classes. How would the compiler know which method we meant to use? Java prevents all that by not providing multiple inheritance.

However, Java does provide a way to get most of the benefits and very few of the problems from multiple inheritance. You can include instances of other classes as fields within your class. That way, your class can access the public (or package, if your class is in the same package) fields and methods within those classes. Because you can't access the private bits and because you can't include abstract classes, you're (if those other classes are well designed) well protected from getting into problems that arise from having more than one ancestor. This technique is sometimes called *composition*, because your new class is composed, in part, of the publicly available bits of other classes. As with all techniques, be sure you need to do it, though. The simpler and cleaner you keep your objects, the easier it is to get your program to work, and the more your fellow developers appreciate your work.

Here's an example of the kind of problem for which composition works really well (with thanks to Jeremy Conner at Uplogix for the idea). Consider a classic monster from horror movies: a wolfman. Typically, a wolfman is more man than wolf (if only because the actors in the furry suits are themselves humans and not wolves). Consequently, we might model our wolfman by making a new class called Wolfman that extends Man (which might itself extend Human and be parallel to Woman) and includes an instance of the Wolf class as one of its fields. Then we can get all the attributes of a man and most of the attributes (anything declared public) from a wolf and have a software model of a wolfman.

Modeling Behavior through Interfaces

Java includes the concept of interfaces. An *interface* is a set of methods (basically, things an object can do) that an object must have if it uses (the keyword in Java is implements) that interface. In particular, a class that implements an interface must implement all the methods within that interface. Let's return to our three concrete classes: Cat, Dog, and Mouse.

Cats are predators and carnivores. Dogs are carnivores (there's some argument that they're omnivores, but we call them carnivores for the sake of our example) and both predators and scavengers. Mice are herbivores and are not predators or scavengers. So, we might create a set of interfaces to model the behavior of the animals we chose. We have the following interfaces: Predator, Scavenger, Carnivore, and Herbivore. If we add bears, we need an Omnivore interface, too.

Abstract Classes

Sometimes, a Java developer writes a class that should never be instantiated. That is, it's a class that will never have an object associated with it. Such a class usually serves as the basis for other classes. Our Mammal class is an example of such a class. All the mammals in the real world are specific types of mammals rather than just mammals. Cats, dogs, mice, humans, whales, and so on are all mammals, of course, but they all have more specific names and more specific traits. So, there's no actual animal that's a generic mammal. Consequently, we don't want anyone to create an instance of our Mammal class, because that would be bad modeling.

Java lets developers declare that a class should never have an instance by using the abstract keyword. In Java, abstract means that the class can still be extended by other classes but that it can never be instantiated (turned into an object). Returning to our example, we can have Mammal be abstract (because there's no such thing as a generic mammal) and still have Cat, Dog, and Mouse extend Mammal (because cats, dogs, and mice are mammals).

The hard part is figuring out when a class should be abstract. Modeling the animal kingdom is a simple example, so it's not hard to see that Mammal should be an abstract class.

The opposite of an abstract class is usually called a *concrete class*. Concrete classes are the default, so there's no keyword for it. In most programs, most classes are concrete classes.

Methods in Abstract Classes

Abstract classes can include abstract methods. Any class that extends a class with an abstract method must implement that method. For example, our Mammal class includes an abstract **speak**() method. Any class that extends Mammal must implement the **speak** method, and that implementation must have the same signature. So, in this case, the implementations must return void and accept no arguments.

Abstract classes can also include regular methods that their descendant classes can use without needing to implement them. Listing 6-1 shows both kinds of methods within the Mammal class.

Listing 6-1. *Methods within an abstract class*

```
package com.apress.java7forabsolutebeginners.examples.animalKingdom;

abstract class Mammal {
  // And here's a method for making the sound.
  // Each child class must implement it.
  abstract void speak();

  // All descendant classes can call this and do
  // not need to implement their own versions of it
  protected void sayWhatIAm() {
    System.out.println("I am a mammal");
  }
}
```

That's a trivial method, but it raises an interesting point. Classes that extend the Mammal class might also have methods with the same signature. Those methods are said to *override* this method. For example, the Cat class might have a **sayWhatIAm** method of its own. Let's suppose it was identical but printed "I am a cat" to System.out. Then, to use the Mammal class's method, we'd have to use the **super** keyword, as shown in Listing 6-2.

■ **Note** I made the sayWhatIAm() method protected so that only descendants of the Mammal class can say they're mammals. If it were public, we might have Snake objects saying they're mammals, and that would be wrong. Being protected forces any overriding methods in descendant classes to also be protected. Consequently, the sayWhatIAm() method in the Cat class has to be protected. That makes perfect sense, though. If we were to add Lion and Tiger classes, we would want them to say they are mammals and cats.

Listing 6-2. *The Cat class with an overridden sayWhatIAm method*

```
package com.apress.java7forabsolutebeginners.examples.animalKingdom;

class Cat extends Mammal {
  // implement the super class's abstract methods
```

```
    private static int numberOfCats;

    Cat() {
        numberOfCats++;
    }

    public static final int getNumberOfCats() {
        return numberOfCats;
    }

    @Override
    protected void sayWhatIAm() {
        System.out.println("I am a cat");
        super.sayWhatIAm();
    }
}
```

If a test program then called a `Cat` object's `sayWhatIAm ()` method, the output would be as shown in Listing 6-3.

Listing 6-3. Output of a Cat object's sayWhatIAm method

```
I am a cat
I am a mammal
```

This is a trivial example, but I hope it gives you a sense of how you can use the characteristics of both a base class and a child class to provide meaningful information and other functionality for your users. The trick is knowing which objects to put at which level. One rule of thumb is to put each object as high in your class hierarchy as you can. That's whyI define the speak method at the `Mammal` level but implement it at the individual animal level.

Static Members

Classes can have *static members*, including fields, methods, and other classes (a class within a class is called an *inner class*). A static member of a class is often called a *class member*. The important thing to know about class members is that only one instance of that member ever exists. If our `Cat` class has a static method, we might have ten different instances of the `Cat` class, but there would only ever be one of that static method. That becomes an issue when each of the members of the `Cat` class want to use that method. The instances end up waiting for each other.

Static members have their uses, though. When you want to be certain that only one of something exists for all the objects that instantiate a particular class, the `static` keyword is how you do it. One obvious use of the `static` keyword is on the `main` method. Imagine if every instance of a program class could start a new program. We would quickly swamp the operating system with programs. A more common and useful use of static members is to implement counters. Suppose we want to keep track of how many `Cat` objects we create. The `Cat` class could then include a static field called `numberOfCats`, and the constructors for the class would increment that field every time we create a `Cat` object. That code would look something like the `Cat` class in Listing 6-4.

Listing 6-4. *Counting Cat objects*

```
class Cat extends Mammal{

  static int numberOfCats;

  Cat() {
    numberOfCats++;
  }
}
```

To get the number of `Cat` objects, we can either implement a method to return the value or we can reference the field and get its value. To reference a static member, we use the name of the class separated from the static member's name by a period, as shown in Listing 6-5.

Listing 6-5 *Referencing a static member*

```
System.out.println(Cat.numberOfCats);
```

However, we should generally prefer the idiom of making the static field private and creating a get method to return that value. Otherwise, we expose the field for other classes to set, and that is probably a bug. Listing 6-6 shows the `Cat` class modified to use the private field pattern (patterns are common idioms in computer science—there are many of them, and they are a worthwhile thing to study if you pursue programming).

Listing 6-6. *The Cat class with a private static field*

```
class Cat extends Mammal{

  private static int numberOfCats;

  Cat() {
    numberOfCats++;
  }

  public static final int getNumberOfCats() {
    return numberOfCats;
  }
}
```

Do you notice that the method is also static? We need only one such method, regardless of how many `Cat` objects we create, so it makes sense for `getNumberOfCats` to be static. We also make it `final`, because there's no reason for child classes to implement their own `getNumberOfCats` methods. Thus, if we have `Tiger` and `Lion` classes extending the `Cat` class, they could not have `getNumberOfCats` methods unless those methods have different arguments.

Polymorphism

Polymorphism, from the Greek poly, for many, and morph, for form, means that the same thing can have different forms. It's a technical term in many fields, including chemistry, biology, and (of course) computer science. Each field defines it in terms relevant to that field of study, but it all boils down to having multiple forms.

In object-oriented computer languages, one kind of polymorphism is the ability of different classes to respond appropriately to the same input. So, our Mammal class might define a speak method. The Cat class would implement the speak method as a meow, the dog as a bark, and the mouse as a squeak. They all implement the same method, but they each do it in their own appropriate way. These methods are said to be overridden. The methods in the child class replace the behavior of the parent class with their own behavior—that is, they override the parent's method.

Another kind of polymorphism (called *overloading*) is having the same behavior mean something different depending on the object passed to the behavior (or method). For example, our Cat object might have two methods called chase, and an instance of Cat would exhibit different behavior for the chase(Tail) method and the chase(Mouse) method. That is, we have methods of the same name, but they have different signatures (one takes a Tail object as its argument and one takes a Mouse object). That's a classic example of method overloading.

Our Animals in Java

Listing 6-7 shows an incomplete definition of the animal classes used as examples earlier in the chapter. When a developer writes this kind of code, the developer is "creating stubs" or "writing stubbed out code." A *stub* means that we created the structure but have left at least some of the details for another time or for someone else to do.

You should put your code in packages. That way, the code in one package won't interfere with the code in other packages. If you put everything in the default package, you soon run into the problem of wanting to call a class or interface by a name you already used. I suggest you get in the habit of putting all your code into packages. The package used throughout this chapter includes a Predator interface. Imagine if want another object model that defined Predator drones (the remote-control aircraft made famous in recent wars). That's exactly the kind of entanglement that makes packages so useful. So we add a package definition for each class and interface. In this case, they are in the same package.

Listing 6-7. *The finished Mammal class*

```
package com.apress.java7forabsolutebeginners.examples.animalKingdom;

abstract class Mammal {
  // And here's a method for making the sound.
  // Each child class must implement it.
  abstract void speak();

  // All descendant classes can call this
  // and do not need to implement their own versions of it
  protected void sayWhatIAm() {
    System.out.println("I am a mammal");
  }
}
```

The Mammal class serves as the basis for our other classes. As we discussed previously, we never want to create a Mammal object, so it's abstract. It also has an abstract method, so every class that extends Mammal has to implement a speak method with the same signature (returns void and accepts no arguments). Finally, it includes an ordinary method, which descendant classes can use (see Listing 6-8).

Listing 6-8. *The finished Cat class*

```java
package com.apress.java7forabsolutebeginners.examples.animalKingdom;

class Cat extends Mammal implements Predator, Carnivore {

  private static int numberOfCats;

  Cat() {
    numberOfCats++;
  }

  public static final int getNumberOfCats() {
    return numberOfCats;
  }

  @Override
  protected void sayWhatIAm() {
    System.out.println("I am a cat");
    super.sayWhatIAm();
  }

  // implement the super class's abstract methods
  @Override
  void speak() {
    System.out.println("The cat says, \"meow.\"");
  }

  // here's our example of overloading
  void chase(Mouse mouse) {
    // chase a mouse
  }
  public void chase (Object tail) {
    // chase one's tail
  }

  // methods for the Predator interface
  @Override
  public void hunt() {
    // go hunting
  }

  // methods for the Carnivore interface
  @Override
  public void eat (Object freshMeat) {
    // eat fresh meat
  }
}
```

Because we use the Cat class throughout the earlier examples, you already know it extends the
Mammal class. As we discussed in the "Modeling Behavior through Interfaces" section, it also implements
the Predator and Carnivore interfaces. After all, cats are predators and carnivores (see Listing 6-9).

103

Listing 6-9. *The finished Dog class*

```
package com.apress.java7forabsolutebeginners .examples.animalKingdom;

class Dog extends Mammal implements Predator, Carnivore, Scavenger {
  // implement the super class's abstract methods
  @Override
  void speak() {
    System.out.println("The dog says, \"bark.\"");
  }
    // methods for the Predator interface
  @Override  public void hunt() {
    // go hunting
  }

  // methods for the Carnivore interface
  @Override  public void eat (Object freshMeat) {
    // eat fresh meat
  }

  // methods for the Scavenger interface
  @Override  public void eat (Object carrion, boolean tooOld) {
    if (tooOld) {
      // don't eat that!
    } else {
      // munch away
    }
  }
}
```

The Dog class also extends Mammal and implements the Predator and Carnivore classes. However, dogs also scavenge for food, so the Dog class also implements the Scavenger Interface.

Now, let's move onto an animal that is still a mammal but that has different behaviors: a mouse. Listing 6-10 defines our Mouse object.

Listing 6-10. *The finished Mouse class*

```
package com.apress.java7forabsolutebeginners .examples.animalKingdom;

class Mouse extends Mammal implements Herbivore{
  // implement the super class's abstract methods
  @Override
  void speak() {
    System.out.println("The mouse says, \"squeak.\"");
  }
    // methods for the Herbivore interface
  @Override  public void eat (Object plantMatter) {
    // eat plants
  }
}
```

As with our other animal objects, the `Mouse` class extends `Mammal`. However, a mouse is not a carnivore, a predator, or a scavenger. Instead, a mouse is an herbivore, so we make our `Mouse` class implement the `Herbivore` interface.

Now let's move onto the interfaces. We start with the Predator interface (see Listing 6-11).

***Listing 6-11.** The Predator interface*

```
package com.apress.java7forabsolutebeginners .examples.animalKingdom;

interface Predator {
  public void hunt();
}
```

All predators hunt, so our `Predator` interface includes a hunt() method. Any class that implements this `Predator` interface must implement a hunt() method with the same signature (void and with no arguments). If we have a `Drone` class that implements a Predator interface, that interface might implement a `launch(Missile hellfire)` method, which is different from a `Predator` interface that suits animals (at least outside the realm of science fiction).

Let's move on to the `Carnivore` interface, shown in Listing 6-12.

***Listing 6-12.** The Carnivore interface*

```
package com.apress.java7forabsolutebeginners .examples.animalKingdom;

interface Carnivore {
  public void eat(Object freshMeat);
}
```

Carnivores eat fresh meat, so we specify an object named `freshMeat` as the argument to the interface's only method.

Compare that to the `Scavenger` interface, shown in Listing 6-13.

***Listing 6-13.** The Scavenger interface*

```
package com.apress.java7forabsolutebeginners .examples.animalKingdom;

interface Scavenger {
  public void eat(Object carrion, boolean tooOld);
}
```

Scavengers eat whatever meat they can find. Of course, one issue is that some meat might be too foul to eat, so we include a boolean argument that we can test for that problem.

Finally, we come to our Herbivore interface, as shown in Listing 6-14.

***Listing 6-14.** The Hervibore interface*

```
package com.apress.java7forabsolutebeginners .examples.animalKingdom;

interface Herbivore {
  public void eat(Object plantMatter);
}
```

The Herbivore interface is parallel to the Carnivore and Scavenger interfaces, but herbivores eat plants, so we specify an object named plantMatter as the only argument.

Finally, here's a program class, called `AnimalVoices`, that lets our animals speak (see Listing 6-15).

Listing 6-15. Getting our animals to speak

```
package com.apress.java7forabsolutebeginners .examples.animalKingdom;

public class AnimalVoices {

  public static void main(String[] args) {
    // create instances of our animals
    Cat cat = new Cat();
    Dog dog = new Dog();
    Mouse mouse = new Mouse();

    // let our animals speak
    cat.speak();
    dog.speak();
    mouse.speak();
  }

}
```

As you can see, all it does is create an instance of each kind of animal and then have each one speak.

A Lesson about Granularity

Five classes and four interfaces might seem like a lot of objects to get three animals to make their appropriate sounds. Honestly, if I were writing a program to produce three lines of text, I'd write just one class. However, the purpose of the animal kingdom example was to show how to model a (not very) complex system in Java.

If I were really writing a system to model the animal kingdom, I'd have many more classes. For starters, if I were doing this for real, I wouldn't pass generic objects to the **eat** methods. I'd have an abstract class called **Food** and concrete classes called **FreshMeat**, **Carrion**, and **PlantMatter** and very likely subclasses from those, too.

If you "chunk up" your program into as many classes and interfaces as possible, you gain two things:

- Extensibility

- Maintainability

Extensibility means that you can easily make your program do more than it does now. In the case of our animal program, we could quickly add more animals and make those animals do more things (such as walk, swim, play, and sleep). If we expand the program, we might also expand the food details such that the **PlantMatter** class has **Nut** and **Grain** subclasses.

Maintainability means that you can easily find the spot where your code is wrong when you find an error. If all your code is in just a few classes (or worst of all, one class), you have a harder time figuring out the problem. Sure, the debugger gets you to the right line, but you won't know whether the problem is in your definition of an animal or your definition of a mammal or your definition of its behavior (such as predator or herbivore). Making multiple classes and interfaces greatly aids debugging because you can see which piece holds the problem spot. In other words, granularity makes it easier to create error-free programs.

Real programs need granularity, and good programmers work to achieve it.

Pass-by-Reference and Pass-by-Value

Pass-by-reference and *pass-by-value* refer to how information is passed from one object to another. Nearly all of the passing of information in Java goes through methods, but information can also go through fields within an object.

Strictly speaking, Java uses only pass-by-value. However, the values it passes differ greatly based on what is passed. For primitives, Java passes a copy of the primitive. So, if you pass an int to a method, the method receives a copy of the int, not the original int. For objects, Java passes a pointer. A *pointer* is the address of an object in memory. This subtle difference trips up many novice Java developers. A few examples clarify (I hope) the issue (see Listing 6-16). I say, "I hope," because this topic gives even seasoned developers fits.

Listing 6-16. *Pass-by-reference and pass-by-value*

```
package com.apress.java7forabsolutebeginners .examples.hello;

public class IntegerWrapper {

  public int objectInt = 0;
}

package com.apress.java7forabsolutebeginners .examples.hello;

public class Hello {

  static int primitiveInt = 0;
  static IntegerWrapper intWrapper = new IntegerWrapper();

  public static void main(String[] args) throws Exception {
    passBy(primitiveInt, intWrapper);
    System.out.println("primitiveInt = " + primitiveInt +
        "; intWrapper.objectInt = " + intWrapper.objectInt);
  }
    public static void passBy(int primitiveInt, IntegerWrapper intWrapper) {
    primitiveInt++;
    intWrapper.objectInt++;
  }
}
```

As you can see, this program has two classes, IntegerWrapper and PassByTest. IntegerWrapper is a way to turn a primitive into an object (and don't ever write objects like this for real, by the way—it's bad form, but it makes sense to keep this illustration as simple as possible). PassByTest demonstrates pass-by-reference and pass-by-value. When we run PassByTest, its output is primitiveInt = 0; intWrapper.objectInt = 1.

When you pass a primitive to a method, the JVM preserves the original value and makes a new primitive (literally, a copy) with the same value for use in the method. The JVM consequently has two values, the original `primitiveInt` field in `PassByTest` and the `primitiveInt` argument to the `passBy` method. Therein lies the heart of the issue: Because the JVM makes a new primitive, the original never gets modified.

Even if the `passBy` method returned the primitive value, it would not change the original value. Until we re-assign the original value, it remains whatever it was originally set to (0 in this case). If we assign the return value of the method to the original primitive, that works. Again, though, we have two different values, and we assign the value of the new one (created by the method) to the old one. Consider the modified `PassByTest` class in Listing 6-17.

Listing 6-17. PassByTest with a return value for the passBy method

```
package com.apress.java7forabsolutebeginners .examples.hello;

public class Hello {

  static int primitiveInt = 0;
  static IntegerWrapper intWrapper = new IntegerWrapper();

  public static void main(String[] args) throws Exception {
    passBy(primitiveInt, intWrapper);
    System.out.println("primitiveInt = " + primitiveInt +
        "; intWrapper.objectInt = " + intWrapper.objectInt);
  }
  public static int passBy(int primitiveInt, IntegerWrapper intWrapper) {
    primitiveInt++;
    intWrapper.objectInt++;
    return primitiveInt;
  }
}
```

The `passBy` method now returns an `int`, but the output remains the same (`primitiveInt` remains 0). I know I've hammered the point repeatedly, but, again, `primitiveInt` in the method is a different primitive than the `primitiveInt` field in the class. Remember, the compiler makes a copy of it when it calls the method.

Now, let's look at what happens to `IntegerWrapper.objectInt`. Because `IntegerWrapper` is an object, the value that gets passed is its address in memory (that is, a pointer to the object). There's only one `IntegerWrapper` object, named `intWrapper`, in memory (because we used the `new` keyword with that class only once). So, any work done on `intWrapper` is done to the same object. Consequently, when we increment `intWrapper.objectInt`, the change makes it back to the `main` method, because the `main` method still looks at the same spot in memory. That is, `intWrapper` continues to be at the same location in memory, and so we change that object where we could not change a primitive.

If all that seems confusing, you're in good company. It stumped me enough that I remember clearly, thirty years later, when I first realized that something (a function in Fortran, in fact) was working on the pass-by-reference model. It's a tricky concept, but you have to master it to be able to program in Java (and many other languages).

Java has a particular reason for passing objects by reference, by the way. Suppose you have a complex object. Such a class might have several fields, and many of those fields might themselves be references to other objects (remember the composition technique), and so on, to any depth you can imagine (object stacks, as such things are called, are often many layers deep). What exactly is the value of such an object, and how much memory and processing time gets chewed up trying to make a temporary copy for every method that gets that object as an argument? And what happens if we use such an object recursively (that is, the object can modify itself)? If you think about those issues for a minute, you see why objects are passed as references (that is, as memory addresses). Otherwise, Java programs would be substantially harder to create and perform more poorly than they could.

Summary

Many books have been written (and no doubt more books will be written) on object modeling. It's a fundamental part of object-oriented programming, and it's easy to fall into bad practices. Mastering object modeling requires both experience and study: experience to see how object models actually work and study to be aware of the issues. This chapter presents one simple example (a few members of the animal kingdom), but it's by no means a complete treatment of object modeling.

Along the way, we learned when to use abstract classes, static and final methods, and static fields. We also learned why we generally want fields to be private and have get methods rather than having the field be visible outside the class.

We also learned a bit about the value of granular programming (also known as "chunking" and modularity and many other similar names). Remember to "chunk" your programs into classes and interfaces, both to make them easier to understand and to make them easier to debug when problems arise.

Finally, we dove into the thorny theoretical issue of pass-by-reference versus pass-by-value. In particular, we learned that Java is strictly pass-by-value. However, some of those values are pointers (that is, memory addresses at which objects reside). Consequently, modifying an object that has been passed modifies the original object, whereas modifying a primitive modifies only a local copy of the primitive rather than the original.

CHAPTER 7

Writing a User Interface

Most of the people who want to develop software get into it to write programs that have rich user interfaces of some sort. That rich user interface might be through a set of windows, such as programs like Word or many games use, or through a web browser. However, a substantial community of developers largely develops programs that have no user interface. They write programs such as device drivers (the software that lets something like a mouse work with a computer), services (programs that provide information to other programs outside of the user interface), and database engines (which usually manage data in such a way that many programs can access that data). So there's plenty of work to do outside of user interfaces. Still, though, the visible part of the job attracts a lot of people to the profession, and there's nothing wrong with that.

This chapter shows you how to develop a user interface with the most commonly used of Java's built-in user-interface toolkits: Java Swing. We start with some simple basics and we end with an implementation of a Minesweeper game. After all, why not have a little fun when we're done? (And I bet a lot of the folks who buy this book would like to write a game. That works for me; I like games, too.)

Java Swing: The Basics

Java Swing is a large toolkit that includes support for all the things that you generally (and some things you don't generally) see in a non-web user interface: windows, buttons (with text, images, both, or neither), option lists, menus, labels, text boxes, text areas, checkboxes, droplists, drawing areas, file-selection dialogs, file save dialogs, other dialogs, and so on. In short, Swing offers all the tools you need to write almost any program. Some specialized programs might require interface objects that Swing doesn't have, but other toolkits probably don't have them, either. Also, Swing does include the ability to make new kinds of interface objects, though that's beyond the scope of this book.

Swing uses the Java Foundation Classes (JFC). The JFC is another toolkit that supports the creation of applications that can run on many different operating systems (such as Windows, Unix, and MacOS). Swing is one of several toolkits supported by JFC. Others include Java2D and the Abstract Window Toolkit (AWT). We use parts of the AWT as we work on our Swing application. For example, Java's Color class is part of the AWT.

Some people dislike Swing, claiming that it's overly complex and slow. Those criticisms fall on any UI toolkit, though. Swing is verbose but not more verbose than other UI toolkits that I've used. When you need to specify a lot of properties (size, font, color, placement on the screen, conditional presence, and so on), it takes a number of lines of code for each object to specify all that. That's the nature of the job, regardless of toolkit. As for speed, Swing can perform as well as other UI toolkits, though you have to know a great deal about the toolkit to get the most from it. Again, that's also true of other UI toolkits. The code in this book is not optimized for speed, by the way. I just show you the basics. To teach you everything about Swing, I'd have to write another (very likely larger) book.

A Basic Swing Application

Swing applications follow a fairly common flow. First, we create a JFrame object. The JFrame object is the main window and holds all the other interface components (buttons, text fields, and so on).

So, let's write a Swing application. The JFrame class lets you create a window, put other components in that window, and associate other windows with the first window. Consequently, creating a JFrame object is often the first step to creating a Swing application. As usual in software development, other ways exist, but we follow one common path, as shown in Listing 7-1.

Listing 7-1. The simplest possible Swing application

```
package com.apress.java7forabsolutebeginners.examples.swingdemo;

import java.awt.Dimension;

import javax.swing.JFrame;

public class SwingDemo {

  private JFrame frame = new JFrame("SwingDemo");

  private void createAndShowGUI() {
    frame.setDefaultCloseOperation(JFrame.EXIT_ON_CLOSE);
    frame.setPreferredSize(new Dimension(200, 200));
    frame.pack();
    frame.setVisible(true);
  }

  public static void main(String[] args) {
    SwingDemo swingDemo = new SwingDemo();
    swingDemo.createAndShowGUI();
  }
}
```

Before we go any further, Figure 7-1 shows our simple application.

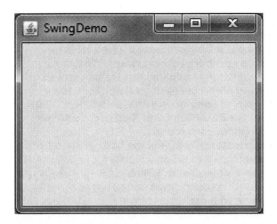

Figure 7-1. *Simple SwingDemo application*

All this program does is create and display an empty window. Let's look at how it does it, though. As you can see, we first create a `JFrame` object, which defines the window. Then, we specify some attributes for that window: size and whether to stop the application when the window closes. After setting those attributes, we prepare the window for display with the `pack` and `setVisible` methods. The `pack` method tells any Swing component that can have children to arrange its children within the component. The `setVisible` method dictates whether a component is visible or hidden. Naturally, for an application's main window, we want it to be visible. Hiding components can work well in some circumstances, though. If you have a window that you want to show sometimes and not other times, leaving the window in the set of windows and setting it to visible or hidden as needed uses a lot less overhead than creating it from scratch every time, especially if the window needs to maintain some content along the way.

Notice the behavior of the `main` method. In particular, notice that it creates an instance of the class that contains it. That's a common idiom for Swing programs. Otherwise, every method in the class must be static, and that's a nuisance (and often just won't work). I prefer to create the instance as soon as possible, to get it out of the way, so I put it in the main method. Other developers prefer to wait until at least one Swing component requires an instance. That's largely a matter of style. The important thing is that you'll almost always need to create an instance of your base class at some point.

■ **Note** A window is not a program. As the `Jframe.EXIT_ON_CLOSE` constant implies, an application does not need to stop because all its windows have been closed. In fact, some applications never have a window in the first place. Device drivers and services almost always run without showing a window.

Before we proceed, let's learn a bit more about JFrame. The first thing that trips up a lot of people is that a JFrame goes into a separate component called .a content pane. You can get the content pane with the `getContentPane()` method. You can also replace a content pane by calling `setContentPane()`. Any class that extends `Container` can serve as a content pane. Swing developers often use a `JPanel` object when they need to replace `JFrame`'s content pane. You can swap sets of content by using `setContentPane`. However, the card layout might work better for hiding and showing different sets of content.

Swing includes the concept of .a "layout." A layout. is an object that defines the relationship between other objects. For example, if you use a BoxLayout object, your components go in a line either horizontally or vertically. A grid layout, on the other hand, creates a layout that looks like a table (a number of cells wide by a number of cells high). Java also has a number of other layouts. We use a number of them in this chapter and later in the book. One handy thing about layouts is that you can use layouts within layouts. For example, you might use a BoxLayout object set to vertical and then use a number of other BoxLayouts, each set to horizontal, to add rows of components to your window. You can achieve a similar effect with a GridLayout object, too, but the BoxLayout with BoxLayout scheme might work better if you have different numbers of objects to put in each row.

I can go on for a long time (probably for a whole book) about all the options available in Swing, but I'll mention just one more that may be of interest to you. Swing includes different looks for programs. If you use the default settings (as I do in this chapter), you get Java's Metal look, which is meant to look the same on all operating systems. To get the native layout for any given operating system, use the SystemLookAndFeel object. If you use SystemLookAndFeel, people who use your software on Windows get a Windows look and feel, whereas users on other operating systems get the look and feel of those operating systems. The down side is that if Java can't figure out the look and feel of the system, your program doesn't work. That's why so many Java programs (especially those written for demonstrations and books) use the default (Metal) look and feel. Still, if you're writing software just for yourself or for a group of users who use the same operating system, and you can be sure that Java supports that operating system's look and feel, you can make your programs look just like the other programs that run on that operating system.

Now, let's do a little more with our program. Let's start by adding a feature many programs have, a menu. Listing 7.2 shows how to add .a menu.

Listing 7-2. A Swing program with a menu

```
package com.apress.java7forabsolutebeginners.examples.swingdemo;

import java.awt.Dimension;
import java.awt.event.ActionEvent;
import java.awt.event.ActionListener;

import javax.swing.JFrame;
import javax.swing.JMenu;
import javax.swing.JMenuBar;
import javax.swing.JMenuItem;

public class SwingDemo implements ActionListener {

    private JFrame frame = new JFrame("SwingDemo");

    private void addMenu(JFrame frame) {
        JMenu file = new JMenu("File");
        file.setMnemonic('F');
        JMenuItem exitItem = new JMenuItem("Exit");
        exitItem.setMnemonic('x');
        exitItem.addActionListener(this);
        file.add(exitItem);
        JMenuBar menuBar = new JMenuBar();
```

```java
      menuBar.add(file);
      frame.setJMenuBar(menuBar);
  }

  private void createAndShowGUI() {
      frame.setDefaultCloseOperation(JFrame.EXIT_ON_CLOSE);
      frame.setPreferredSize(new Dimension(200, 200));
      addMenu(frame);
      frame.pack();
      frame.setVisible(true);
  }

  public static void main(String[] args) {
      SwingDemo swingDemo = new SwingDemo();
      swingDemo.createAndShowGUI();
  }

  @Override
  public void actionPerformed(ActionEvent e) {
      if (e.getActionCommand().equals("Exit")) {
          System.exit(0);
      }
  }
}
```

Again, before we discuss how and why it works, let's see what it looks like. Figure 7-2 shows our additions.

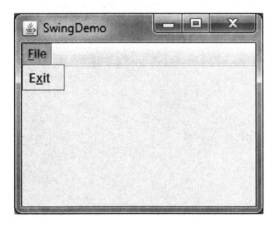

Figure 7-2. SwingDemo with a menu

That listing shows why some people complain that Swing is verbose. We added a lot of code just to add a menu with a single item. We can manage that problem, though, by using good software design and coding practices. Feel free to write helper classes (for example, the `ActionListener` can be its own class; here's a place to apply the design principles we covered in Chapter 6, "Object-Oriented Programming"), and you should always be careful to make each method serve a well-defined purpose. As your programs get larger, good design and good coding become ever more important. Indeed, good design is a developer's primary skill (though we often keep the designs simple in this book to make easier-to-read examples).

So, let's look at what we had to add to get a menu. We encapsulated the menu code in a separate method (a good practice) called `addMenu`. As you can see, it first creates a menu called "File," then it creates a menu item called "Exit," and finally, it creates a menu bar to hold the menu item and attaches that menu bar to the `JFrame` object. If we created another menu object and added it to the menu bar, we'd have another top-level menu object. For example, the word processor I'm using to write this book has a File menu, an Edit menu, a Format menu, and so on. Each top-level menu is visible in the menu bar and contains one or more menu items. .The `createAndShowGUI` method (which is the controlling method in the program) then calls the `addMenu` method.

The other big addition that we need to make a menu work is an `ActionListener`. In this case, we made the program class itself the `ActionListener` by implementing the `ActionListener` interface. More complex programs often have a separate class (or several classes) serve as listeners. A *listener*, as its name implies, monitors (listens to) the events in the program and lets you specify that something should be done when a certain event happens. In this case, we want the program to stop when someone chooses `Exit` from the `File` menu, so we check for that event and exit when it happens. Java offers a number of listeners, including mouse, keyboard, and many other listeners, all of which extend the `EventListener` interface. We'll add another listener in the next iteration of our SwingDemo program.

Let's add a few other commonly used components: a button, a label, a text area, and a separate child window called a dialog. In software development, a dialog (or dialog box) is a separate window that serves a simple, well-defined purpose, such as displaying information or letting the user choose a file. All those little windows that pop up to ask whether you want to do something in the Windows operating system are probably the best known (and least loved) dialog boxes. Listing 7-3 shows the expanded code for all these new components.

Figure 7-3 shows what our modified program looks like when we're done.

Figure 7-3. *SwingDemo with more features*

Listing 7-3. A more complex Swing program

```java
package com.apress.java7forabsolutebeginners.examples.swingdemo;

import java.awt.Component;
import java.awt.Dimension;
import java.awt.event.ActionEvent;
import java.awt.event.ActionListener;
import java.awt.event.MouseEvent;
import java.awt.event.MouseListener;

import javax.swing.BoxLayout;
import javax.swing.JButton;
import javax.swing.JFrame;
import javax.swing.JLabel;
import javax.swing.JMenu;
import javax.swing.JMenuBar;
import javax.swing.JMenuItem;
import javax.swing.JOptionPane;
import javax.swing.JPanel;
import javax.swing.JTextArea;

public class SwingDemo implements ActionListener, MouseListener {

    private JFrame frame = new JFrame("SwingDemo");
    private JPanel panel = new JPanel();
    private JButton sayButton = new JButton("I say!");
    private JLabel sayLabel = new JLabel("Say something:");
    private JTextArea sayText = new JTextArea();

    private void addMenu(JFrame frame) {
        JMenu file = new JMenu("File");
        file.setMnemonic('F');
        JMenuItem exitItem = new JMenuItem("Exit");
        exitItem.setMnemonic('x');
        exitItem.addActionListener(this);
        file.add(exitItem);
        JMenuBar menuBar = new JMenuBar();
        menuBar.add(file);
        frame.setJMenuBar(menuBar);
    }

    private void arrangeComponents(JFrame frame) {
        panel.setLayout(new BoxLayout(panel, BoxLayout.Y_AXIS));
        sayText.setPreferredSize(new Dimension(200, 50));
        sayText.setAlignmentX(Component.CENTER_ALIGNMENT);
        sayLabel.setAlignmentX(Component.CENTER_ALIGNMENT);
        sayButton.setAlignmentX(Component.CENTER_ALIGNMENT);
        sayButton.addMouseListener(this);
        panel.add(sayLabel);
        panel.add(sayText);
```

117

```java
    panel.add(sayButton);
    frame.add(panel);
}
  private void createAndShowGUI() {
    frame.setDefaultCloseOperation(JFrame.EXIT_ON_CLOSE);
    addMenu(frame);
    arrangeComponents(frame);
    frame.pack();
    frame.setVisible(true);
}

public static void main(String[] args) {
    SwingDemo swingDemo = new SwingDemo();
    swingDemo.createAndShowGUI();
}

@Override
public void actionPerformed(ActionEvent e) {
    if (e.getActionCommand().equals("Exit")) {
        System.exit(0);
    }
}

@Override
public void mouseClicked(MouseEvent e) {
}

@Override
public void mouseEntered(MouseEvent e) {
}

@Override
public void mouseExited(MouseEvent e) {
}

@Override
public void mousePressed(MouseEvent e) {
}

@Override
public void mouseReleased(MouseEvent e) {
    if (e.getSource() == sayButton) {
        JOptionPane.showMessageDialog(frame, sayText.getText(),
            "You said", JOptionPane.PLAIN_MESSAGE);
    }
}
}
```

Getting big, isn't it? Actually, no. It's a much bigger program than most of what we've done so far, but it's still not as big as many real programs. Managing complexity is a big part of software development. As mentioned previously, good design and good coding practices let you manage the complexity of your code and still produce robust programs. I hammer on this point, by the way, because it is crucial to good software development.

In this case, we've managed the additional complexity by adding an arrangeComponents method. That method lets you associate all the components with a JPanel and then add the panel to the frame. Without a panel, the frame would have no place to put the components, so JFrame and JPanel often go hand in hand. As usual, other ways exist, but a JFrame object with one or more JPanel objects is common in Swing applications.

In a more complex program, multiple methods (and probably classes) would handle all the components. In larger Swing programs, it's common practice to have each window be defined by its own class. In such systems, another class (or set of classes), called a controller, determines which window (or windows) should be visible and which one should have focus. Our little program isn't that complex, though, so one class will do.

We also had to implement the MouseListener interface, so that the program can tell when someone clicks on the button. The MouseListener interface requires five methods, but we use only one of them. Other programs might need to distinguish between when a mouse button is pressed and when it is released (for enabling behavior such as drag and drop or drawing a box in a drawing program), but our little program just needs to know that the user clicked the button. Note the line where a mouse listener is added to the button. Each component that you want to handle an event has to have an event listener added to it. When you have multiple objects listening for events, you have to figure out which object the user chooses and make your program respond accordingly. The getSource method lets us do that. You'll see a great deal more of that kind of decision making, both with menus and with buttons, in the next example.

▪ **Tip**   If you need to detect whether a mouse button has been clicked, use the mouseReleased method instead of the mouseClicked method. In many JVMs, mouseClicked doesn't work well (in particular, it misses some clicks, which is frustrating for the user), whereas mouseReleased is more reliable. This happens because mouse motion interrupts the mouse listener (Java has a separate listener interface for monitoring mouse motion). So, if you twitch just a little bit while clicking the button, you lose the mouse click.

A Larger Swing Application

As it happens, I like Minesweeper and similar games, so I thought I'd write my own Minesweeper game to serve as a larger, more real example of a Swing application. In addition to being one of my favorite games, MineSweeper makes a good sample because it uses a mouse listener and an action listener. It's also the kind of application that benefits from having both a program class and a number of additional classes to handle various bits of functionality.

Before we get started, let's think about the design of such a program. Table 7-1 describes the various classes that comprise the MineSweeper program.

Table 7-1. *MineSweeper classes*

Class Name	Description
MineSweeper	The program class. It contains the user interface (Swing) elements and has links to the game's functionality (which is in the other classes).
MineField	Models a minefield. Contains Mine objects.
Mine	Models an individual mine.
MineIcon	Defines and makes available the mine icons.
MineSweeperActionListener	Listens for menu actions.
MineSweeperMouseListener	Listens for mouse actions that affect the play area (left clicks and right clicks).
MineSweeperHelper	Convenience class that contains the game's logic.

Let's start with the program class (MineSweeper). After listing 7-4, I'll describe the flow of control through the class (in other words, the logic of it) and describe each method. Compared to other things we've done, it's a big and complex class. For now, read through it, even if it doesn't seem to make sense. Then we'll work through it in detail. Listing 7-4 shows the MineSweeper class. Before we get into the listing, though, let's see what we're going to get from the MineSweeper class, in Figure 7-4.

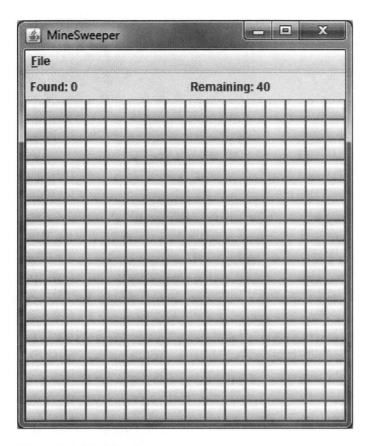

Figure 7-4. *The MineSweeper program*

Listing 7-4. *The MineSweeper class*

```
package com.apress.java7forabsolutebeginners.examples.MineSweeper;

import java.awt.Component;
import java.awt.Dimension;
import java.awt.GridLayout;

import javax.swing.BorderFactory;
import javax.swing.BoxLayout;
import javax.swing.ButtonGroup;
import javax.swing.JButton;
import javax.swing.JFrame;
import javax.swing.JLabel;
import javax.swing.JMenu;
import javax.swing.JMenuBar;
import javax.swing.JMenuItem;
import javax.swing.JPanel;
```

```java
import javax.swing.JRadioButtonMenuItem;
import javax.swing.border.Border;

public class MineSweeper {

  int columns = 8;
  int rows = 8;
  int numberOfMines = 10;

  JFrame frame = new JFrame("MineSweeper");
  JPanel minePanel = new JPanel();
  JLabel minesRemainingLabel = new JLabel("Remaining:");
  JLabel minesFoundLabel = new JLabel("Found: 0");
  JButton[][] mineButtons;
  Dimension buttonSize = new Dimension(20, 20);

  MineField mineField;
  MineSweeperMouseListener mouseListener;
  MineSweeperActionListener actionListener;
  MineSweeperHelper helper;

  public MineSweeper() {
    helper = new MineSweeperHelper(this);
    actionListener = new MineSweeperActionListener(this, helper);
    mouseListener = new MineSweeperMouseListener(this, helper);
    init();
  }

  void init() {
    mineButtons = new JButton[rows][columns];
    for (int i = 0; i < rows; i++) {
      for (int j = 0; j < columns; j++) {
        JButton currentButton = new JButton();
        mineButtons[i][j] = currentButton;
        currentButton.setPreferredSize(buttonSize);
        currentButton.setMaximumSize(buttonSize);
        currentButton.setMinimumSize(buttonSize);
        currentButton.addMouseListener(mouseListener);
        currentButton.setEnabled(true);
        currentButton.setText("");
        currentButton.setIcon(null);
      }
    }
    minePanel.setLayout(new GridLayout(rows, columns));
    for (int i = 0; i < rows; i++) {
      for (int j = 0; j < columns; j++) {
        minePanel.add(mineButtons[i][j]);
      }
    }
    mineField = new MineField(rows, columns, numberOfMines);
  }
```

```java
private void addAndArrangePanels(JFrame frame) {
  Border paddingBorder = BorderFactory.createEmptyBorder(5,5,5,5);
  JPanel controlPanel = new JPanel();
  minesFoundLabel.setBorder(paddingBorder);
  minesFoundLabel.setAlignmentX(Component.LEFT_ALIGNMENT);
  minesRemainingLabel.setAlignmentX(Component.RIGHT_ALIGNMENT);
  minesRemainingLabel.setBorder(paddingBorder);
  minesRemainingLabel.setText("Remaining: " + mineField.getMinesRemaining());
  controlPanel.add(minesFoundLabel);
  controlPanel.add(minesRemainingLabel);
  GridLayout gridLayout = new GridLayout(1,2);
  controlPanel.setLayout(gridLayout);
  frame.getContentPane().add(controlPanel);
  frame.getContentPane().add(minePanel);
}

private void addMenu(JFrame frame) {
  JMenu file = new JMenu("File");
  file.setMnemonic('F');
  JMenuItem newItem = new JMenuItem("New Game");
  newItem.setMnemonic('n');
  newItem.addActionListener(actionListener);
  file.add(newItem);
  ButtonGroup sizeOptions = new ButtonGroup();
  JRadioButtonMenuItem smallOption = new JRadioButtonMenuItem("Small (8 x 8, 10 mines)");
  smallOption.setMnemonic('s');
  smallOption.addActionListener(actionListener);
  sizeOptions.add(smallOption);
  file.add(smallOption);
  JRadioButtonMenuItem mediumOption =
      new JRadioButtonMenuItem("Medium (16 x 16, 40 mines)");
  mediumOption.setMnemonic('m');
  mediumOption.addActionListener(actionListener);
  sizeOptions.add(mediumOption);
  file.add(mediumOption);
  JRadioButtonMenuItem largeOption =
      new JRadioButtonMenuItem("Large (16 x 32, 100 mines)");
  largeOption.setMnemonic('l');
  largeOption.addActionListener(actionListener);
  sizeOptions.add(largeOption);
  file.add(largeOption);
  JMenuItem exitItem = new JMenuItem("Exit");
  exitItem.setMnemonic('x');
  exitItem.addActionListener(actionListener);
  file.add(exitItem);
  JMenuBar menuBar = new JMenuBar();
  menuBar.add(file);
  frame.setJMenuBar(menuBar);
}
```

```
    private void createAndShowGUI() {
      frame.setDefaultCloseOperation(JFrame.EXIT_ON_CLOSE);
      frame.getContentPane()
          .setLayout(new BoxLayout(frame.getContentPane(), BoxLayout.Y_AXIS));

      addAndArrangePanels(frame);
      addMenu(frame);

      frame.pack();
      frame.setVisible(true);
    }

    public static void main(String[] args) {
      MineSweeper mineSweeper = new MineSweeper();
      mineSweeper.createAndShowGUI();
    }
  }
```

MineSweeper does the same things as the other Swing classes we've already written, and it does quite a bit more, as you just saw. So let's step through exactly what it's doing. We'll start where you just stopped: at the bottom, with the main method. As you learned in Chapter 1, "Writing Your First Java Program," the main method is the entry point for a program. Listing 7-5 shows the main method.

Listing 7-5. *MineSweeper's main method*

```
  public static void main(String[] args) {
    MineSweeper mineSweeper = new MineSweeper();
    mineSweeper.createAndShowGUI();
  }
```

The main method doesn't do much. It creates an instance of the MineSweeper class, which is a handy way to avoid having to use nothing but static objects and methods throughout the class. Creating a new object calls the constructor for that object's class. In the other classes we've seen so far, the constructors have done nothing (and we've not coded them, relying on the default constructors for our objects). The MineSweeper class, however, needs a true constructor. Listing 7-6 shows the constructor.

Listing 7-6. *MineSweeper's constructor*

```
  public MineSweeper() {
    helper = new MineSweeperHelper(this);
    actionListener = new MineSweeperActionListener(this, helper);
    mouseListener = new MineSweeperMouseListener(this, helper);
    init();
  }
```

The MineSweeper constructor first creates a helper object by instantiating (a fancy word for creating an object) the MineSweeperHelper class. We have to do that first, so that we can pass the helper object to our two listener objects. The next two lines create instances of the MineSweeperActionListener and MineSweeperMouseListener classes. Those classes monitor the menu and the minefield (respectively) for mouse clicks. We could have had those listeners here in the MineSweeper class (in fact, we originally had that functionality in the MineSweeper class). Instead, we decided to have the MineSweeper class handle just the user interface definition and push all the other tasks off to other classes. That's the kind of design decision that you'll often face as you develop your programs. In this case, both my editor (Ewan) and my technical reviewer (Massimo) suggested splitting the functionality, and they were right. (Thanks, guys.) Even relatively simple (and yes, MineSweeper is pretty simple) software benefits from being reviewed by others, which is something to keep in mind when you do your own programming.

You probably noticed that all the classes created by the constructor take the MineSweeper instance itself (through the `this` keyword) as an argument. For now, don't concern yourself with that detail. You'll see why that happens when we cover those classes.

Finally, the `MineSweeper` constructor calls the `init` method, which appears (again) in Listing 7-7.

Listing 7-7. MineSweeper's init method

```
void init() {
  mineButtons = new JButton[rows][columns];
  for (int i = 0; i < rows; i++) {
    for (int j = 0; j < columns; j++) {
      JButton currentButton = new JButton();
      mineButtons[i][j] = currentButton;
      currentButton.setPreferredSize(buttonSize);
      currentButton.setMaximumSize(buttonSize);
      currentButton.setMinimumSize(buttonSize);
      currentButton.addMouseListener(mouseListener);
      currentButton.setEnabled(true);
      currentButton.setText("");
      currentButton.setIcon(null);
    }
  }
  minePanel.setLayout(new GridLayout(rows, columns));
  for (int i = 0; i < rows; i++) {
    for (int j = 0; j < columns; j++) {
      minePanel.add(mineButtons[i][j]);
    }
  }
  mineField = new MineField(rows, columns, numberOfMines);
}
```

The init method creates the two-dimensional array of small buttons that is the user interface to the minefield. (The minefield itself is a more abstract object that contains the information about where the mines are a subtle but meaningful distinction that we delve into a bit more later in the chapter.) It then adds all those buttons to the JPanel object that holds the minefield buttons. Finally, it creates the actual minefield. (Again, the buttons are the way we let the player access the set of information that is the minefield.)

▨ **Note** The init method gets called both when the user starts the application and when the user starts a new game. That's why it replaces the existing instance of the `MineField` class with a new instance.

After the constructor and the init method are done setting up the game, the main method passes control to the next method in the chain of execution: createAndShowGUI. Listing 7-8 shows the createAndShowGUI method.

Listing 7-8. MineSweeper's createAndShowGUI method

```
private void createAndShowGUI() {
  frame.setDefaultCloseOperation(JFrame.EXIT_ON_CLOSE);
  frame.getContentPane()
      .setLayout(new BoxLayout(frame.getContentPane(), BoxLayout.Y_AXIS));

  addAndArrangePanels(frame);
  addMenu(frame);

  frame.pack();
  frame.setVisible(true);
}
```

The createAndShowGUI method sets up and shows the JFrame object. Remember that a JFrame object is a window. So we define the details of the program's window and then show it. Let's take it line by line from here. The first line indicates that closing the window should also exit the program (stopping a program and removing it from the operating system's list of running programs is often called "exiting a program"). The second line sets the layout. In this case, it uses a BoxLayout object that places controls in a line vertically. Notice that we have to get the content pane to be able to set the layout. Next, we pass execution (that is, the current work being done by the program) to the addAndArrangePanels method (which we get to next). When that's done, execution returns to this method. Then, we pass execution to yet another method called addMenu. Notice that both of those methods take the JFrame object as argument, which tells us that those methods do more of the work of setting up the window. In fact, they do most of that work. Finally, we get to the last two lines, which directly affect the JFrame object. The line that calls the pack method on the JFrame object (that is, the frame.pack(); line) tells the JVM to organize all the controls in the JFrame object. The last line calls the setVisible method on the JFrame object, which is Java's way of saying to make the window visible to the user. You can keep windows in memory and make them visible or invisible. This gives better performance than re-specifying a window when you need to hide a window.

Now let's look at the addAndArrangePanels method, which appears in listing 7-9.

Listing 7-9. MineSweeper's addAndArrangePanels method

```
private void addAndArrangePanels(JFrame frame) {
  Border paddingBorder = BorderFactory.createEmptyBorder(5,5,5,5);
  JPanel controlPanel = new JPanel();
  minesFoundLabel.setBorder(paddingBorder);
  minesFoundLabel.setAlignmentX(Component.LEFT_ALIGNMENT);
  minesRemainingLabel.setAlignmentX(Component.RIGHT_ALIGNMENT);
  minesRemainingLabel.setBorder(paddingBorder);
  minesRemainingLabel.setText("Remaining: " + mineField.getMinesRemaining());
  controlPanel.add(minesFoundLabel);
  controlPanel.add(minesRemainingLabel);
  GridLayout gridLayout = new GridLayout(1,2);
  controlPanel.setLayout(gridLayout);
```

```
    frame.getContentPane().add(controlPanel);
    frame.getContentPane().add(minePanel);
}
```

You might ask, "Panels? What panels?" Well, it happens that the MineSweeper program uses two JPanel objects. One panel holds the score panel and the other holds the minefield. Remember the BoxLayout object with the vertical axis? It dictates that one panel is over the other. In this case, the panel that shows the scores (called controlPanel) is above the minefield (called minePanel). Again, let's go through it one line at a time.

The first line creates a Border object that has 5 pixels of padding on all four sides. We use that Border object to keep our labels from bumping into the other things in the window. The second line creates a new JPanel object called controlPanel, which holds our labels. So why not create the panel that holds the minefield here? Because we need it elsewhere, so we have to create it in the class variables at the top of the class. The third line sets the padding for the minesFoundLabel object, which tells the player how many mines they've marked so far. (Of course, the player might be wrong; that's part of the fun.) The fourth line sets the alignment of the minesFoundLabel to the left, which makes it appear on the left side of the panel. The fifth line sets the alignment of the minesRemainingLabel, which tells the player how many mines have yet to be found, such that the label is on the right side of the panel. The sixth line uses our border definition to add a border to the minesRemainingLabel. The seventh line sets the text of the minesRemainingLabel. So why didn't we set the value of the minesFoundLabel? Because we don't need to concatenate two strings together to set that one and we can't be sure how many mines the player has chosen to have in the game. The next two lines add our labels to the controlPanel object. Then, we create a GridLayout object, which we use to control the placement of the two labels. In this case, we create a small grid with just one row and two cells (one for each label). Finally, we add the two panels to the JFrame object. At this point, all the controls that appear in the window have been defined and their relationships to one another have also been defined.

▓ **Note** Creating a component, setting its attributes, and adding the component to a container is the normal idiom for setting up user interfaces in Swing (and other user interface frameworks as well). You'll do a lot of that if you write many applications that have user interfaces. Remember that a container is also a component, so you'll often add one component to another component and then add that set of components to yet another component. You can see that here in the addAndArrangePanels method when we add labels to a JPanel object and then add the JPanel object to the JFrame object.

Now that we have the components in the window defined, let's add a menu, so that a player can start a new game, set the size of the game, and exit the game. We do all that in the AddMenu method, which appears in Listing 7-10.

Listing 7-10. MineSweeper's addMenu method

```
private void addMenu(JFrame frame) {
    JMenu file = new JMenu("File");
    file.setMnemonic('F');
    JMenuItem newItem = new JMenuItem("New Game");
    newItem.setMnemonic('n');
```

```
        newItem.addActionListener(actionListener);
        file.add(newItem);
        ButtonGroup sizeOptions = new ButtonGroup();
        JRadioButtonMenuItem smallOption = new JRadioButtonMenuItem("Small (8 x 8, 10 mines)");
        smallOption.setMnemonic('s');
        smallOption.addActionListener(actionListener);
        sizeOptions.add(smallOption);
        file.add(smallOption);
        JRadioButtonMenuItem mediumOption =
            new JRadioButtonMenuItem("Medium (16 x 16, 40 mines)");
        mediumOption.setMnemonic('m');
        mediumOption.addActionListener(actionListener);
        sizeOptions.add(mediumOption);
        file.add(mediumOption);
        JRadioButtonMenuItem largeOption =
            new JRadioButtonMenuItem("Large (16 x 32, 100 mines)");
        largeOption.setMnemonic('l');
        largeOption.addActionListener(actionListener);
        sizeOptions.add(largeOption);
        file.add(largeOption);
        JMenuItem exitItem = new JMenuItem("Exit");
        exitItem.setMnemonic('x');
        exitItem.addActionListener(actionListener);
        file.add(exitItem);
        JMenuBar menuBar = new JMenuBar();
        menuBar.add(file);
        frame.setJMenuBar(menuBar);
    }
```

The addMenu method is larger than some of the programs we've written so far. As I mentioned at the start of the chapter, one common complaint about Swing is that it is overly verbose (which means that it takes a lot of code to do what seems like not much work). Again, that's an unfair criticism because other user-interface frameworks suffer from the same problem. Being able to set a lot of options to make your program do all kinds of things means there are a lot of attributes to set, which means a lot of code. That's the nature of user-interface development. You get used to it after you create a few programs that have graphical user interfaces (GUIs).

So, let's look at the addMenu method in detail. The method follows a repetitious pattern, so we describe the pattern rather than describe every line (after all, it *is* a big method). The first line creates a JMenu object named "file." If our program also had an Edit menu (such as a word processor might have), we would have another JMenu object. So, to Swing, a menu is one of the menus in the larger menu structure (which we get to near the bottom of the method). After creating the File menu object, we start creating JMenuItem objects. Each JMenuItem object defines one of the choices in this particular menu. For each menu item, we specify a name (such as "New Game" or "Exit"), set a mnemonic character (which lets the player control the menu with the keyboard), add an ActionListener object (the same action listener for all of them, in this case), and then add the menu item to the file menu object. Towards the bottom of the method, we create a JMenuBar object. A JmenuBar object probably corresponds more closely to what you think of when someone says, "menu," because a JMenuBar object defines the whole menu across the top of a program. Once we have our JMenuBar object, we add the file menu object to it and, finally, add the whole menu to our window (again, defined by our JFrame object).

Now that we're through all the methods, we should look at the fields in the MineSweeper class. The fields are the variables at the top of the class. Rather than make you flip all the pages between here and there, Listing 7-11 shows the field definitions.

Listing 7-11. *MineSweeper's fields*

```
int columns = 8;
int rows = 8;
int numberOfMines = 10;

JFrame frame = new JFrame("MineSweeper");
JPanel minePanel = new JPanel();
JLabel minesRemainingLabel = new JLabel("Remaining:");
JLabel minesFoundLabel = new JLabel("Found: 0");
JButton[][] mineButtons;
Dimension buttonSize = new Dimension(20, 20);

MineField mineField;
MineSweeperMouseListener mouseListener;
MineSweeperActionListener actionListener;
MineSweeperHelper helper;
```

The rest of the `MineSweeper` class and the other classes that comprise the program use these values. The three int values at the top control the size of the game and the number of mines. They have default values (the values of the small size of the game) so that the game can load a version of the game when the player starts the MineSweeper application. The `JFrame`, `JPanel`, `JLabel`, `JButton`, and `Dimension` objects help us define the user interface. The last four give us a way to refer to the other classes that we use to make the program work.

To sum up our trip through MineSweeper class, we can make a few general observations about the whole class. The most interesting thing about this class is programmatically creating a lot of buttons and then figuring out which one the user selected. Another interesting thing is the ability to replace the existing minefield and all its buttons with a new minefield and buttons when the user wants a new game (because of winning or losing or choosing to abandon the current game). The `validate` methods on the `minePanel` and `frame` objects make that possible. After the existing buttons have been removed and new buttons added, the `validate` methods tells the program to redraw the minefield panel and all its buttons. If your own applications need to know which mouse button the user pressed, use the `MouseEvent.getButton` method, as we did here. In this case, we check only for the left button and treat anything else as a right click (even though it could be some other button, such as the middle button).

Now let's move to the problems. This version of Minesweeper is an example, so it's far from perfect. For one thing, rather than figure out which other buttons should be revealed when an empty spot is clicked, the code cycles through the all the mines. I did that because the `MineField` class already has a `cascade` method for figuring out which neighboring locations would clear because of click. Also, I made no attempt to optimize performance (though it runs as well as the Windows Minesweeper game on my Windows laptop). Also, as you can see, I didn't bother to solve the problem of making the first click never hit a mine. If you want to tackle that problem, by the way, populate the mine field after the user clicks the first mine button (that's called late loading). Finally, I'm no artist, so the icons I created aren't much to look at. They're ours, though, so we don't have to worry about copyrights to use them. Feel free to create or find your own.

I separate the `MineField` and `Mine` classes from the user interface because I might want to use those classes as the underpinnings of a Minesweeper game that does not use Swing. In particular, I might write an Android version of Minesweeper, just for fun (it certainly wouldn't be a money maker, because many

Minesweeper apps already exist for Android—most of my projects are for fun and my own learning). Also, it's the kind of abstraction that makes for good design. When the real-world situation you model has discrete objects, it's good practice to create a class for each of those objects. In this case, a mine is a discrete real-world object (to which the game adds another layer of abstraction, in fact), so a `Mine` class is a good choice. The same applies to a minefield, so the `MineField` class is also a good design idea. Now, let's move on to the `MineField` class. Like the `MineSweeper` class, it's a bigger class than anything else we've seen earlier in the book. Again, please read through it as closely as you can, but don't be concerned if parts of it don't make sense right now. We take it apart method by method after you see the whole thing. Listing 7-12 shows the entire `MineField` class.

Listing 7-12. The MineField class

```java
package com.apress.java7forabsolutebeginners.examples.MineSweeper;

public class MineField {

  private Mine[][] mineField;
  private int rows;
  private int columns;
  private int mines;
  private int minesFound = 0;
  private int minesRemaining;
  private int emptiesRemaining;
  enum gameState {WIN, LOSE, CONTINUE};

    MineField(int rows, int columns, int mines) {
    this.rows = rows;
    this.columns = columns;
    this.mines = mines;
    minesRemaining = mines;
    emptiesRemaining = rows * columns - mines;
    mineField = new Mine[rows][columns];
    init();
    populate();
  }

  private void init() {
    for (int i = 0; i < rows; i++){
      for (int j = 0; j < columns; j++) {
        mineField[i][j] = new Mine();
      }
    }
  }
    gameState resolveClick(int x, int y, boolean left) {
    for (int i = 0; i < rows; i++){
      for (int j = 0; j < columns; j++) {
        if (i == x && j == y) {
          Mine thisMine = mineField[i][j];
          if (left) {
            if (thisMine.getFlagState() ==
```

```
                Mine.flagState.MINE) {
              return gameState.CONTINUE;
          }
          if (thisMine.isCleared())
            return gameState.CONTINUE;
          if (thisMine.hasMine()) {
            return gameState.LOSE;
          } else {
            return cascade(i, j);
          }
        } else {
          Mine.flagState state =
            thisMine.setFlagState();
          if(state == Mine.flagState.MINE) {
            minesFound++;
            minesRemaining--;
          } else if(state == Mine.flagState.SUSPECT) {
            minesFound--;
            minesRemaining++;
          }
        }
      }
    }
  }
  return gameState.CONTINUE;
}

private void populate() {
  populate(0);
}

private void populate(int mineCount) {
  int currentCount = mineCount;
  double mineChance = (double) mines / (double) (rows * columns);
  for (int i = 0; i < rows; i++) {
    for (int j = 0; j < columns; j++) {
      Mine thisMine = mineField[i][j];
      if (!thisMine.hasMine()) {
        if (Math.random() < mineChance) {
          thisMine.setMine();
          currentCount++;
          if (currentCount == mines) {
            return;
          }
        }
      }
    }
  }
  if (currentCount < mines) {
    populate(currentCount);
  }
}
```

```
    int getMinesFound() {
      return minesFound;
    }

    int getMinesRemaining() {
      return minesRemaining;
    }

    private gameState cascade(int x, int y) {
      if (x < 0 || y < 0 || x >= rows || y >= columns) {
        return gameState.CONTINUE;
      }
      Mine thisMine = mineField[x][y];
      if (thisMine.hasMine()) {
        return gameState.CONTINUE;
      }
      if (!thisMine.isCleared()) {
        thisMine.clear();
        emptiesRemaining--;
        if (emptiesRemaining == 0) {
          return gameState.WIN;
        }
      }
      if (countAdjacentMines(x, y) > 0) {
        return gameState.CONTINUE;
      } else{
        for (int i = x - 1; i <= x + 1; i++) {
          for (int j = y - 1; j <= y + 1; j++) {
            if (i < 0 || j < 0 || i >= rows || j >= columns) {
              continue;
            } else if (!mineField[i][j].isCleared()) {
              cascade(i, j);
            }
          }
        }
      }
      return gameState.CONTINUE;
    }

    int countAdjacentMines(int x, int y) {
      int count = 0;
      for (int i = x - 1; i <= x + 1; i++) {
        for (int j = y - 1; j <= y + 1; j++) {
          if (i == x && j == y) {
            continue;
          } else if (i < 0 || j < 0 || i >= rows || j >= columns) {
            continue;
          } else if (mineField[i][j].hasMine()) {
            count++;
          }
        }
      }
    }
```

```
    return count;
  }

  boolean getMineCleared(int x, int y) {
    return mineField[x][y].isCleared();
  }
    Mine.flagState getMineFlag(int x, int y) {
    return mineField[x][y].getFlagState();
  }

  boolean isMine(int x, int y) {
    return mineField[x][y].hasMine();
  }
}
```

Let's start at the top, with the fields (remember, a variable at the class level is called a field). Listing 7-13 shows the fields in the MineField class.

Listing 7-13. *The MineField class's fields*

```
private Mine[][] mineField;
private int rows;
private int columns;
private int mines;
private int minesFound = 0;
private int minesRemaining;
private int emptiesRemaining;
enum gameState {WIN, LOSE, CONTINUE};
```

First, we have a two-dimensional array that holds the locations of the mines. Then we get a bunch of integer values to tell us how many rows, columns, and mines this instance of the game should have. Then we get more int values to tell us the state (number of mines found, number of mines remaining, and empty spaces remaining) of the current game. We add a minesRemaining field to avoid having to type mines - minesFound repeatedly. The emptiesRemaining field is more interesting, because it lets us know when the user has won. Finally, we have a tri-state enumeration that tells us the current state of the whole game—specifically, whether the player has won, the player has lost, or the player can continue the current game.

▓ **Note** The gameState enumeration is not private (meaning it is visible to all the other classes in the package) because the other classes use its values in various places, as we see later.

The MineField class has a constructor (used by the init method in the MineSweeper class). Listing 7-14 shows the MineField constructor.

Listing 7-14. The MineField construcor

```
MineField(int rows, int columns, int mines) {
  this.rows = rows;
  this.columns = columns;
  this.mines = mines;
  minesRemaining = mines;
  emptiesRemaining = rows * columns - mines;
  mineField = new Mine[rows][columns];
  init();
  populate();
}
```

Like most constructors, the `MineField` constructor first populates the fields with the values of the current game. Then it calls a method called `init` (which we examine next). Finally, it calls the populate method that has no constructors (there are two populate methods—we go over why that is shortly). The pattern of a constructor doing some simple work and then calling other methods to do more complex work is common, by the way. It offers a way to isolate complexity, which makes the code easier to read and easier to debug when problems arise.

Now let's look at the `init` method, shown in Listing 7-15.

Listing 7-15. The MineField init method

```
private void init() {
  for (int i = 0; i < rows; i++){
    for (int j = 0; j < columns; j++) {
      mineField[i][j] = new Mine();
    }
  }
}
```

As you can see, it's a simple method. It populates the minefield with the right number of Mine objects. The two populate methods do the heavy lifting of figuring out where the mines reside. If you're a clever reader (and I know you are), you're wondering how there can be a Mine object in every possible location; we tackle that mystery when we get to the Mine object itself.

For now, let's press on into the two populate methods., which I've put together in Listing 7-16.

Listing 7-16. The two populate methods

```
private void populate() {
  populate(0);
}

private void populate(int mineCount) {
  int currentCount = mineCount;
  double mineChance = (double) mines / (double) (rows * columns);
  for (int i = 0; i < rows; i++) {
    for (int j = 0; j < columns; j++) {
      Mine thisMine = mineField[i][j];
      if (!thisMine.hasMine()) {
        if (Math.random() < mineChance) {
          thisMine.setMine();
```

```
              currentCount++;
              if (currentCount == mines) {
                return;
              }
            }
          }
        }
      }
    }
    if (currentCount < mines) {
      populate(currentCount);
    }
  }
```

So why two populate methods? The first one is a convenience method that saves the trouble of providing an argument. In this case, it's not all that convenient, because we call only the convenience method once. You can rightfully say that we should have used just one method. However, we use this pattern so often that it's essentially a habit. More importantly, it gives us a chance to talk about this useful pattern.

So, again, why two methods? It's a useful technique in a number of situations. If you're exposing methods to other objects (meaning the methods are not private), multiple methods of the same name let developers (including you) call the same method with different parameters. Then each of those methods calls some other method that applies the parameters. In other cases, the simpler method gets used multiple times to make coding a bit easier (by not having to specify parameters that rarely change every time).

Now let's talk about what the two populate methods do. The simple populate method calls the more complex populate method with an argument (which is the value needed to start the process of populating the minefield). That initial value is the number of mines that have been placed so far. That's why the initial argument is 0.

The complex version of the populate method keeps a count (the currentCount variable) of the mines placed so far. To figure out whether any given spot has a mine, the method uses the random number generator to compare against the chance of a mine being in any one spot. That chance is the number of possible spots divided by the number of mines.

If we happen to get to the required number of mines before going through the whole array, we can stop. The if statement in the middle of the method accomplishes that goal. On the other hand, if we go through the whole array and don't get to the required number of mines, we call the populate method again. Let me repeat that bit: We call the method we're in again. That's called recursion, and I dedicate a whole chapter to that relatively advanced topic later in the book. Recursion. is one of my favorite programming techniques, and you can do some interesting things with it. For now, though, let's finish a MineSweeper game.

If we do have to re-enter the method, the second pass will go through the array again until we finally have the required number of mines. In theory, this process could require more than two passes. In testing, though, no more than two passes were ever needed, and the first pass never produced fewer than seven mines. This algorithm gives a slight weighting to the top left corner of the minefield, but I think that's an acceptable problem.

So, the populate methods get a little tricky, but they do solve the problem of how to randomly populate a minefield. Let's press on to other methods.

The next two methods, getMinesFound and getMinesRemaining, return the values of fields. So let's skip describing them in any further detail. The method after those two, though, is another complex bit of code that requires some explanation. Listing 7-17 shows the cascade method.

Listing 7-17. The MineField cascade method

```
private gameState cascade(int x, int y) {
  if (x < 0 || y < 0 || x >= rows || y >= columns) {
    return gameState.CONTINUE;
  }
  Mine thisMine = mineField[x][y];
  if (thisMine.hasMine()) {
    return gameState.CONTINUE;
  }
  if (!thisMine.isCleared()) {
    thisMine.clear();
    emptiesRemaining--;
    if (emptiesRemaining == 0) {
      return gameState.WIN;
    }
  }
  if (countAdjacentMines(x, y) > 0) {
    return gameState.CONTINUE;
  } else{
    for (int i = x - 1; i <= x + 1; i++) {
      for (int j = y - 1; j <= y + 1; j++) {
        if (i < 0 || j < 0 || i >= rows || j >= columns) {
          continue;
        } else if (!mineField[i][j].isCleared()) {
          cascade(i, j);
        }
      }
    }
  }
  return gameState.CONTINUE;
}
```

The cascade method handles the hardest task, which is figuring out whether multiple locations should be cleared when one location is cleared. It uses a simple version of the well-known flood fill algorithm, checking for adjacent clear locations rather than pixels of the same color (as you would expect from a flood fill in a paint program). It works by checking the location the player clicked (not right-clicked), checking every location next to (including diagonally) that location, checking all the locations next to those locations, and so on, until we finally run out of locations to check. To make that algorithm work requires recursion again. As you can see near the bottom of the method, the cascade method calls itself.

Given that a large area without mines can result in a single click clearing a lot of locations, the cascade method might end up calling itself quite a number of times. I haven't tested the method for the purpose of seeing how often it is called, but we would not be surprised to see 100 calls in a worst-case scenario. If you are interested in knowing that, add a counter variable (it has to be an argument to the method), increment it each time you enter the method, and print that value to the console. Then, when you play a game, you see how many calls to the cascade method happen.

Another bit of complexity that crops up in the cascade method is the need to check for boundaries. If the current location is at the edge of the game area, checking an adjacent location can result in an **ArrayOutOfBounds** exception, which wouldn't be much fun. So we have an **if** statement check all four boundaries and not call the **cascade** method again if doing so would result in an impossible location.

Finally, you probably notice that the cascade method returns one of the values from the gameState enumeration. Most of the time, that's gameState.CONTINUE. However, it is possible for a cascade event to clear the board and win the game, so the method can also return `gameState.WIN`.

The `MineField` class has one last non-trivial method, called `countAdjacentMines`. Listing 7-18 shows the `countAdjacentMines` method.

Listing 7-18. *The MineSweeper countAdjacentMines method*

```java
int countAdjacentMines(int x, int y) {
  int count = 0;
  for (int i = x - 1; i <= x + 1; i++) {
    for (int j = y - 1; j <= y + 1; j++) {
      if (i == x && j == y) {
        continue;
      } else if (i < 0 || j < 0 || i >= rows || j >= columns) {
        continue;
      } else if (mineField[i][j].hasMine()) {
        count++;
      }
    }
  }
  return count;
}
```

When a player clears a location that does not contain a mine, we have to show the number of adjacent mines in that location. To do that, we need a method of counting the mines adjacent to any given location. As with the **cascade** method, we have to check for the edges of the playing field, and we use identical code to do that. Other than that, the `countAdjacentMines` method checks each adjacent (including diagonals) location and adds up the number of mines found.

The Mine class defines an individual location. You might think it's misnamed, because it doesn't correspond only to locations that have mines. To that end, we thought about changing the name to Location. Then it occurred to us that, when Explosive Ordnance Disposal specialists (those folks are real heroes, by the way) check for explosives, they assume every location is mined. So, in a fit of sophistry, I left the name as Mine. Listing 7-19 shows the Mine class.

Listing 7-19. *The Mine class*

```java
package com.apress.java7forabsolutebeginners.examples.MineSweeper;

public class Mine {

  enum flagState {UNKNOWN, MINE, SUSPECT};
    private boolean isCleared = false;
  private boolean hasMine = false;
  private flagState flag = flagState.UNKNOWN;
      boolean hasMine() {
    return hasMine;
  }
```

```java
  void setMine() {
    hasMine = true;
  }

  boolean isCleared() {
    return isCleared;
  }

  void clear() {
    isCleared = true;
  }

  flagState getFlagState() {
    return flag;
  }

  flagState setFlagState() {
    if (flag == flagState.UNKNOWN) {
      flag = flagState.MINE;
      return flagState.MINE;
    }
    if (flag == flagState.MINE) {
      flag = flagState.SUSPECT;
      return flagState.SUSPECT;
    }
    if (flag == flagState.SUSPECT) {
      flag = flagState.UNKNOWN;
      return flagState.UNKNOWN;
    }
    return flagState.UNKNOWN;
  }
}
```

The `Mine` class keeps track of whether a location has a mine, whether the location has been cleared, and whether the user has flagged the location as having a mine, being a suspect (usually marked by a question mark icon in minesweeper games), or being unknown (which means not having an icon in the game). The only complexity is in the `setFlagState` method, which toggles through the states rather than accepting an argument to set the flag state. That behavior models the user's behavior of cycling through flags by right-clicking on a minefield location.

Now we can move on to the `MineSweeperHelper` class, which contains miscellaneous methods that the game needs. Though not as large as the `MineSweeper` and `MineField` classes, it's still a large class when compared to earlier work. Again, read through it and do your best to understand it (now that you know how the rest of the program works, you can probably do pretty well with it), and then we examine it in detail. Listing 7-20 shows the `MineSweeperHelper` class.

Listing 7-20. *The MineSweeperHelper class*

```java
package com.apress.java7forabsolutebeginners.examples.MineSweeper;

import java.awt.Color;
```

```
import javax.swing.JButton;
import javax.swing.JOptionPane;

public class MineSweeperHelper {

  private MineSweeper mineSweeper;

  public MineSweeperHelper(MineSweeper mineSweeper) {
    this.mineSweeper = mineSweeper;
  }

  void updateLabels() {
    mineSweeper.minesFoundLabel.setText("Found: " + mineSweeper.mineField.getMinesFound());
    mineSweeper.minesRemainingLabel.setText("Remaining: " +
        mineSweeper.mineField.getMinesRemaining());
  }

  void updateButtons() {
    for (int i = 0; i < mineSweeper.rows; i++) {
      for (int j = 0; j < mineSweeper.columns; j++) {
        if (mineSweeper.mineField.getMineCleared(i, j) == true) {
          mineSweeper.mineButtons[i][j].removeMouseListener(mineSweeper.mouseListener);
          mineSweeper.mineButtons[i][j].setBackground(Color.WHITE);
          int count = mineSweeper.mineField.countAdjacentMines(i, j);
          if (count > 0) {
            mineSweeper.mineButtons[i][j].setIcon(MineIcon.getNumberIcon(count));
          }
        } else {
          if (mineSweeper.mineField.getMineFlag(i, j) == Mine.flagState.MINE) {
            mineSweeper.mineButtons[i][j].setIcon(MineIcon.getMineIcon());
          } else if (mineSweeper.mineField.getMineFlag(i, j) == Mine.flagState.SUSPECT) {
            mineSweeper.mineButtons[i][j].setIcon(MineIcon.getSuspectIcon());
          } else {
            mineSweeper.mineButtons[i][j].setIcon(null);
          }
        }
      }
    }
  }

  void showAll() {
    for (int i = 0; i < mineSweeper.rows; i++) {
      for (int j = 0; j < mineSweeper.columns; j++) {
        boolean mine = mineSweeper.mineField.isMine(i, j);
        if (mine) {
          mineSweeper.mineButtons[i][j].setIcon(MineIcon.getMineIcon());
        } else {
          JButton thisButton = mineSweeper.mineButtons[i][j];
          thisButton.removeMouseListener(mineSweeper.mouseListener);
          thisButton.setBackground(Color.WHITE);
          thisButton.setIcon(null);
          int count = mineSweeper.mineField.countAdjacentMines(i, j);
```

```
            if (count > 0) {
              thisButton.setIcon(MineIcon.getNumberIcon(count));
            }
          }
        }
      }
    }
  }

  void endGame(boolean won) {
    showAll();
    String wonOrLost;
    int option;
    if (won) {
      wonOrLost = "You won!";
    } else {
      wonOrLost = "You lost.";
    }
    option = JOptionPane.showConfirmDialog(mineSweeper.frame, wonOrLost
        + " Play again?", wonOrLost,
      JOptionPane.YES_NO_OPTION);
    if (option == 1) {
      System.exit(0);
    } else {
      newGame(mineSweeper.rows, mineSweeper.columns);
    }
  }

  void newGame(int previousRows, int previousColumns) {
    for (int i = 0; i < previousRows; i++) {
      for (int j = 0; j < previousColumns; j++) {
        mineSweeper.minePanel.remove(mineSweeper.mineButtons[i][j]);
      }
    }
    mineSweeper.init();
    mineSweeper.minePanel.validate();
    mineSweeper.frame.validate();
    mineSweeper.frame.pack();
    updateLabels();
  }
}
```

The MineSweeperHelper class has a constructor, as shown in Listing 7-21.

Listing 7-21. *The MineSweeperHelper constructor*

```
public MineSweeperHelper(MineSweeper mineSweeper) {
  this.mineSweeper = mineSweeper;
}
```

This constructor doesn't do much, but what it does is critically important. All the methods in the class work on an instance of the MineSweeper class, so we must have an instance for them. The constructor gives us that instance. As we saw in the constructor for the MineSweeper class, the

MineSweeper class passes itself (with the this keyword) to this class (and to the other utility classes that do work on its behalf). That's a common idiom for helper classes: The helper has to have a link back to the object it's helping to be able to do anything.

Let's examine the next method: updateLabels. Listing 7-22 shows the updateLabels method.

Listing 7-22. *The MineSweeperHelper updateLabels method*

```
void updateLabels() {
  mineSweeper.minesFoundLabel.setText("Found: " + mineSweeper.mineField.getMinesFound());
  mineSweeper.minesRemainingLabel.setText("Remaining: " +
      mineSweeper.mineField.getMinesRemaining());
}
```

It doesn't get much simpler than that. The updateLabels has the simple task of updating the labels that show how many mines have been found and how many mines remain to be found. Remember that those values are based on the player's guesses, not the actual values. The player could be wrong, which would make the numbers wrong. That's part of the fun.

The updateButtons method does a bit more, including placing the numbers on the grid, which we explore in a bit more detail after the listing. Listing 7-23 shows the updateButtons method.

Listing 7-23. *The MineSweeperHelper updateButtons method*

```
void updateButtons() {
  for (int i = 0; i < mineSweeper.rows; i++) {
    for (int j = 0; j < mineSweeper.columns; j++) {
      if (mineSweeper.mineField.getMineCleared(i, j) == true) {
        mineSweeper.mineButtons[i][j].removeMouseListener(mineSweeper.mouseListener);
        mineSweeper.mineButtons[i][j].setBackground(Color.WHITE);
        int count = mineSweeper.mineField.countAdjacentMines(i, j);
        if (count > 0) {
          mineSweeper.mineButtons[i][j].setIcon(MineIcon.getNumberIcon(count));
        }
      } else {
        if (mineSweeper.mineField.getMineFlag(i, j) == Mine.flagState.MINE) {
          mineSweeper.mineButtons[i][j].setIcon(MineIcon.getMineIcon());
        } else if (mineSweeper.mineField.getMineFlag(i, j) == Mine.flagState.SUSPECT) {
          mineSweeper.mineButtons[i][j].setIcon(MineIcon.getSuspectIcon());
        } else {
          mineSweeper.mineButtons[i][j].setIcon(null);
        }
      }
    }
  }
}
```

The updateButtons method runs through the whole grid, replacing any cleared buttons with either empty spaces or numbers and setting the mine and suspect icons on any locations the player has marked as either a mine or a suspect. As you can see from the listing 7-23, that takes a number of if statements, some of them nested inside other if statements. Let's start with the first if statement (the first line inside the for loops). If the location has been cleared, it removes the mouselistener for that location, so that further clicks on that location won't do anything. Then it sets the background color to white and puts the proper icon image (which might be no image at all if no mines are adjacent to the location) in the location. If the mine has not been cleared, we enter the outer else block. I say, "outer," because it contains other else blocks (after if blocks, of course). Because the location has not been cleared, we have to make sure the mine and suspect icons are properly set. Finally, if the player has removed (or never set) the mine and suspect icons on this location, we have to make sure no icon is present. That's why we set the location's icon to null in that last line (not counting the lines with the closing braces).

In essence, the updateLabels method manages the appearance of the minefield, setting the colors and icons for all the locations. There's a good design tip in there for you: Always make sure each method has a single, well-defined task. If a method has to do several things, break it up into several methods and have one method do nothing but (or at least not much more than) call the others. We see an example of this kind of method when we get to the newGame method.

Next up, we get to the showAll method, shown in Listing 7-24.

Listing 7-24. *The MineSweeperHelper showAll method*

```
void showAll() {
  for (int i = 0; i < mineSweeper.rows; i++) {
    for (int j = 0; j < mineSweeper.columns; j++) {
      boolean mine = mineSweeper.mineField.isMine(i, j);
      if (mine) {
        mineSweeper.mineButtons[i][j].setIcon(MineIcon.getMineIcon());
      } else {
        JButton thisButton = mineSweeper.mineButtons[i][j];
        thisButton.removeMouseListener(mineSweeper.mouseListener);
        thisButton.setBackground(Color.WHITE);
        thisButton.setIcon(null);
        int count = mineSweeper.mineField.countAdjacentMines(i, j);
        if (count > 0) {
          thisButton.setIcon(MineIcon.getNumberIcon(count));
        }
      }
    }
  }
}
```

The showAll method .has the simple task of revealing everything and removing the mouse listener from all the locations. It gets called only when the game ends, whether the player won or lost. Why show everything if the player won? The player might not have set mine icons on all of the locations that have mines and might even have won in spite of being wrong. We want a complete representation of the true state of the game at the end, so we clear and set the proper number icons (including no icon) for all the locations that don't have mines and set the mine icon for all the locations that do have mines. If the player won, doing so confirms the player's accuracy. If the player lost, showing the true state of the game reveals mistakes, possibly letting the player learn to better play the game.

Notice that there's no instance of the MineIcon class, but we can get icons out of it anyway. We see how that works when we get to the MineIcon class. For now, let's move on to the endGame method. Listing 7-25 shows the endGame method.

Listing 7-25. The MineSweeperHelper endGame method

```
void endGame(boolean won) {
  showAll();
  String wonOrLost;
  int option;
  if (won) {
    wonOrLost = "You won!";
  } else {
    wonOrLost = "You lost.";
  }
  option = JOptionPane.showConfirmDialog(mineSweeper.frame, wonOrLost
          + " Play again?", wonOrLost,
      JOptionPane.YES_NO_OPTION);
  if (option == 1) {
    System.exit(0);
  } else {
    newGame(mineSweeper.rows, mineSweeper.columns);
  }
}
```

As we saw in the description of the `showAll` method, the `endGame` method calls the `showAll` method. Then it shows the player a dialog box to indicate whether the player won or lost and ask the player whether to play again. To show the dialog box, we use the `JOptionPane` class, which is one way to show a dialog box in Swing. They probably call it `JOptionPane` because it has a bunch of different options. If you examine the JavaDoc for `JOptionBox`, you see that it has a number of constructors, each of which creates a different kind of dialog box. For this case, we want a box with a message, a Yes button, a No button, and the capability to let us know which button the player clicked. To do all that, we create a String object to hold the message (either "You won!" or "You lost.") and define an int value to hold the return value of the `JOptionPane` object. The return value indicates which button the user clicked, with 0 being "Yes" and 1 being "No." Finally, if the user chose "No" (return value of 1), we exit the program with an exit code of 0 (which means the program shut down normally, rather than as the result of an error). If the user chose "Yes," we call the `newGame` method, which is the next method. Listing 7-26 shows the `newGame` method.

Listing 7-26. The MineSweeper newGame method

```
void newGame(int previousRows, int previousColumns) {
  for (int i = 0; i < previousRows; i++) {
    for (int j = 0; j < previousColumns; j++) {
      mineSweeper.minePanel.remove(mineSweeper.mineButtons[i][j]);
    }
  }
  mineSweeper.init();
  mineSweeper.minePanel.validate();
  mineSweeper.frame.validate();
  mineSweeper.frame.pack();
  updateLabels();
}
```

As we saw in the description of the `updateButtons` method, when a method needs to call a bunch of other methods, it's best for the calling method to not do too much more than that, and the things it does do should be simple. Otherwise, you risk having a hard method to understand and to debug. Also, because a method with that problem is overly complex, it's exactly the kind of place where errors arise. So not only is such a method hard to debug, but it's likely that you have to debug it—a double whammy.

In the case of the newGame method, it performs one simple task (removing all the buttons from the minefield panel), and then calls a chain of other methods that do the work of setting up a new game and updating the interface. In particular, it calls the init method in the MineSweeper class, which makes a new MineField object and sets up all the buttons in the play area. Then it validates the minePanel object in the MineSweeper class, which ensures that all the old buttons won't appear and that the new buttons created by the init method will appear. Then it validates the JFrame object, which forces it to correctly accept the changed minePanel object. (Think of the validate method on Swing objects as a mechanism for ensuring that any changes are shown to the user.) Then it calls the pack method on the JFrame object, which finishes the job of refreshing our changed minefield interface. Finally, it updates the labels to their starting values (which were set by the init method).

That's a lot to do, but we manage it by having methods that do clearly defined bits of it for us, rather than lumping it all together in one spot, which would, again, be hard to understand, hard to debug, and (worst of all) more likely to produce errors. Remember: If you have to struggle to figure out what a method is doing, it probably needs to be multiple methods. On the other hand, it might also mean that you have a design problem (probably a badly thought-out set of classes). Either way, take hard-to-understand code as a sign of a problem and think of a way to make it easy to understand.

Now let's look at an unusual class, the MineIcon class, shown in Listing 7-27.

Listing 7-27. *The MineIcon class*

```java
package com.apress.java7forabsolutebeginners.examples.MineSweeper;

import javax.swing.Icon;
import javax.swing.ImageIcon;

public class MineIcon {

    private static Icon mineIcon = new ImageIcon("C:\\Projects\\MineSweeper\\mine.png");
    private static Icon suspectIcon = new ImageIcon("C:\\Projects\\MineSweeper\\question.png");
    private static Icon oneIcon = new ImageIcon("C:\\Projects\\MineSweeper\\one.png");
    private static Icon twoIcon = new ImageIcon("C:\\Projects\\MineSweeper\\two.png");
    private static Icon threeIcon = new ImageIcon("C:\\Projects\\MineSweeper\\three.png");
    private static Icon fourIcon = new ImageIcon("C:\\Projects\\MineSweeper\\four.png");
    private static Icon fiveIcon = new ImageIcon("C:\\Projects\\MineSweeper\\five.png");
    private static Icon sixIcon = new ImageIcon("C:\\Projects\\MineSweeper\\six.png");
    private static Icon sevenIcon = new ImageIcon("C:\\Projects\\MineSweeper\\seven.png");
    private static Icon eightIcon = new ImageIcon("C:\\Projects\\MineSweeper\\eight.png");

    static Icon getMineIcon() {
        return mineIcon;
    }

    static Icon getSuspectIcon() {
        return suspectIcon;
    }

    static Icon getNumberIcon(int mineCount) {
        if (mineCount == 1) return oneIcon;
        if (mineCount == 2) return twoIcon;
```

```
      if (mineCount == 3) return threeIcon;
      if (mineCount == 4) return fourIcon;
      if (mineCount == 5) return fiveIcon;
      if (mineCount == 6) return sixIcon;
      if (mineCount == 7) return sevenIcon;
      if (mineCount == 8) return eightIcon;
      return null;
   }
}
```

Notice that every member, both fields and methods, is static. We do that because there's no point in loading the icon images more than once. Because being static is handy for the icons, we also make the methods static. Consequently, we never need to create an instance of the MineIcon class. To get an icon, we can use the syntax for calling a class method. (Remember that a class method belongs to the class, not to any instance of the class.) That syntax is the name of the class, a period, and the name and arguments of the method, such as MineIcon.getMineIcon();.

Static methods are fairly common. You can use them for any task that doesn't require an instance of the containing class. Even classes that consist entirely of static methods are fairly common. As with the MineIcon class, they provide functionality that doesn't need an object of any sort to work. They either offer utility methods (such as formatting String objects in special ways needed by a particular application) or return items (such as our icons) that don't require any other input to find. It might seem odd, because you've never seen it before, but it gives you another tool in your programming toolkit.

Hang in there. We're almost done with the code for the MineSweeper program. We have just the two classes that listen for user actions (mouse clicks and menu actions) left to go. Let's keep going with the MineSweeperMouseListener class, shown in Listing 7-28.

Listing 7-28. *The MineSweeperMouseListener class*

```java
package com.apress.java7forabsolutebeginners.examples.MineSweeper;

import java.awt.event.MouseEvent;
import java.awt.event.MouseListener;

import javax.swing.JButton;

public class MineSweeperMouseListener implements MouseListener {

   private MineSweeper mineSweeper;
   private MineSweeperHelper mineSweeperHelper;

   public MineSweeperMouseListener(MineSweeper mineSweeper, MineSweeperHelper helper) {
      this.mineSweeper = mineSweeper;
      mineSweeperHelper = helper;
   }

   @Override
   public void mouseClicked(MouseEvent e) {
   }
```

```
@Override
public void mouseEntered(MouseEvent e) {
}

@Override
public void mouseExited(MouseEvent e) {
}

@Override
public void mousePressed(MouseEvent e) {
}

@Override
public void mouseReleased(MouseEvent e) {
  JButton clickedButton = (JButton) e.getSource();
  for (int i = 0; i < mineSweeper.rows; i++) {
    for (int j = 0; j < mineSweeper.columns; j++) {
      if (clickedButton == mineSweeper.mineButtons[i][j]) {
        MineField.gameState state;
        if (e.getButton() == MouseEvent.BUTTON1) {
          state = mineSweeper.mineField.resolveClick(i,j, true);
          if (state == MineField.gameState.CONTINUE) {
            if (mineSweeper.mineField.getMineFlag(i, j) == Mine.flagState.UNKNOWN) {
              clickedButton.removeMouseListener(this);
            }
          }
        } else {
          state = mineSweeper.mineField.resolveClick(i,j, false);
        }
        if (state == MineField.gameState.WIN) {
          mineSweeperHelper.endGame(true);
        } else if (state == MineField.gameState.LOSE){
          mineSweeperHelper.endGame(false);
        } else {
          mineSweeperHelper.updateButtons();
        }
      }
    }
  }
  mineSweeperHelper.updateLabels();
}
}
```

As we saw in the MineSweeperHelper class, the MineSweeperMouseListener class has a constructor that it uses to get an instance of the MineSweeper class. It also gets an instance of the MineSweeperHelper class. Both of those classes need to listen for mouse clicks, so the MineSweeperMouseListener class has to have instances of both classes. The only other method that does anything is the mouseReleased method. As we learn earlier, using the mouseReleased method is more reliable than using the mouseClicked method, thanks to the problem of mouse motion wiping out the click event.

The mouseClicked method runs through all the buttons until it finds the button on which the player clicked. If the player clicked the left mouse button, the method calls the resolveClick method in the MineField class to see whether the player hit a mine. If not, the resolveClick method figures out whether the game is over (because the player won or lost) or the game should continue. If the user clicked any other button (most likely the right button), this method still calls the `resolveClick` method, but with the button flag indicating that a button other than the left button was clicked. The `resolveClick` method then toggles the mine, suspect, and unknown icons on that location. Finally, the `mouseClicked` method uses the value returned by the `resolveClick` method to end the game (the player won or lost) or continue the game. If the game didn't end, we update the buttons in the minefield. Finally, once all the other processing has been done, the `mouseClicked` method updates the labels.

The `MineSweeperMouseListener` class isn't complex, but it is worth moving this functionality into its own class, to simplify the `MineSweeper` class. It also follows the design principle that each object should have a clear purpose. In this case, we create a class with the clear mission of listening for clicks in the minefield, and removing that functionality (and moving other bits to other classes) lets the MineSweeper focus purely on showing the user interface.

Let's finish up this long journey through the MineSweeper game by looking at the last class in the MineSweeper package. Listing 7-29 shows the `MineSweeperActionListener` class.

Listing 7-29. *The MineSweeperActionListener class*

```
package com.apress.java7forabsolutebeginners.examples.MineSweeper;

import java.awt.event.ActionEvent;
import java.awt.event.ActionListener;

public class MineSweeperActionListener implements ActionListener {

  private MineSweeper mineSweeper;
  private MineSweeperHelper mineSweeperHelper;

  public MineSweeperActionListener(MineSweeper mineSweeper, MineSweeperHelper helper) {
    this.mineSweeper = mineSweeper;
    mineSweeperHelper = helper;
  }


  @Override
  public void actionPerformed(ActionEvent e) {
    if (e.getActionCommand().equals("Exit")) {
      System.exit(0);
    }
    if (e.getActionCommand().equals("New Game")) {
      mineSweeperHelper.newGame(mineSweeper.rows, mineSweeper.columns);
      return;
    }
    if (e.getActionCommand().equals("Small (8 x 8, 10 mines)")) {
      int previousRows = mineSweeper.rows;
      int previousColumns = mineSweeper.columns;
      mineSweeper.rows = 8;
      mineSweeper.columns = 8;
      mineSweeper.numberOfMines = 10;
      mineSweeperHelper.newGame(previousRows, previousColumns);
      return;
    }
```

```
    if (e.getActionCommand().equals("Medium (16 x 16, 40 mines)")) {
      int previousRows = mineSweeper.rows;
      int previousColumns = mineSweeper.columns;
      mineSweeper.rows = 16;
      mineSweeper.columns = 16;
      mineSweeper.numberOfMines = 40;
      mineSweeperHelper.newGame(previousRows, previousColumns);
      return;
    }
    if (e.getActionCommand().equals("Large (16 x 32, 100 mines)")) {
      int previousRows = mineSweeper.rows;
      int previousColumns = mineSweeper.columns;
      mineSweeper.rows = 16;
      mineSweeper.columns = 32;
      mineSweeper.numberOfMines = 100;
      mineSweeperHelper.newGame(previousRows, previousColumns);
      return;
    }
  }
}
```

Similar to the MineSweeperMouseListener class, the MineSweeperActionListener has to have both a MineSweeper object and a MineSweeperHelper object. To that end, it has a constructor that provides those two objects. The only method in the class (remember that a constructor isn't a method, though it looks a lot like one) is the actionPerformed method, which implements the only method defined by the ActionListener interface.

The actionPerformed method listens for menu events and either exits the game or starts a new game. In the case of starting a new game, it can either start a new game with the current settings (size of the playing field and number of mines) or start a new game with new settings. For a new game with a different size, the actionPerformed method gets the size of the current playing field, sets the size of the new playing field (by setting values in the MineSweeper object), and then calls the newGame method in the MineSweeperHelper object. Remember that the newGame method first removes the existing buttons that comprise the playing field. That's why we have to get the current size of the playing field.

As with the MineSweeperMouseListener class, the MineSweeperActionListener is a simple class. Again, though, it conforms to good design principles by having a clear purpose, and it helps simplify the MineSweeper class (which was getting cluttered before we split it into five classes).

Now that we've made it through the whole MineSweeper program, let's see what we get when we're done, in the form of a finished game in Figure 7-5.

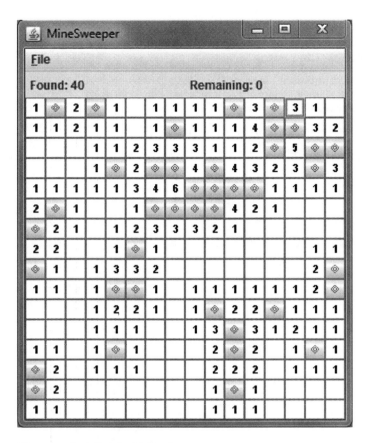

Figure 7-5. *A finished MineSweeper game*

Summary

In this chapter, you saw a number of Swing applications, of steadily increasing complexity, culminating in a larger application that implements our own version of a common and popular game. It made for a long chapter and a lot of code, but it shows our first real-world example. We create several more real applications as we proceed throughout the rest of the book, but none of them are as large as the MineSweeper game.

In the course of writing those applications, we saw that:

- Swing applications can become verbose (a problem that plagues all user-interface frameworks).

- The starting point for a Swing application is a `JFrame` object, because it gives us a window.

- The place to add components is in the content pane.

- The normal idiom for working with Swing components is to create a component, set whatever attributes we need to set on it (to customize it for our purpose), and then add that component to another component.

- It can be handy to move the mouse and menu listeners (and keyboard listeners, if we needed them) out to their own classes, to simplify a large class and to let each class focus on a single, clear purpose.

- It can be handy to have a helper class, to again simplify a large class.

- All the members of a class can be static and how to use such a class.

The best way (and only real way, in my opinion) to learn to program is to program. So go write a Swing application or two of your own.

CHAPTER 8

Writing and Reading Files

Writing data to and reading data from files are common tasks for almost any kind of program. Even simple games, such as our MineSweeper game, can benefit from storing information in a file and retrieving it later. (MineSweeper could store the size of game the player last chose and keep track of the best time for each size.) Java provides an extensive collection of classes and interfaces for dealing with files (and associated objects such as directories and drives). The heart of it all is the aptly named and often-used `java.io.File` class. "io" stands for input/output.

Working with File Objects

The first thing to know about working with `java.io.File` (I'll call it "`File`" from here on) objects is that a `File` object is *not* a file. A `File` object in Java is an object that contains various bits of information about a file. The distinction might seem meaningless, but it's very important. Consider the following bit of code: `File myFile = new File();` That code does not create an empty file on your system. Instead, it creates an object within your program. For the sake of comparison, let's look at code that creates an empty file on your system. Notice how we have to create a file, with the `createNewFile()` method, after we create the file object.

Note To get the code in Listing 8-1 and Listing 8-2 to work, you must first create a directory called test on your C drive.

Figure 8-1 shows my test directory (which I created just for this code) before running Listing 8-1. It's not the most thrilling image, but I thought you should see the "before" image to go with Figure 8-2 (which shows the "after" image).

Figure 8-1. A test directory

Listing 8-1. Creating an empty file

```java
package com.apress.java7forabsolutebeginners.examples;

import java.io.File;

public class FileTest {

    public static void main(String[] args) {
        String fileName = "C:\\test\\myFile.txt";
        File myFile = new File(fileName);
        try {
            myFile.createNewFile();
        } catch (Exception e) {
            System.out.println("Couldn't create " + myFile.getPath());
        }
        System.out.println("Created " + myFile.getPath());
    }
}
```

If you have a `test` directory on your C drive, that program creates an empty text file called `myFile.txt` in that directory. Figure 8-2 shows the results on my Windows laptop.

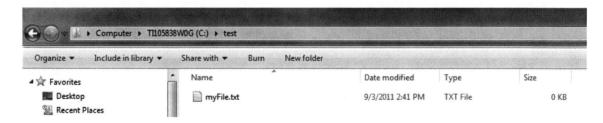

Figure 8-2. Test directory with our file

Let's examine the code. First, notice that we have double backslashes (which are escape sequences that insert a single backslash) for path separators. Using double backslashes is actually bad practice. It assumes we're running on a Windows (or perhaps DOS) system. But what happens when someone runs our program on a Unix or Linux system or a Mac? The JVM might figure it out and use the right characters, but we can't count on such things. Instead, we should specify a file name by using Java's path specifiers, as shown in listing 8-2.

Second, notice that we must handle an exception to work with a File object. Nearly all the methods in the various Input/Output classes and interfaces throw an IOException. As we learned when we covered the basics of exceptions in Chapter 2, "Java Syntax," Java objects generally throw exceptions whenever something beyond the bounds of your program might cause a problem. In the case of methods that deal with files, your program cannot anticipate all the things that can go wrong on the file system. You might inadvertently specify a directory or drive that does not exist or specify an invalid file name. For example, my laptop has no Z drive. So, if I try to create Z:\\test\\myFile.txt, the program fails. Listing 8-2 shows how to create a file with a path that works on any operating system (so long as a JVM exists for that operating system).

Listing 8-2. Creating an empty file with path specifiers

```
package com.apress.java7forabsolutebeginners.examples;

import java.io.File;

public class FileTest {

    public static void main(String[] args) {
        String fileName = "C:" + File.separator +
                "test" + File.separator + "myFile.txt";
        File myFile = new File(fileName);
        try {
            myFile.createNewFile();
        } catch (Exception e) {
            System.out.println("Couldn't create " + myFile.getPath());
        }
        System.out.println("Created " + myFile.getPath());
    }
}
```

Now, no matter what system we run the program on, we get a proper path for our file. If everything else works (the C drive exists, the test directory exists, our program has permission to write a file in that location, and so on), we get a new and empty text file where we expect it.

Opening a File

You probably can't get by with just writing new files all the time, so you should know how to open a file that already exists, too. What opening a file really amounts to is creating a File object that corresponds to a file on the file system. Then, through that File object, you can do various things to the contents of the file. We get to manipulating contents later; for now, let's just get a File object for an existing file. Because we already created myFile.txt, let's get a File object for that file. To make sure we actually found a file, we use the exists() method to check for a file, as shown in see Listing 8-3.

Listing 8-3. Getting a File object for an existing file

```
package com.apress.java7forabsolutebeginners.examples;

import java.io.File;

public class FileTest {

    public static void main(String[] args) {
        String fileName = "C:" + File.separator +
                "test" + File.separator + "myFile.txt";
        File myFile = new File(fileName);
        System.out.println(fileName + " exists? " + myFile.exists());
    }
}
```

Notice how the creation of a File object is the same, regardless of whether the file exists or not. As we saw earlier in this chapter, a File object is not a file. A File object is a path specification (which might or might not exist on the file system) and some other information that might or might correspond to an actual file. Just specifying a path and creating a new File object for it does not create a new file or prove an existing file exists. To do that, we have to take further steps, as shown in Listings 8-1 and 8-2 (where we used the createnewFile() method) and Listing 8-3 (where we used the exists() method).

Deleting a File

Sometimes, you need to delete a file, too. The process parallels that of creating a new or finding an existing file. Listing 8-4 shows the simplest way to do it.

Listing 8-4. Deleting a file

```
package com.apress.java7forabsolutebeginners.examples;

import java.io.File;
import java.io.IOException;

public class FileTest {

  public static void main(String[] args) throws IOException {
    String fileName = "C:" + File.separator +
        "test" + File.separator + "myFile.txt";
    File myFile = new File(fileName);
    if(!myFile.exists()) {
      throw new IOException("Cannot delete " + fileName
          + " because" + fileName + " does not exist");
    } else {
      myFile.delete();
    }
    System.out.println(fileName + " exists? " + myFile.exists());
  }
}
```

You don't need to check for the file after you delete it, by the way. If the operation fails, you get an error message. We put in the print statement so that the program would produce some output and let us know it's done. Figure 8-3 shows the output (in Eclipse's console window) if the program finds a file named `myFile.txt` in the `test` directory and removes it.

Figure 8-3. *Output for a successful file deletion*

Figure 8-4 shows the output (in Eclipse's console window) if the program cannot find and remove a file named `myFile.txt` in the test directory.

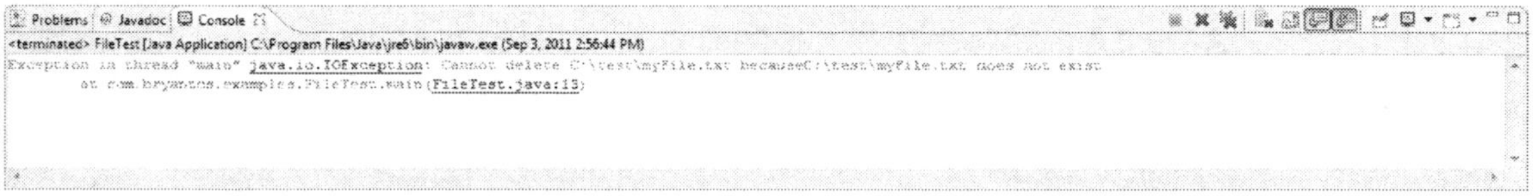

Figure 8-4. *Output for a failed file deletion*

Working with Temporary Files

Temporary files give us a way to store data that we might want at some point but don't want right now and that we don't to keep after the program exits. For example, most word processors keep a temporary file open while you work on a document. That file serves a number of purposes, including offering a way to recover at least most of your work if the program crashes. The temporary file gets removed only if the program exits normally, so a crash leaves a file that contains your work, which can be handy indeed.

The `File` class provides a few methods specifically for dealing with temporary files. These methods let you create multiple temp files without having to think of a new name for each one. Instead, you specify a prefix (at least three characters long), a suffix (which is `.tmp` if you set the suffix to `null`), and (optionally) a directory. If you don't specify a directory, the JVM creates your files in the system's temp directory. On most systems, the default temp directory is a subdirectory of your user directory.

So, let's look at how to create a batch of temporary files in Listing 8-5.

Listing 8-5. *Creating temp files*

```java
package com.apress.java7forabsolutebeginners.examples;

import java.io.File;

public class FileTest {

    public static void main(String[] args) {
```

```
        String tempDirectoryName = "C:" + File.separator + "test";
        File tempDirectory = new File(tempDirectoryName);
        for (int i = 0; i < 10; i++) {
            try {
                File thisFile =
                        File.createTempFile("tmp", null, tempDirectory);
            } catch (Exception e) {
                System.out.println("Couldn't create temp file " + i);
            }
        }
        System.out.println("Done creating temp files");
    }
}
```

The createTempFile method guarantees that each temp file created during the life of the program will be different. It doesn't guarantee that the file names will mean anything to a human. Listing 8-6 shows the names of the files that program created in our **test** directory.

Listing 8-6. *Temp file names*

```
tmp1672349819571008723.tmp
tmp3234113842230809615.tmp
tmp5343720775549909618.tmp
tmp6194798942830449846.tmp
tmp7016714774703888253.tmp
tmp720922773409895465.tmp
tmp7634665877605496722.tmp
tmp7730975525106591320.tmp
tmp7990076292249445444.tmp
tmp8048303951856646489.tmp
```

Figure 8-5 shows the temp files after they've been created in my test directory.

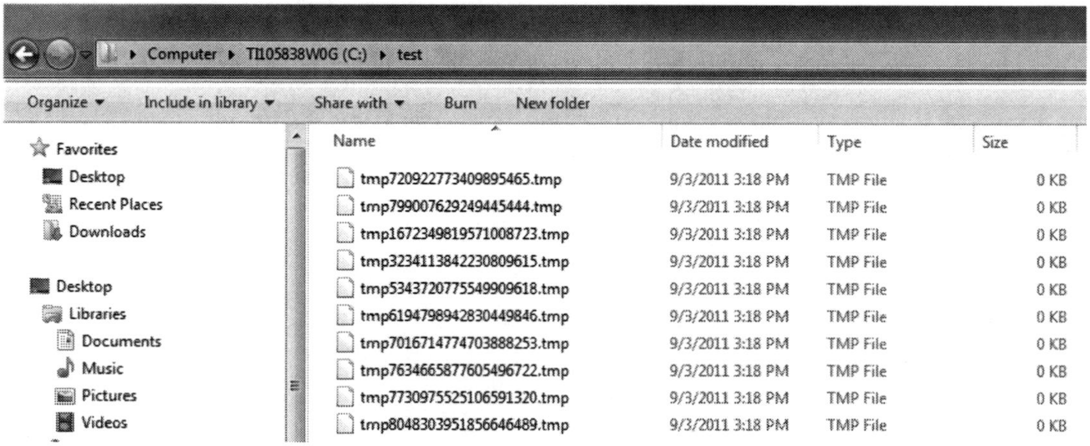

Figure 8-5. *Temp files in the test directory*

Some systems create files and leave them on the system for a long time (usually until a user deletes them, often through a program's user interface rather than through the file system). For example, Windows Live Mail stores each mail message as a separate file, for example. Still, we usually want to delete any temp files that we might create. (Otherwise, they don't really seem like temp files.) All we have to do to get rid of any temp files we create is add one line, as in Listing 8-7.

Listing 8-7. Removing temp files

```
package com.apress.java7forabsolutebeginners.examples;

import java.io.File;

public class FileTest {

    public static void main(String[] args) {
        String tempDirectoryName = "C:" + File.separator + "test";
        File tempDirectory = new File(tempDirectoryName);
        for (int i = 0; i < 10; i++) {
            try {
                File thisFile =
                    File.createTempFile("tmp", null, tempDirectory);
                thisFile.deleteOnExit();
            } catch (Exception e) {
                System.out.println("Couldn't create temp file " + i);
            }
        }
        System.out.println("Done creating temp files");
    }
}
```

The deleteOnExit() method tells the JVM to remove the file (or directory or set of directories and files) associated with a particular File object when the program exits. In this case, the files don't exist for long. However, in a program that does more, the temp files might linger for quite a while as the program does whatever it does. Consider a game, for example, that's storing various information in temp files. Those files exist until you stop playing.

Creating a Directory

Sometimes, you need to create a directory in which to put the files you create. As it happens, the File class defines both directories and files. (You saw an example of that in the programs that deal with temporary files, earlier in this chapter, when we use a File object to specify our test directory.) Remember that a File object is a path with some other information. The path can be to either a file or a directory. Listing 8-8 shows a simple program that creates a directory.

Listing 8-8. *Creating a directory*

```
package com.apress.java7forabsolutebeginners.examples;

import java.io.File;

public class FileTest {

    public static void main(String[] args) {
        String testDirectoryName = "C:" + File.separator + "test";
        File testDirectory = new File(testDirectoryName);
        try {
            testDirectory.mkdir();
        } catch (Exception e) {
            System.out.println("Couldn't create a directory called "
                    + testDirectoryName);
            System.exit(1);
        }
        System.out.println("Created a directory called " + testDirectoryName);
    }
}
```

Note that we use the `mkdir` method rather than the `createNewFile` method. Windows, requires that we give special permission to write into the root of the C: drive. Any attempt to create a file called `C:\test` on the system would fail. (If we change the path to `C:\temp\test`, we would get a file called `test` (with no extension) in our `test` directory.) However, we can create a new directory as a child of the root directory, so the `mkdir` method works.

You can also create multiple directories, in the form of a longer path to a particular location. Suppose we want to create a directory called `C:\test\test2\test3`. We can use the `mkdirs` method (note the s on the end) to do so, as shown in Listing 8-9 (with the line that specifies the path and the `mkdirs` line highlighted).

Listing 8-9. *Creating multiple directories*

```
package com.apress.java7forabsolutebeginners.examples;

import java.io.File;

public class FileTest {

    public static void main(String[] args) {
        String testDirectoryName = "C:" + File.separator + "test" +
                File.separator + "test2" + File.separator + "test3";
        File testDirectory = new File(testDirectoryName);
        try {
            testDirectory.mkdirs();
        } catch (Exception e) {
            System.out.println("Couldn't create a directory called "
                    + testDirectoryName);
            System.exit(1);
        }
```

```
      System.out.println("Created a directory called " + testDirectoryName);
    }
  }
```

Notice the System.Exit(1) command. That line makes the program stop (to be more precise, it terminates the currently running Java Virtual Machine) if something bad happens. By convention (and an old convention, at that), an exit code of 0 indicates that a program stopped normally (that is, without error). Any other value indicates some kind of error. In the days before detailed exception messages (and still today in some systems), a cryptic number was all a person got when a program failed. Then someone would have to look up the number in a list of error codes to find out what happened. Good system operators knew large numbers of these codes by heart. Developers are happy to get more meaningful output these days.

As usual, you can see the name of the directory in Eclipse's console. I've also included a screenshot of the file system after the program runs, just to show that it works. Figure 8-6 shows the directories in the path field of Windows Explorer on my system.

Figure 8-6. Result of creating three nested directories

Deleting a Directory

Similarly, you might need to delete a directory at some point. As you probably expect by now, the code for doing so is remarkably similar to the code for creating a directory, as shown in Listing 8-10.

Listing 8-10. Deleting a directory

```java
package com.apress.java7forabsolutebeginners.examples;

import java.io.File;

public class FileTest {

  public static void main(String[] args) {
    String testDirectoryName = "C:" + File.separator + "test";
    File testDirectory = new File(testDirectoryName);
    if (testDirectory.exists()) {
      testDirectory.delete();
      System.out.println("Deleted a directory called " + testDirectoryName);
    } else {
      System.out.println("Couldn't delete " + testDirectory
          + " because it does not exist");
    }
  }
}
```

Deleting Multiple Directories

If you use the mkdirs method and the JVM can't create the final directory, it might create some of the directories along the way. That's a problem, so you need to check for each directory in the chain and remove it. For that reason, paths are sometimes stored as a collection of individual values (perhaps in an array of String objects), so that they can be worked through programmatically. In cases where not making empty directories matters (and it always matters, because it's bad form to clutter up the user's drive), it's best to store the bits of the path as a collection and create each one individually, stopping and removing any directories that get created if one fails. Consequently, we wouldn't use the mkdirs method if we care about removing path fragments after a failed directory creation attempt. Listing 8-11 shows a small program to create directories until one fails and then remove any that might be created along the way.

> ▓ **Note** If you still have a directory called test on your C drive, remove it before running the code in Listing 8-11.

Listing 8-11. Rolling back directories when creating a path fails

```java
package com.apress.java7forabsolutebeginners.examples;

import java.io.File;

public class FileTest {

  public static void main(String[] args) {
    String currentPath = "C:";
    // a double colon is illegal on my Windows machine, so this fails
    String[] pathParts = {"test", "test2", "test3::fail"};
    for (String pathPart: pathParts) {
      currentPath += File.separator + pathPart;
      File testDirectory = new File(currentPath);
      if (!testDirectory.mkdir()) {
        System.out.println("Failed to create " + testDirectory
            + "; removing all created directories");
        removePathByParts("C:", pathParts);
      } else {
        System.out.println("Created " + testDirectory);
      }
    }
  }

  private static void removePathByParts(String pathStart, String[] pathParts) {
    String currentPath = pathStart;
    String[] paths = new String[pathParts.length];
    // First, build an array of possible paths
```

160

```
    for (int pathCounter = 0; pathCounter < pathParts.length; pathCounter++) {
      currentPath += File.separator + pathParts[pathCounter];
      paths[pathCounter] = currentPath;
    }
    // Then work backwards, checking for the existence of each path
    // and deleting each one if we find it
    for (int pathCounter = pathParts.length - 1; pathCounter >= 0;
          pathCounter--) {
      File currentFile = new File(paths[pathCounter]);
      if (currentFile.delete()) {
        System.out.println("Removed " + currentFile);
      }
    }
  }
}
```

As you can see, fixing a failed `mkdirs` run takes a bit of doing. (Of course, there might be better ways to solve this problem.) Ever have a software installation fail and then notice that you have directories left behind? It's because rolling back a path is a pain in almost every programming language, and some folks don't bother, even for commercial software.

Figure 8-7 shows the output from trying to create a directory with an impossible name and the p_____ ____ the directory creation options.

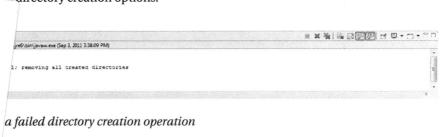

1: removing all created directories

a failed directory creation operation

Writing and Reading Content

We covered quite a bit of ground without ever writing or reading a single byte to or from a file. It often happens in software development that you must invest the time to understand one thing before you can understand another thing. Nearly all fields of study have enough complexity to require learning prerequisite information, and software development works that way, too. As Bill Cosby once quipped, "I had to tell you that joke before I could tell you this joke."

Merrily Down the Stream

In Java (and some other languages), reading from and writing to a file relies on the use of a structure called a *stream*. A stream is the data going to or coming from the file with some metadata (that is, data about the data) to indicate information such as how many bytes are available (in a file being read), whether the data is inbound or outbound, the file descriptor for the file in question, and so on. We do a bit more with streams (because we use a different kind of stream) when we process XML files in the next chapter. For now, just remember that a stream is the data structure that holds the content going to or coming from our file.

Reading a File's Content

Before we can get much further, we first need a file that contains some content. So, let's set up a test case. Copy the content from Listing 8-12 (a few lines from Shakespeare's play, *Hamlet*) into a text file called Hamlet.txt and put the file in your C:\test directory.

Listing 8-12. *Original contents of Hamlet.txt*

```
To sleep: perchance to dream: ay, there's the rub;
For in that sleep of death what dreams may come
When we have shuffled off this mortal coil,
Must give us pause: there's the respect
That makes calamity of so long life
```

(Feel free to use your own favorite bit of content if you don't like mine. For our purposes right now, all we need is some text.)

Now that we have a file with some content, we can read that content into memory with a program. To read a file's content, a Java developer generally reaches for a FileInputStream object. Listing 8-13 shows a simple program to read a file and repeat the contents in the console:

Listing 8-13. *Putting hamlet.txt in the console.*

```java
package com.apress.java7forabsolutebeginners.examples;

import java.io.File;
import java.io.FileInputStream;
import java.io.FileNotFoundException;
import java.io.IOException;

public class ReadFile {

    public static void main(String[] args) {
        // Specify the file
        String fileName = "C:" + File.separator + "test"
            + File.separator + "Hamlet.txt";
        File hamletFile = new File(fileName);
        // Set up a byte array to hold the file's content
        byte[] content = new byte[0];
        try {
            // Create an input stream for the file
            FileInputStream hamletInputStream = new FileInputStream(hamletFile);
            // Figure out how much content the file has
            int bytesAvailable = hamletInputStream.available();
            // Set the content array to the length of the content
            content = new byte[bytesAvailable];
            // Load the file's content into our byte array
            hamletInputStream.read(content);
            // Close the stream
            hamletInputStream.close();
        } catch (FileNotFoundException fnfe) {
            System.out.println("Couldn't find a file called " + fileName);
```

```
        } catch (IOException ioe) {
            System.out.println("Couldn't read from a file called " + fileName);
        }
        // Convert our content to a String
        // and write it out to the console
        System.out.print(new String(content));
    }
}
```

Let's examine that program. After doing what we already know how to do (finding a file), we first set up a data structure (a byte array) to hold the content of the file. Then we set up a `try-catch` block to handle the exceptions that can arise when working with files. We could handle both kinds of exceptions by handling just `Exception` (the parent object of both `FileNotFoundException` and `IOException`), but then we won't know what went wrong. More detail (up to a point) is generally better when diagnosing a problem.

Within our `try-catch` block, we create a stream object to hold the content of the file and then read the content of the stream into our byte array. Then we close the stream. In this simple case, we don't need to close the stream. The JVM does that for us when the program exits. However, closing files as soon as you can is a good habit to have. Each open file forces the operating system to provide an object called a file handle. Enough open files can greatly degrade a computer's performance, crash your program, or even crash the operating system.

After we have the contents of the file in memory, we can do something with it. In this case, we cast it into a `String` object and send the `String` object to the console, thus mirroring the contents of our file. We can potentially do many other things with the contents of a file. A word processing program would display the content to the user so that the user can modify the content, a game might initialize certain values (perhaps the size of the map and how aggressive the opponent is), and so on.

Writing a File's Content

Writing to a file works in much the same way as reading from a file. We get a stream, put the content we want to write to the file in the stream, write that content to the file, and then close the stream. Listing 8-14 shows a program that does just that. It's a little more complex but still straight-forward. For fun and so that we can be sure something happens when we compare the file before and after we run the program, we reverse the file's content along the way.

Listing 8-14*. Writing to hamlet.txt*

```
package com.apress.java7forabsolutebeginners.examples;

import java.io.File;
import java.io.FileInputStream;
import java.io.FileNotFoundException;
import java.io.FileOutputStream;
import java.io.IOException;

public class WriteFile {
```

```java
    public static void main(String[] args) {
        // Specify the file
        String fileName = "C:" + File.separator + "test"
            + File.separator + "Hamlet.txt";
        File hamletFile = new File(fileName);
        // Set up a byte array to hold the file's content
        byte[] content = new byte[0];
        try {
            // Create an input stream for the file
            FileInputStream hamletInputStream = new FileInputStream(hamletFile);
            // Figure out how much content the file has
            int bytesAvailable = hamletInputStream.available();
            // Set the content array to the length of the content
            content = new byte[bytesAvailable];
            // Load the file's content into our byte array
            hamletInputStream.read(content);
            // Close the stream
            hamletInputStream.close();
        } catch (FileNotFoundException fnfe) {
            System.out.println("Couldn't find a file called " + fileName);
        } catch (IOException ioe) {
            System.out.println("Couldn't read from a file called " + fileName);
        }
        // Reverse the contents of our array, just so we'll
        // know we did something to the file's content
        reverseByteArray(content);
        try {
            // Create a stream for our output
            FileOutputStream hamletOutputStream
                = new FileOutputStream(hamletFile);
            // Write our output to our stream
            // (and thus to our file)
            hamletOutputStream.write(content);
            // Close the output stream
            hamletOutputStream.close();
        } catch (FileNotFoundException fnfe) {
            System.out.println("Couldn't find a file called " + fileName);
        } catch (IOException ioe) {
            System.out.println("Couldn't write to a file called " + fileName);
        }
    }

    private static void reverseByteArray(byte[] inBytes) {
        int inLength = inBytes.length;
        for (int i = 0; i < inLength >> 1; i++) {
            byte temp = inBytes[i];
            inBytes[i] = inBytes[inLength - i - 1];
            inBytes[inLength - i - 1] = temp;
        }
    }
}
```

Before we proceed with reviewing the file, let's examine the `reverseByteArray` method. It does what's called *in-place reversing*, because we modify the original object without using any additional memory. Because we use the same memory area that the object already modifies, it's said to be "in-place." We can do that because Java passes memory addresses rather than values for objects (such as an array). We can't do it for a primitive, because Java passes copies of values for primitives. Many developers prefer in-place operations because they consume less memory and generally perform more quickly than code that makes copies of things and then modifies the copies.

This particular reversing algorithm works from both ends of the input at once, by the way. Although you might think we have to worry about whether we have an even number or odd number of bytes, we don't actually need to concern ourselves with that detail. If we start with an even number of bytes, we walk down the array to the middle and swap the center two bytes. With an odd number of bytes, the byte at the center simply never moves. Also, shifting to the right by one is a smidgeon faster than dividing by two. Combined with working from both ends at once and doing the reversal in place (that is, by not creating an additional array to hold intermediate results), this reversing algorithm is about as fast as a reversing algorithm can be, making it a handy trick to remember.

Alternately, we can reverse the contents of the file by using Java's StringBuffer class. To do so, we have to convert the content variable to a String object, create an instance of the StringBuffer class, call the reverse method on the StringBuffer object, and convert the result of StringBuffer.reverse back into a byte array. Listing 8-15 shows that alternate way to reverse the contents of a byte array.

Listing 8-15. *Another way to reverse a byte array*

```
String contentString = content.toString();
StringBuffer sb = new StringBuffer(contentString);
sb.reverse();
content = sb.toString().getBytes();
```

I showed you another way to reverse the contents of a byte to demonstrate that there's almost always another way to do things and to illustrate an issue you should know about: Conversion is expensive. The code in Listing 8-15 does a number of conversions (both of the `toString` methods and the `getBytes` method are conversions). Conversions consume both time and memory, though, so you can optimize your code by using an algorithm that doesn't demand conversions. Conversely, the `reverseByteArray` method does all of its work with bytes and never tries to convert to another type, so it ties up fewer resources (memory) and runs more quickly. Try to remember to not convert between types unless you must.

Now examine the contents of `hamlet.txt`. You find it's completely reversed, as shown in Listing 8-16.

Listing 8-16. *Hamlet in reverse*

```
efil gnol os fo ytimalac sekam tahT
tcepser eht s'ereht :esuap su evig tsuM
,lioc latrom siht ffo delffuhs evah ew nehW
emoc yam smaerd tahw htaed fo peels taht ni roF
;bur eht s'ereht ,ya :maerd ot ecnahcrep :peels oT
```

So now you see how to open a file, read its content, and replace (and reverse) that content. We can also modify the file's content rather than replace it. One simple operation is to append our new content to the existing content. To do so, we need to specify that we want to append to the file when we open it, by using a different `File` constructor. To get it to print nicely, we also put a newline character (`'\n'`) between the original and the reversed content. Listing 8-17 shows the code with the additional and changed lines highlighted.

Listing 8-17. Appending rather than replacing

```java
package com.apress.java7forabsolutebeginners.examples;

import java.io.File;
import java.io.FileInputStream;
import java.io.FileNotFoundException;
import java.io.FileOutputStream;
import java.io.IOException;

public class WriteFile {

    public static void main(String[] args) {
        // Specify the file
        String fileName = "C:" + File.separator + "test"
            + File.separator + "Hamlet.txt";
        File hamletFile = new File(fileName);
        // Set up a byte array to hold the file's content
        byte[] content = new byte[0];
        try {
            // Create an input stream for the file
            FileInputStream hamletInputStream = new FileInputStream(hamletFile);
            // Figure out how much content the file has
            int bytesAvailable = hamletInputStream.available();
            // Set the content array to the length of the content
            content = new byte[bytesAvailable];
            // Load the file's content into our byte array
            hamletInputStream.read(content);
            // Close the stream
            hamletInputStream.close();
        } catch (FileNotFoundException fnfe) {
            System.out.println("Couldn't find a file called " + fileName);
        } catch (IOException ioe) {
            System.out.println("Couldn't read from a file called " + fileName);
        }
        // Reverse the contents of our array, just so we'll
        // know we did something to the file's content
        reverseByteArray(content);
        try {
            // Create a stream for our output
            FileOutputStream hamletOutputStream
                = new FileOutputStream(hamletFile, true);
            // Write a newline character to separate the
            // original content from the new content.
            hamletOutputStream.write('\n');
            // Write our output to the file output stream
            // (and thus to our file)
            hamletOutputStream.write(content);
```

```
            // Close the output stream
            hamletOutputStream.close();
            System.out.println("New contents of hamlet.txt written");
        } catch (FileNotFoundException fnfe) {
            System.out.println("Couldn't find a file called " + fileName);
        } catch (IOException ioe) {
            System.out.println("Couldn't write to a file called " + fileName);
        }
    }

    private static void reverseByteArray(byte[] inBytes) {
        int inLength = inBytes.length;
        for (int i = 0; i < inLength >> 1; i++) {
            byte temp = inBytes[i];
            inBytes[i] = inBytes[inLength - i - 1];
            inBytes[inLength - i - 1] = temp;
        }
    }
}
```

And now we have *Hamlet* going forwards and backwards in Listing 8-18.

Listing 8-18. *Original and reversed content*

```
To sleep: perchance to dream: ay, there's the rub;
For in that sleep of death what dreams may come
When we have shuffled off this mortal coil,
Must give us pause: there's the respect
That makes calamity of so long life
efil gnol os fo ytimalac sekam tahT
tcepser eht s'ereht :esuap su evig tsuM
,lioc latrom siht ffo delffuhs evah ew nehW
emoc yam smaerd tahw htaed fo peels taht ni roF
;bur eht s'ereht ,ya :maerd ot ecnahcrep :peels oT
```

Summary

Software developers often need to work with files, and Java has a rich set of classes that let us do so. As we saw, we use the File class to work with files and directories, and we use streams (FileInputStream objects and FileOutputStream objects) to read and write files. We learned a number of things about File, FileInputStream, and FileOutputStream objects:

- A File object can represent a directory structure defined by a path.

- A File object is not a file or directory. It is an object that represents a file or directory.

- The file or directory represented by a File object does not necessarily exist.

- A failed attempt to create directories can leave unwanted directories, so we need to clean up after a failed directory creation operation.

- `FileInputStream` objects and `FileOutputStream` objects use byte arrays to read from and write to files.

- We can load the content of a FileInputStream object into a FileOutputStream object by using a byte array.

Working with directories, files, and the contents of files might not be the most exciting kind of programming, but it's often necessary. As you continue your programming career (whether as a professional or as a hobbyist), you'll almost certainly work with files on a regular basis.

As ever, I encourage you to write a few programs of your own. Here are a couple of ideas to tackle:

- Read the contents of one file and put them in another file.

- Read all the file names within a directory and put them in a file.

- Add full path names to the names of the files in the previous idea.

- Create all the files listed in a file.

- Create all the files listed in a file, but with a different path for each file.

■ **Tip**   As you test files, read and write only from files within a test directory, as we do in this chapter. That lessens the risk that you'll accidently change a file that could cause a problem. Also, test often, to be sure the files you work with end up in the right places and have the right contents.

Writing and Reading XML

XML stands for Extensible Markup Language. You might think it would be "eXtensible Markup Language," but it's not. Odd acronym aside, XML rates inclusion in a book for beginning programmers because, as your software-development career (whether as a hobbyist sqor a professional) continues, you'll inevitably run into XML in all sorts of places. It's used to store documents, from the contents of a single web page to the contents of entire sets of encyclopedias. It's also used to transmit data between applications, whether the servers running those applications are halfway around the world or in the same room. It's even used (with Cascading Style Sheets) to display information in web browsers. Every company I've worked for over the last dozen years, and every application I've written (at least those applications more serious and substantial than Minesweeper), has made at least some use of XML.

Although a specialized language called XSLT (Extensible Stylesheet Language Transformation) exists specifically for processing XML, Java is also a very popular language for dealing with XML. Also, one of the best and most popular XSLT processors, called Saxon, is coded in Java. Java is especially handy for working with XML because it includes a number of packages intended specifically for processing (reading, writing, and transforming) XML. The two most common packages (largely because they are included in Java) are DOM (Document Object Model) and SAX (Simple API for XML). You can use DOM to read and write XML. SAX only reads (or, more properly, parses) XML. For writing XML, though, you can also create a `String` object and write that to your file. Done correctly, writing `String` objects offers the lowest overhead (in both memory and speed) for producing XML. This chapter will cover writing XML from DOM and from `String` objects, and reading XML with DOM and SAX.

The Structure of XML

Before you get to processing the stuff, you should see what XML looks like and learn a bit about its nature. First off, know that XML, while called a language, isn't a language in the same sense as Java. XML is a storage format, and it offers no processing capabilities of its own. It has no looping structure, no way to specify variables or data types (except that a program might use a bit of XML as a variable or data type, but that's not the same as what Java does). So, XML is really just text that has been organized in a particular way.

The root of any XML document is a single element. That element can have any number of other elements as children, and each of these children can have any number of children, and so on, resulting in a hierarchical structure of arbitrary complexity and depth (which is to say that an XML document can be of any size and have elements nested to any depth). Also, each element can have any number of attributes. However, attributes cannot have children, so most of the content, in most XML documents, comes from the elements.

Before going any further, take a look at the smallest possible XML file.

Listing 9-1. The Smallest Possible XML File

```
<?xml version="1.0" encoding="UTF-8"?>
<elementName/>
```

I have worked with systems that had many such files, as each directory in a set of directories meant to contain the output of a complex process had to have at least one file. Consequently, we had a bunch of XML files with content as follows: `<?xml version="1.0" encoding="UTF-8"?><placeholder/>`You can see the exact syntax shortly. Until then, a more meaningful example will help to clarify things. Here's one of my favorite poems, encoded as an XML document.

Listing 9-2. An Example of XML

```
<?xml version="1.0" encoding="UTF-8"?>
<poem title="The Great Figure" author="William Carlos Williams">
  <line>Among the rain</line>
  <line>and lights</line>
  <line>I saw the figure 5</line>
  <line>in gold</line>
  <line>on a red</line>
  <line>fire truck</line>
  <line>moving</line>
  <line>tense</line>
  <line>unheeded</line>
  <line>to gong clangs</line>
  <line>siren howls</line>
  <line>and wheels rumbling</line>
  <line>through the dark city</line>
</poem>
```

The first line, the document specifier, indicates that this document is an XML document and specifies the version (1.0, which is the most often used version, and suffices for most purposes) and the encoding. Document specifiers always begin with <? and end with ?>. This way, they can't be confused with XML elements. Most systems that can process XML will work with documents that don't have a document specifier, but a document without one isn't strictly an XML file—it's just a collection of characters that happen to look like an XML file. That may seem like an arbitrary and trivial distinction, but your XML document may be rejected for just that reason by some systems, so it's good to get in the habit of always including a document specifier. The encoding indicates the character set that applies to the content. UTF-8 is a large set that includes most of the characters available in non-Asian languages (including English, Greek, Spanish, Russian, and many others). The Asian languages (Chinese, Japanese, Vietnamese, and others) use pictographs (that is, an image that corresponds to a word). The Asian character sets are consequently very large and tricky to manipulate. For the sake of simplicity, we'll stick to UTF-8 and documents in English.

The next line contains the root element. The first element in any XML file is that document's root element. All other elements, no matter how deeply nested, are descendants of the root. The root element, poem, contains two attributes, **title** and **author**. The root element also contains all the **line** elements, which make up the body of the poem.

Note the syntax for each element. Each one begins with an opening tag (`<poem>` or `<line>`) and ends with a closing tag (`</poem>` or `</line>`). The basic rule is that the names within the tags have to match (and there are various restrictions about which characters can be used, but just about any English word works). Other than that, opening tags always start with a left angle character (<) and end with a right angle character(>). Ending tags always begin with a left angle character and a forward slash (</) and end

with a right angle character (>). Elements can also be empty, in which case they can take one of two forms: a beginning tag and an ending tag with nothing between them, or a special empty element tag. For example, an empty line element can be represented as either `<line></line>` or `<line/>`. That second structure provides a handy shortcut that saves some typing. If the poem included a blank line (such as a line between stanzas in a longer poem), you could represent a blank line that way.

▓ **Note** XML is case-sensitive. `<POEM>`, `<Poem>`, and `<poem>` are all different elements, so `<POEM></poem>` would cause an XML parser to throw an error.

A poem offers an example of a fairly traditional document encoded as XML. Consider an example of data transmitted between systems as XML.

Listing 9-2. *XML As Data*

```xml
<?xml version="1.0"?>
<soap:Envelope
    xmlns:soap="http://www.w3.org/2001/12/soap-envelope"
    soap:encodingStyle="http://www.w3.org/2001/12/soap-encoding">
  <soap:Body xmlns:w="http://www.noaa.gov/weather">
    <w:GetTemperature>
      <w:Location>78701</w:Location>
    </w:GetTemperature>
  </soap:Body>
</soap:Envelope>
```

Look closely at the document specifier. In this case, it doesn't indicate encoding. The default encoding for XML is UTF-8, so you can omit the specifier when you are going to use UTF-8 characters. Then you have a root element named soap:Envelope. The specifier and the root element constitute the minimum content for an XML file, but that wouldn't make a very useful message between systems. So this example also contains a bit of data (the zip code for a particular city).This XML document represents a request for data from one system to another system. (I invented it from scratch, by the way; NOAA may use something else entirely.) In particular, it's a request to get the temperature in Austin, TX. Note the indentation. When XML is meant to be read by humans, it's customarily indented, such that each level of elements is farther to the right than its parent level. When creating a stream to send to another system, all the white space between elements is generally removed, resulting in the whole document being on one line. That's tough to read for a human, but it saves bandwidth, and a computer doesn't find it hard to read.

▓ **Note** "Document" is the normal way to refer to any instance of XML, whether it encodes an actual document or some arbitrary bit of data—XML originally comes from the publishing industry, and it retains some of that industry's terminology.

SOAP stands for Simplified Object Access Protocol. It's a common way for systems to pass data back and forth. One system makes a request, and another system sends a corresponding response, which may trigger yet another request. The system that processes the request, and produces a response, may then send a request. In this fashion the systems "play tag" with one another, until the data is properly transmitted (or an error condition indicates that the systems should stop trying). Inter-system and inter-process communication can get much more complex than a simple request-response cycle, but that's beyond the scope of this book.The purpose of this kind of protocol (SOAP is one of many such standards) is to provide separate systems a way to communicate that has as few dependencies as possible on the operating system or language. One system might be a Windows server running an application written in C++, while another system might be a Linux server running a Java application, and yet another system might be a supercomputer running an ADA application. Provided the other system can recognize the request and generate an appropriate response, anything else is irrelevant. This makes SOAP, and similar protocols, very useful to software developers. You can create all kinds of systems and make them talk to one another. The Internet is the plumbing, but SOAP messages, and similar content, constitute the water in the pipes (or the information in the network, to abandon the metaphor). Requests and responses (the latter, in particular) can be very large, by the way. I once created a system that shared insurance policy information with a national insurance clearing house. The responses in that system were very large— often several megabytes of data. (Honestly, had I designed that system, I would have sent a response that specified a location from which the other system could download a file containing the policy. Huge responses can be problematic. The longer the message, the higher the chance for corrupted data, and it's sometimes useful to store data for a time. It wasn't my decision to make, though.)

The `xmlns:soap` attribute specifies the namespace for SOAP, so that any system receiving it can recognize what kind of message it is (assuming the system knows about SOAP at all). (XMLNS stands for XML NameSpace.) The `encodingStyle` element (itself a member of the soap namespace) specifies the exact version of SOAP being used. The `soap:Body` namespace specifies a (fictional, in this case) namespace for weather information. Note that each namespace has an alias (`soap` or `w`, in this document). The aliases save the trouble of typing out the namespace for each element and, more importantly, reduces the number of bytes going down the pipe. The relatively simple poem example has no namespace declaration, which means that it uses the default XML namespace. Every XML element has a namespace, even if it's only the default. In the SOAP example, you can see that a single XML document can contain elements from multiple namespaces (a Microsoft Word document contains as many as 14 different namespaces, just to show how complex things can get). Namespaces let different organizations use the same elements without trampling one another when they get into the same document. For example, if another organization produced weather information, they'd have their own namespace, to prevent collisions with the `noaa` namespace.

XML and Streams

A stream is a collection of data meant to be read sequentially. That is, a stream is meant to be read one byte at a time. It is generally said that such a block of data is serialized (meaning that it is ready to be transmitted and read serially, which is another way to say one byte at a time).In Java (and in other many other languages), XML is processed as streams. Reading XML is done by parsing `InputStream` objects, and writing XML is generally done by creating `StreamResult` objects. When creating XML with `String` objects, the result is often still exported as an `OutputStream`, as some other process needs to receive a stream to do its part in a larger process. For example, many systems produce large documents. In these systems, you can create XML by using `String` objects, create an `OutputStream` from the result, and send that stream as an `InputStream` to another object, which would produce a PDF file. The PDF file serves as the final document, to be stored on a server, printed, or both.

As you saw in Chapter 8, Java uses **Stream** objects for reading from, and writing to, files. Since you're already processing **Stream** objects, saving an XML document as a file is a natural and easy task. Reading an existing file as a stream also makes loading an XML file straightforward. So, there are streams in, streams out, and streams between the steps of larger processes. Fortunately, Java makes working with streams easy.

DOM and SAX

DOM (Document Object Model) and SAX (Simplified API for XML) have their strengths and weaknesses. As with most data-related problems, knowing which one to use comes down to knowing your data. If you need to work with relatively small documents, DOM works well, as it loads the entire XML data stream into memory, making it fast (again, provided the document is small). SAX, on the other hand, uses only enough memory to process the current element (called a node), which makes it capable of handling documents of any size. I've used SAX to parse the contents of books as long as 2,000 pages. The down side of SAX is that you can't reach much of the document at once, as little of it is in memory. Also, SAX only works with incoming XML documents; it doesn't write XML.

So, remember to use DOM for small XML sources and SAX for larger XML sources. If you're uncertain if the XML input will be large or small, use SAX. Of course, whether a document is large or small depends on how much memory is available for processing the document. If your program can run on a computer with plenty of memory all to itself, you can use DOM to load fairly large documents. However, if your program has to share a server with other processes, or has to run on a small device (such as a phone), memory will be limited and your options will be reduced. Finally, if your application has to process multiple documents at once (perhaps for multiple users), the memory for each process will be greatly reduced. The more constrained the memory available to the application, the more you should lean toward SAX. As an example, I recently worked on an application that would trigger an arbitrary number of transforms to create sets of documents. In practice, each set contained about 15 documents. Also, multiple users could start document-production runs at the same time, leading to as many as 50 documents being processed at the same time, all with 8 MB of RAM. We definitely needed to use SAX.

Writing XML

As mentioned above, you can write XML with the DOM package or by writing **String** objects. If you just need to write an XML file, writing strings works well enough (and it is the fastest way to create XML). On the other hand, if you need to pass your XML output to a process that requires an XML header, and perhaps even needs to ensure that the XML conforms to a schema, you might want to consider using DOM.

Before you get to writing XML, you first need a data source to provide the content that you want to turn into XML. Here is a simple class that provides the content of the poem used earlier ("The Great Figure," by William Carlos Williams).

Listing 9-3. *A Poem As a Data Source*

```
package com.bryantcs.examples.xml;

import java.util.ArrayList;
```

```java
public class Poem {

  private static String title = "The Great Figure";
  private static String author ="William Carlos Williams";
  private static ArrayList<String> lines = new ArrayList<String>();

  static {
    lines.add("Among the rain");
    lines.add("and lights");
    lines.add("I saw the figure 5");
    lines.add("in gold");
    lines.add("on a red");
    lines.add("fire truck");
    lines.add("moving");
    lines.add("tense");
    lines.add("unheeded");
    lines.add("to gong clangs");
    lines.add("siren howls");
    lines.add("and wheels rumbling");
    lines.add("through the dark city");
  }

  public static String getTitle() {
    return title;
  }

  public static String getAuthor() {
    return author;
  }

  public static ArrayList<String> getLines() {
    return lines;
  }
}
```

As you can see, it's a pretty simple representation of a poem. Notice that it's also entirely static. Some classes consist entirely of static members, but those classes usually define sets of helper methods (string manipulation specialized for a particular application is a common use for that kind of helper class). A class with static data, though, usually indicates that someone hasn't thought through a problem very well. This kind of thing usually belongs in a file. For our purposes, though, this slightly odd class will serve well enough.

Writing XML with DOM

Here's the code for writing an XML file with DOM, given the Poem class as the data source:

Listing 9-4. *Writing XML with DOM*

```java
package com.bryantcs.examples.xml;

import java.io.File;
```

```java
import java.io.FileNotFoundException;
import java.io.FileOutputStream;
import java.io.IOException;
import java.io.StringWriter;

import javax.xml.parsers.DocumentBuilder;
import javax.xml.parsers.DocumentBuilderFactory;
import javax.xml.parsers.ParserConfigurationException;
import javax.xml.transform.OutputKeys;
import javax.xml.transform.Transformer;
import javax.xml.transform.TransformerConfigurationException;
import javax.xml.transform.TransformerException;
import javax.xml.transform.TransformerFactory;
import javax.xml.transform.dom.DOMSource;
import javax.xml.transform.stream.StreamResult;

import org.w3c.dom.Document;
import org.w3c.dom.Element;
import org.w3c.dom.Text;

public class WriteWithDOM {

  public static void main (String args[]) {
    // Create an empty Document
    Document doc = createDocument();

    // Create the XML
    createElements(doc);

    // Create a String representation of the XML
    String xmlContent = createXMLString(doc);

    // Write the XML to a file
    writeXMLToFile(xmlContent);
  }

// Here's where we create the (empty for now) XML document  private static Document
createDocument() {
    Document doc = null;
    try {
      DocumentBuilderFactory dbfac = DocumentBuilderFactory.newInstance();
      DocumentBuilder docBuilder = dbfac.newDocumentBuilder();
      doc =  docBuilder.newDocument();
      doc.setXmlStandalone(true);
    }
    catch(ParserConfigurationException pce) {
      System.out.println("Couldn't create a DocumentBuilder");
      System.exit(1);
    }
    return doc;
  }
```

```
    // Here's where we add content to the XML document    private static void
createElements(Document doc) {
    // Create the root element
    Element poem = doc.createElement("poem");
    poem.setAttribute("title", Poem.getTitle());
    poem.setAttribute("author", Poem.getAuthor());

    // Add the root element to the document
    doc.appendChild(poem);

    // Create the child elements
    for (String lineIn : Poem.getLines() ) {
      Element line = doc.createElement("line");
      Text lineText = doc.createTextNode(lineIn);
      line.appendChild(lineText);
      // Add each element to the root element        poem.appendChild(line);
    }
  }

  // Here's where we convert the DOM object
  // into a String that contains XML    private static String createXMLString(Document doc) {
    // Transform the DOM to a String
    Transformer transformer = null;
    StringWriter stringWriter = new StringWriter();
    try {
      TransformerFactory transformerFactory =
        TransformerFactory.newInstance();
      transformer = transformerFactory.newTransformer();
      transformer.setOutputProperty(OutputKeys.OMIT_XML_DECLARATION,
        "no");
      transformer.setOutputProperty(OutputKeys.INDENT, "yes");

      // Create a string to contain the XML from the Document object
      stringWriter = new StringWriter();
      StreamResult result = new StreamResult(stringWriter);
      DOMSource source = new DOMSource(doc);
      transformer.transform(source, result);
    } catch (TransformerConfigurationException e) {
      System.out.println("Couldn't create a Transformer");
      System.exit(1);
    } catch (TransformerException e) {
      System.out.println("Couldn't transform DOM to a String");
      System.exit(1);
    }
    return stringWriter.toString();
  }

  // Here's where we turn the String holding the XML
  // into a file    private static void writeXMLToFile(String xmlContent) {
    String fileName = "C:" + File.separator + "test"
    + File.separator + "domoutput.xml";
    try {
```

```
        File domOutput = new File(fileName);
        FileOutputStream domOutputStream
            = new FileOutputStream(domOutput, true);
        domOutputStream.write(xmlContent.getBytes());
        domOutputStream.close();
        System.out.println(fileName + " was successfully written");
    } catch (FileNotFoundException fnfe) {
        System.out.println("Couldn't find a file called " + fileName);
        System.exit(1);
    } catch (IOException ioe) {
        System.out.println("Couldn't write to a file called " + fileName);
        System.exit(1);
    }
  }
}
```

▓ **Tip**   Use a `StringBuilder` object to create a string whenever you need to append strings onto other strings. If you use the string concatenation operator (+), the JVM creates a new String object but also keeps the previous String object in memory, which quickly consumes a great deal of memory. Modern JVMs have gotten better about handling this problem, but it remains an issue, and good practice dictates using StringBuilder when you have more than one or two concatenations to do.

As you can see, I've carved it up into a few methods to cleanly and clearly separate the parts of the algorithm. That's a practice you'll see many developers follow, and it's good to embrace this when code complexity reaches a certain level. Every programmer has a different threshold for when they think a long method should become multiple methods. My own threshold is pretty low. A method doesn't have to get very long before I start itching to split it. In this case, splitting the code also lets me handle the `Exception` objects thrown by each step separately.

The process for creating XML with DOM is fairly straightforward:

1.   Create an empty `Document` object (the top-level DOM object that contains everything else). That's done in the `createDocument` method.

2.   Create the elements and attributes (and their children, grandchildren, and so on, as needed) and add the elements and attributes to the Document object. The `createElements` method performs this step.

3.   Convert the contents of the DOM object to a `String` object. The `createXMLString` method does this step for you.

4.   Write the `String` object to the target (a file in this case). The `writeXMLToFile` method creates your file and puts your XML into the file.

Writing XML with Strings

Here's the code to produce the same output by writing out a **String** object.

Listing 9-5. *Writing XML with Strings*

```java
package com.bryantcs.examples.xml;

import java.io.File;
import java.io.FileNotFoundException;
import java.io.FileOutputStream;
import java.io.IOException;

public class WriteWithStrings {

  public static void main(String[] args) {
    String xmlContent = createXMLContent();
    writeXMLToFile(xmlContent);
  }

  private static String createXMLContent() {
    // write the first line
    StringBuilder sb = new StringBuilder();
    sb.append("<?xml version=\"1.0\" encoding=\"UTF-8\"?>");     sb.append("<poem title=\"");
    sb.append(Poem.getTitle());
    sb.append("\" author=\"");
    sb.append(Poem.getAuthor());
    sb.append("\">\n");
    // write the middle lines
    for (String lineIn : Poem.getLines()) {
      sb.append("<line>");
      sb.append(lineIn);
      sb.append("</line>\n");
    }
    // write the last line
    sb.append("</poem>");
    return sb.toString();
  }

  private static void writeXMLToFile(String xmlContent) {
    String fileName = "C:" + File.separator + "test"
    + File.separator + "domoutput.xml";
    try {
      File domOutput = new File(fileName);
      FileOutputStream domOutputStream
          = new FileOutputStream(domOutput, true);
      domOutputStream.write(xmlContent.getBytes());
      domOutputStream.close();
      System.out.println(fileName + " was successfully created");
    } catch (FileNotFoundException fnfe) {
      System.out.println("Couldn't find a file called " + fileName);
```

```
      System.exit(1);
    } catch (IOException ioe) {
      System.out.println("Couldn't write to a file called " + fileName);
      System.exit(1);
    }
  }
}
```

As you can see, the code is substantially simpler and easier to follow. It also performs more quickly. Again, it doesn't have some of the output features from DOM (no XML header, for example), but it works if you just need a simple XML document.

Reading XML

To read XML, you can use either DOM or SAX. As mentioned earlier in this chapter, DOM is handy when you can be sure that your XML content will fit into the memory you have available. However, DOM fails when the input is too large. SAX, on the other hand, can handle any amount of input. For SAX, you need only as much memory as the largest element needs (usually not much, unless you're doing something such as processing large images or items where a single element can contain a large amount of data).

Reading XML with DOM

Here's the source for a program that reads XML with DOM. For this program to work, you need to create a file named poemsource.xml and put it in your C:\test (on Windows) or C:/test (on Unix or Linux) directory. You can use the contents of the domoutput.xml file as the contents of the poemsource.xml file.

Listing 9-6. Reading XML with DOM

```
package com.bryantcs.examples.xml;

import java.io.File;
import java.io.IOException;

import javax.xml.parsers.DocumentBuilder;
import javax.xml.parsers.DocumentBuilderFactory;
import javax.xml.parsers.ParserConfigurationException;

import org.w3c.dom.Document;
import org.w3c.dom.Element;
import org.w3c.dom.NamedNodeMap;
import org.w3c.dom.Node;
import org.w3c.dom.NodeList;
import org.xml.sax.SAXException;
```

```
public class ReadWithDOM {

  public static void main(String[] args) {
    String fileName = "C:" + File.separator + "test"
    + File.separator + "poemsource.xml";
    writeFileContentsToConsole(fileName);
  }

  // Write the contents of the file to the console  private static void
writeFileContentsToConsole(String fileName) {
    // Create a DOM Document object    Document doc = createDocument(fileName);
    // Get the root element    Element root = doc.getDocumentElement();
    // Create a StringBuilder object that describes the root element    StringBuilder sb = new
StringBuilder();    sb.append("The root element is named: \"" + root.getNodeName() + "\"");
    sb.append(" and has the following attributes: ");
    NamedNodeMap attributes = root.getAttributes();
    for (int i = 0; i < attributes.getLength(); i ++) {
      Node thisAttribute = attributes.item(i);
      sb.append(thisAttribute.getNodeName());
      sb.append (" (\"" + thisAttribute.getNodeValue() + "\")");
      if (i < attributes.getLength() - 1) {
        sb.append(", ");
      }
    }
    // Write the description of the root element to the console    System.out.println(sb);

    // Work through the children of the root
    // First, get a list of the child nodes    NodeList nodes =
doc.getElementsByTagName("line");
    for (int i = 0; i < nodes.getLength(); i++) {
      // Process each element in turn    Element element = (Element) nodes.item(i);
      System.out.println("Found an element named \"" +
      // By writing its name and content to the console (System.out)
element.getTagName() + "\"" +
        " with the following content: \"" +
        element.getTextContent() + "\"");
    }
  }

  // Create a DOM Document object from a file  private static Document createDocument(String
fileName) {
    Document doc = null;
    try {
      // Get the file     File xmlFile = new File(fileName);
      // Create document builder factory     DocumentBuilderFactory dbfac =
DocumentBuilderFactory.newInstance();
      // Create a document builder object     DocumentBuilder docBuilder =
dbfac.newDocumentBuilder();
      // Load the document by parsing the file with the document builder    doc =
docBuilder.parse(xmlFile);
      // Indicate that this document is self-contained    doc.setXmlStandalone(true);
    }
```

```
  // Deal with the possible exceptions    catch (IOException ioe) {
    System.out.println("Couldn't open file: " + fileName);
    System.exit(1);
  }
  catch (SAXException se) {
    System.out.println("Couldn't parse the XML file");
    System.exit(1);
  }
  catch(ParserConfigurationException pce) {
    System.out.println("Couldn't create a DocumentBuilder");
    System.exit(1);
  }
  // Finally return the Document object
  // that we built from the file    return doc;
  }
}
```

In this case, we just create a `Document` object, read through each line of the input, and describe the content in the console. Naturally, you'll probably want to do something more than describe your input in the console, but this example shows you how to read a file. One thing to note is that each `Element` object is really a `Node` object (the `Element` interface extends the `Node` interface). Due to the way DOM has been implemented, you sometimes need to work with both `Element` objects and `Node` objects, as I had to do here when working with the attribute values.

Reading XML with SAX

SAX uses an interface called `ContentHandler` to expose parsing events that you can then intercept in your own code to do whatever processing you want to do for each parsing event. The SAX packages also provide a default implementation of `ContentHandler`, called `DefaultHandler`. `DefaultHandler` does nothing with each event, because doing nothing is the default behavior. However, you can override the methods in `DefaultHandler` to do whatever you like. The advantage of extending `DefaultHandler` is that you can override just the methods you care about and leave the rest alone. In the example I've used here, I didn't need many of the methods in `DefaultHandler`, so I didn't override them.

If you look at the names of the methods, you can see why SAX uses so little memory to process XML. It triggers an event for the beginning and end of each part of an XML document, be it the document itself or an element. So, all the parser has to put in memory is the name (and some other details) about the element, and a list of the element's children. It doesn't have to put the element's content into memory until it gets to the characters method, which is the method that handles an element's character content. Most elements don't have vast amounts of text content (one exception is when someone stores an image in an XML element, as Word documents do), so the memory used to process the text usually isn't much.

To show you how to read a simple XML document and describe its contents in the console, I first created a class (called `XMLToConsoleHandler`) that extends `DefaultHandler` and overrides the handful of methods I need to use when capturing the contents of an XML file. Here's the `XMLToConsoleHandler` class:

Listing 9-7. *XMLToConsolHandler*

```
package com.bryantcs.examples.xml;

import org.xml.sax.Attributes;
import org.xml.sax.SAXException;
```

```java
import org.xml.sax.helpers.DefaultHandler;

public class XMLToConsoleHandler extends DefaultHandler {

    // The characters method handles the actual content of an element  @Override
    public void characters(char[] content, int start, int length) throws SAXException {
        // Describe the content in the console    System.out.println("Found content: " + new
String(content, start, length));  }

    // The endDocument method lets us do something
    // when the parser reaches the end of the document  @Override
    public void endDocument() throws SAXException {
        // Announce in the console that we found the end of the document
System.out.println("Found the end of the document");   }

    // The endElement method lets us do something
    // when the parser reaches the end of an element  @Override
    public void endElement(String arg0, String localName, String qName)
        throws SAXException {
        // Announce in the console that we found the end of an element
System.out.println("Found the end of an element named \"" + qName + "\"");
    }

    // The startDocument lets us do something
    // when we find the top of the document  @Override
    public void startDocument() throws SAXException {
        // Announce in the console that we found the beginning of the document
System.out.println("Found the start of the document");
    }

    // The startElement method lets us do something
    // when we reach the beginning of an element  @Override
    public void startElement(String uri, String localName, String qName,
        Attributes attributes) throws SAXException {
        // Create a StringBuilder object to contain our description of this element
StringBuilder sb = new StringBuilder();
        // Add the name of the element    sb.append("Found the start of an element named \"" +
qName + "\"");
        // See if the element has any attributes    if (attributes != null &&
attributes.getLength() > 0) {
            sb.append(" with attributes named ");
            // If we do find attributes, describe each one    for (int i = 0; i <
attributes.getLength(); i++) {
                String attributeName = attributes.getLocalName(i);
                String attributeValue = attributes.getValue(i);
                sb.append("\"" + attributeName + "\"");
                sb.append(" (value = ");
                sb.append("\"" + attributeValue + "\"");
                sb.append(")");
```

```
        // If we're not at the end of the attributes,
        // add a comma, for proper formatting        if (i < attributes.getLength() - 1) {
          sb.append(", ");
        }
      }
    }
    // Describe the element in the console    System.out.println(sb.toString());
  }
}
```

Again, we're using a **StringBuilder** to avoid creating an excess of **String** objects in memory. The only complexity comes when we work through any attributes that may be present, and most of the code is really just for "pretty printing" (a phrase that programmers often use when referring to code that formats output to be easily read by humans).

Let's look at the class that uses the **XMLToConsoleHandler** class to write to the console. Again, you need to have a file named poemsource.xml in the C:\test (on Windows) or C:/test (on Unix or Linux) directory. You can use the contents of the domoutput.xml file as the contents of the poemsource.xml file. Here's that class:

Listing 9-8. ReadWithSAX

```
package com.bryantcs.examples.xml;

import java.io.File;
import java.io.IOException;

import javax.xml.parsers.ParserConfigurationException;
import javax.xml.parsers.SAXParser;
import javax.xml.parsers.SAXParserFactory;

import org.xml.sax.SAXException;

public class ReadWithSAX {

  public static void main(String[] args) {
    String fileName = "C:" + File.separator + "test"
        + File.separator + "poemsource.xml";
    getFileContents(fileName);
  }

  private static void getFileContents (String fileName) {
    try {
    // Make an instance of our handler       XMLToConsoleHandler handler = new
XMLToConsoleHandler();
      // Get a parser factory       SAXParserFactory factory = SAXParserFactory.newInstance();
      // Get a parser      SAXParser saxParser = factory.newSAXParser();
      // And now parse the file with our handler       saxParser.parse(fileName, handler );
```

```
    // Deal with the possible exceptions      } catch(IOException ioe) {
      System.out.println("Couldn't open " + fileName + " for parsing");
    } catch(ParserConfigurationException pce) {
      System.out.println("Failed to create a SAX parser ");
    } catch(SAXException saxe) {
      System.out.println("Failed to parse an XML file");
    }
  }
}
```

Simple, isn't it? One of the joys of SAX is that it's simple to implement. Create a handler, create a parser, and pass your input and handler to the factory. Consequently, the exception-handling code is longer than the code that does the work. Of course, this arrangement is really masking the fact that the complexity is in the handler class. Still, carving up your code so that complexity is isolated to a single class is exactly the right way to use an object-oriented language such as Java.

A Word about Factory Classes

You may have noticed that to get a `DocumentBuilder` object, you had to use a `DocumentBuilderFactory` object. Similarly, to get a `SAXParser` object, you had to use a `SAXParserFactory` object. The factory pattern is often used in Java (and other object-oriented languages, such as C++) to permit the creation of objects that have varying attributes. For example, the `SAXParserFactory` class includes a way to specify a separate validator object, to ensure that the XML conforms to a schema (which is a definition of what a set of data should contain).

The factory pattern is a handy way to present a group of very similar objects that vary only by having some features turned on or off. Otherwise, you'd have to have a class for every possible combination of features. In some cases, that would be a lot of very similar classes. The factory pattern offers an easy-to-use and easy-to-understand solution to that problem. Consequently, Java has a number of factory objects in its standard libraries. You can also create your own factory classes. When you find yourself needing to create many very similar (but slightly different) objects, consider creating a factory for them.

Summary

Well, that was a whirlwind tour of how to use Java to work with XML. Several good books have been written about the subject, as there's a great deal more complexity than what's been presented here. Still, this chapter should prepare you for when you have to read and write XML files or streams.

In particular, we covered the basics of Java's two main ways to deal with XML: the Document Object Model (DOM) and the Simplified API for XML (SAX). You learned that DOM offers great performance because it loads the entire document into memory. However, loading the entire document into memory is also DOM's biggest problem, as large documents may exceed the available memory. SAX, on the other hand, can handle any amount of XML (including gigabyte-size streams of data), but it requires making a custom handler class for each kind of XML document.

Finally, you looked at the nature of factory classes and learned about why they exist, and when you might want to use them.

CHAPTER 10

Animation

Animation involves an image that changes over time. It's interesting (to us, anyway, but we love etymology) that *animation* outside of computer science means "bestowing of life." Animated images certainly seem to have more life than still images.

Timing Is Everything

The essence of animation is timing. An animated image changes every so often. Usually, that's very often (many times a second), but an image that changes once a minute (such as a clock) is still animated, though it might not be much fun to watch. To give you an idea of how often an animated image can change, let's look at some common animation speeds that most of us see every day, usually without even thinking of them as being animated images.

A standard TV signal (STV, the predecessor to HDTV) shows a new image (approximately) 30 times a second. That is, an STV signal has a frame rate of 30 per second. *Frame rate* is a key term in animation, in computing in general, and in other industries. You've seen what it means in animation. For computing in general, "frame rate" refers to how often a program processes all of its inputs and produces all of its outputs. The classic example is software that steers a vehicle. If the vehicle is a freighter at sea, a low frame rate (such as once a minute) might suffice. For an automated lander (for the moon or Mars), a frame rate approaching 100 times per second might be necessary. Such a system is said to work at a certain *hertz*, which is the technical term for how many times a second a process repeats. Hertz is used in many industries, including the electronics industry. Finally, for video games, animation is generally measured in frames per second (FPS), which is the same as hertz but is an industry-specific term.

To get back to common frame rates (or FPS), a standard TV shows 30 frames per second. Most movies are filmed at 24 FPS (though this is rapidly changing to 60 FPS). NTSC (the standard television signal format in the United States and the predecessor to HDTV) works at 60 FPS (but it's interlaced, meaning the screen is divided into lines and alternating sets of lines are shown 30 times per second each). Many other countries (including most of Europe) use 50 FPS (interlaced) for standard television. The ATSC standard (essentially the HDTV standard used in the United States) shows between 24 and 60 frames per second, depending on several factors. More recent HDTV devices claim frame rates as high as 240. Finally, most computer monitors operate between 75 and 85 hertz, meaning 75 to 85 frames per second.

That last rate is generally the one most important to programmers (though game console programmers have to concern themselves with TV frame rates, too). We can make animation systems that can show hundreds of frames per second, but there's no point in doing so. No monitor can show that many frames per second. Consequently, a monitor's hertz is the practical limit on computer-generated animation. In fact, not only is trying for a frame rate higher than the monitor's hertz pointless, it might do harm, by tying up the system such that it can't do other work (either for your process or for other processes).

In creating samples for this chapter, we chose frame rates between 4 and 25 FPS. That might seem low, but it's adequate for the sake of examples. A low frame rate might even help you understand how animation works, as you can then see it happen. If you watch the sprite animation example closely, you can see the individual images being drawn.

By the way, humans (and cats, dogs, and anything else with non-mechanical eyes) don't see the world as frames going by every so often. Being analog, the human eye and brain respond to a steady input of light, motion, and color. The question that usually concerns game makers and other animators (such as the folks who re-create car accidents for use in court rooms) is at what rate can the viewers feel like they're seeing something realistic (which, again, is not the same as seeing something real). That number varies hugely according to a number of factors, such as resolution, light/dark balance of the content on the screen, the lighting in the viewer's area, the visual acuity of the viewer (which is itself dictated by a number of variables, such as age, fatigue, experience with animation, and so on).

So what is the right FPS for your application? The only real way to know is to put it in front of several different potential users and ask them if it looks good. Also, if you do a lot of animation, you'll probably develop a feel for the right frame rate. Finally, game makers often concern themselves with what the competition is doing. If their games run at 75 FPS, your game better be able to do that, too, or have a good reason for not doing so.

Animation: A Simple Example

Let's start with the basics: getting an object to move from one side of the screen to the other. My friends in the game industry say this is the "Hello, World" stage of game development. To do it, we create two classes: a field for the object to cross and a frame to be the main program. (We could do it in a single class, but Swing makes a separate drawing field easier to do.) Listing 10-1 shows the program class (called ScootBall because a ball scoots across the screen).

Listing 10-1. *The ScootBall class*

```
package com.bryantcs.examples.animation;

import java.awt.BorderLayout;
import java.awt.Color;
import java.awt.Dimension;
import java.awt.FlowLayout;
import java.awt.event.ActionEvent;
import java.awt.event.ActionListener;

import javax.swing.JButton;
import javax.swing.JFrame;
import javax.swing.JMenu;
import javax.swing.JMenuBar;
import javax.swing.JMenuItem;
import javax.swing.JPanel;
```

```java
public class ScootBall implements ActionListener {

  private static final long serialVersionUID = 1L;

  ScootBallPanel scootBallPanel = new ScootBallPanel();
  JFrame frame = new JFrame("ScootBall");
  JPanel buttonPanel=new JPanel(new FlowLayout(FlowLayout.CENTER));
  JButton scootButton=new JButton("Scoot");
  Thread animationThread = null;

  private void addMenu(JFrame frame) {
    JMenu file = new JMenu("File");
    file.setMnemonic('F');
    JMenuItem exitItem = new JMenuItem("Exit");
    exitItem.setMnemonic('x');
    exitItem.addActionListener(this);
    file.add(exitItem);
    JMenuBar menuBar = new JMenuBar();
    menuBar.add(file);
    frame.setJMenuBar(menuBar);
  }

  private void createAndShowGUI() {
    addMenu(frame);
    frame.setDefaultCloseOperation(JFrame.EXIT_ON_CLOSE);
    frame.getContentPane().setLayout(new BorderLayout());
    scootButton.addActionListener(this);
    buttonPanel.add(scootButton);
    scootBallPanel.setPreferredSize(new Dimension(400, 200));
    scootBallPanel.setBackground(Color.WHITE);
    frame.getContentPane().add(scootBallPanel,BorderLayout.CENTER);
    frame.getContentPane().add(scootBallPanel);
    frame.getContentPane().add(buttonPanel,BorderLayout.SOUTH);
    frame.pack();
    frame.setVisible(true);
  }

  public static void main(String[] args) {
    ScootBall scootBall = new ScootBall();
    scootBall.createAndShowGUI();
  }

  // The actionPerformed method listens for actions taken by the user
  public void actionPerformed(ActionEvent e) {
    // If the user chooses Exit, then exit
    if (e.getActionCommand().equals("Exit")) {
      System.exit(0);
    }
    // Since we didn't exit, check for whether the user clicked the Scoot button
    // and ignore the click if a ball is already moving. If not, start one moving.
    if (e.getActionCommand().equals("Scoot") && scootBallPanel.isAnimating() == false) {
      scootBallPanel.reset();
```

```
         animationThread = new Thread(scootBallPanel);
         scootBallPanel.setAnimating(true);
         animationThread.start();
      }
   }
}
```

The key to the this class is the **actionPerformed** method. It checks for which action the user has chosen and starts the animation if the user selects the Scoot button (and if the ball isn't already being drawn). The animation is accomplished through the **ScootBallPanel** class. Because **ScootBallPanel** implements the **Runnable** interface (meaning it can be run in its own thread), we have a means to let it know when to start drawing the ball. Note that we create a new thread each time the Scoot button is pressed, letting any previous thread go to garbage collection. That's a simple way to restart an animation process.Listing 10-2 shows the **ScootBallPanel** class.

Listing 10-2. *The ScootBallPanel class*

```
package com.bryantcs.examples.animation;

import java.awt.Color;
import java.awt.Graphics;

import javax.swing.JPanel;


public class ScootBallPanel extends JPanel implements Runnable {

  private static final long serialVersionUID = 1L;
  private boolean animating = false;
  private int xPosition = 5;


  public boolean isAnimating() {
    return animating;
  }

  public void setAnimating(boolean animating) {
    this.animating = animating;
  }

  public void reset() {
    xPosition = 5;
  }

  public void paint (Graphics g) {
    int width = this.getSize().width;
    int height = this.getSize().height;
    super.paintComponent(g);
```

```
    if (animating) {
      g.setColor(Color.RED);
      g.fillOval(xPosition, height / 2, 10 ,10);
      xPosition += 20;
      if (xPosition > width) {
        animating = false;
      }
    }
  }

  // The run method controls how often the screen
  // gets redrawn and so controls the frame rate
  public void run() {
    while(animating) {
      try {
        Thread.sleep(40);
        this.repaint();
      } catch (InterruptedException ie) {
        return;
      }
    }
  }
}
```

Those two classes create a program that looks like the image in Figure 10-1.

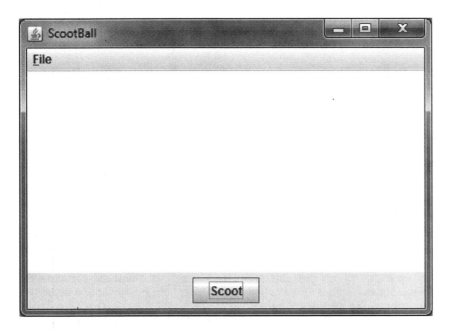

Figure 10-1. ScootBall starting state

The heart of the `ScootBallPanel` class is the `run` method, which implements the corresponding `run` method in the `Runnable` interface. All it does is run through a continuous loop, sleeping a while and then repainting the panel. How long it sleeps dictates the frame rate. In this case, it sleeps for 40 milliseconds, producing a frame rate of about 25. I wrote, "about," because the repainting takes some time, yielding a frame rate a bit less than 25. We see how to get a more exact frame rate in the next example.

The paint method draws the ball on the screen, each time at a new position, until that position exceeds the width of the panel. In particular, the call to `super.paintComponent(g)` redraws the panel to its original state (a blank white box). The remaining lines then draw the ball. Figure 10-2 shows a ball scooting across the screen.

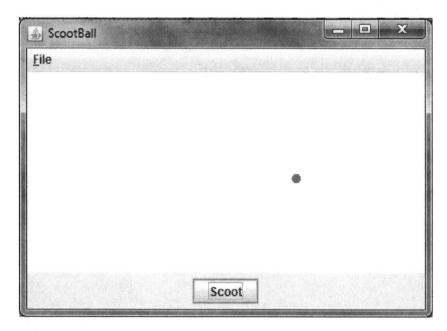

Figure 10-2. *Scootball in actionScootball is not much of a program, but it demonstrates the basics of animation: drawing an updated image every so often (generally some number of times per second). Let's move on to a slightly more complicated (and thus more interesting) example.*

Animating Multiple Items

This example shows one way to animate multiple items at once. In this case, we use an object-oriented approach to the problem (Java is an object-oriented language, after all). In particular, we create a class for the things we want to animate and then create multiple instances of that class. Being a simple example, we use the same class for all the animating items. However, you can use the same technique to animate different kinds of objects. For example, a tank (an instance of one class) might shoot a bullet (an instance of a different class) at a bunker (an instance of a third class).

The trick is to have each object draw itself and then iterate through them, letting each one draw itself in turn. In that way, the calling class needs to know nothing about how to draw the objects and can focus on the timing and user interface. This kind of organization embodies one of the principles of object-oriented programming, encapsulation, and embodies a primary goal of nearly all software systems, separation of concerns (meaning that each different thing a program can do should be handled by a different part of the program). Those principles are part of the advantage of object-oriented programming, because they make designing programs and finding errors much easier. We get to finding errors in the next chapter.

To illustrate how to animate multiple objects at the same time, we create a simple fireworks program. When the user clicks the **Go** button, it draws fireworks on the screen, in sets of four. Figure 10-3 shows the Fireworks program in action.

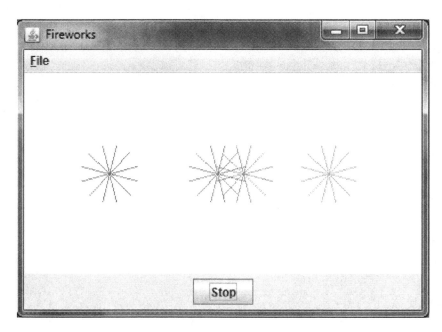

Figure 10-3. *The Fireworks program in action*

By the way, even with a simple animation program such as Fireworks, a screenshot does not do it justice. It's the nature of animation that no static image of part of the animation can compare to the actual animation. So please run the programs in this chapter to see how they really look. I hope you've been running the programs in the book all along, but, if not, you need to do so in this chapter if you want to have a real sense of what they do. I suggest you then customize the programs to create your own versions and ultimately your own original animations.

The `Fireworks` class works similarly to the `ScootBall` class, except for one important difference: the `Fireworks` class uses a `Timer` object to control the animation. The `Timer` class provides instances an easy way to trigger a process (not just animations, but any process) every so often. Because the timer is independent of the drawing process, we get much closer to a frame rate of exactly 25 frames per second (once every 40 milliseconds). Also, the timer simplifies both this class and the drawing panel class, because we no longer have to manage threads. The program still uses threads, but the `Timer` class does that work for us. For those reasons, using a `Timer` object is much better than making your own thread and setting it to sleep for some amount of time. (I showed you the other way so that you'd know it exists, but use `Timer` objects for your own animations.).Listing 10-3 shows the `Fireworks` class.

Listing 10-3. The Fireworks class

```java
package com.bryantcs.examples.animation;
import java.awt.BorderLayout;
import java.awt.Color;
import java.awt.Dimension;
import java.awt.FlowLayout;
import java.awt.event.ActionEvent;
import java.awt.event.ActionListener;

import javax.swing.JButton;
import javax.swing.JFrame;
import javax.swing.JMenu;
import javax.swing.JMenuBar;
import javax.swing.JMenuItem;
import javax.swing.JPanel;
import javax.swing.Timer;

public class Fireworks implements ActionListener {

    private static final long serialVersionUID = 1L;

    FireworksPanel fireworksPanel = new FireworksPanel();
    JFrame frame = new JFrame("Fireworks");
    JPanel buttonPanel=new JPanel(new FlowLayout(FlowLayout.CENTER));
    JButton actionButton=new JButton("Go");
    boolean animating = false;
    // Here's the timer, which checks for user actions
    // and, if the animation is running, redraws the
    // screen. It does both 25 times per second
    // (1000 milliseconds divided by 40).
    Timer timer = new Timer(40, this);

    private void addMenu(JFrame frame) {
        JMenu file = new JMenu("File");
        file.setMnemonic('F');
        JMenuItem exitItem = new JMenuItem("Exit");
        exitItem.setMnemonic('x');
        exitItem.addActionListener(this);
        file.add(exitItem);
        JMenuBar menuBar = new JMenuBar();
        menuBar.add(file);
        frame.setJMenuBar(menuBar);
    }

    private void createAndShowGUI() {
        addMenu(frame);
        frame.setDefaultCloseOperation(JFrame.EXIT_ON_CLOSE);
        frame.getContentPane().setLayout(new BorderLayout());
        actionButton.addActionListener(this);
        buttonPanel.add(actionButton);
        fireworksPanel.setPreferredSize(new Dimension(400, 200));
```

```
      fireworksPanel.setBackground(Color.WHITE);
      frame.getContentPane().add(fireworksPanel,BorderLayout.CENTER);
      frame.getContentPane().add(fireworksPanel);
      frame.getContentPane().add(buttonPanel,BorderLayout.SOUTH);
      frame.pack();
      frame.setVisible(true);
  }

  public static void main(String[] args) {
    Fireworks fireworks = new Fireworks();
    fireworks.createAndShowGUI();
  }

  // This method listens to the timer. The
  // program goes through it every 40th of a
  // second, giving us a Hertz or frame rate of 25.
  public void actionPerformed(ActionEvent e) {
    if (e.getActionCommand() != null) {
      // Check for the user choosing Exit
      // from the file menu and exit if so
      if (e.getActionCommand().equals("Exit")) {
        System.exit(0);
      }
      // Check for the Go button being clicked and, if so,
      // start the animation and set the button to Stop
      if (e.getActionCommand().equals("Go")) {
        animating = true;
        timer.start();
        actionButton.setText("Stop");
      }
      // Check for the Stop button being clicked and, if so,
      // stop the animation and set the button to Go
      if (e.getActionCommand().equals("Stop")) {
        animating = false;
        timer.stop();
        actionButton.setText("Go");
      }
    }
    // If the animation is running (the user has
    // clicked Go but not Stop), repaint the window
    // which is how we create the animation).
    if (animating){
      fireworksPanel.repaint();
    }
  }
}
```

Now let's look at the Fireworks drawing panel. The use of a `Timer` object in the Fireworks class simplifies this class, too. We no longer need to implement the `Runnable` interface, have a `run` method, or specify when to repaint. Again, the `Timer` class does all that for us, letting us focus on drawing the collection of objects we want on the panel. Listing 10-4 shows the `FireworksPanel` class.

Listing 10-4. *The FireworksPanel class*

```java
package com.bryantcs.examples.animation;

import java.awt.Graphics;

import javax.swing.JPanel;

public class FireworksPanel extends JPanel{

  private static final long serialVersionUID = 1L;
  private Firework[] fireworks = new Firework[4];

  FireworksPanel() {
    init();
  }

  void init() {
    for (int i = 0; i < 4; i++) {
      fireworks[i] = new Firework((int)(Math.random()
        * this.getWidth()), this.getHeight(), 30);
    }
  }

  public void reset() {
    init();
  }

  public void paint (Graphics g) {
    super.paintComponent(g);
    for (int i = 0; i < 4; i++) {
      if (fireworks[i].isDone()) {
        fireworks[i] = new Firework((int)(Math.random()
          * this.getWidth()), this.getHeight(), 30);
      }
      fireworks[i].draw(g);
    }
  }
}
```

All the `FireworksPanel` class really does is manage the set of objects we want to draw, so let's look at the class that defines the individual objects. The `Firework` class uses a random color to draw a line halfway up the screen and then creates a burst of a dozen evenly spaced lines. Conceptually, it's simple, but it takes a bit of code to get the math right. Listing 10-5 shows the Firework class.

Listing 10-5. *The Firework class*

```java
package com.bryantcs.examples.animation;

import java.awt.Color;
import java.awt.Graphics;
```

```java
public class Firework {

  private int startX, startY, burstX, burstY, burstStep, currentStep, panelHeight, steps;
  Color color;

  // It takes a fair bit of setup work to figure out
  // * the starting location
  // * the bursting location
  // * which step we're on
  // * the total number of steps
  Firework(int x, int height, int ticks) {
    panelHeight = height;
    steps = ticks;
    startX = x;
    startY = height;
    burstX = x;
    burstY = height >> 1;
    burstStep = ticks >> 1;
    currentStep = 0;
    color = new Color((int)(Math.random() * 0xFFFFFF));
  }

  void draw(Graphics g) {
    Color drawColor = color;
    g.setColor(drawColor);
    int height = panelHeight - panelHeight / steps * currentStep;
    // the origin is at the top of the screen, so we check for being in
    // the bottom half by checking to see if the current height is larger
    // than the burst height. It seems backwards, but that's how it works.
    if (height > burstY) {
      // if we are in the bottom half of the panel, just draw
      // the line that represents the firework shell going up.
      g.drawLine(startX, startY, burstX, height);
    }

    if(currentStep >= burstStep) {
      // When we reach the bursting point, draw 12 lines in a circle.
      // For that, we need a tiny bit of trigonometry.
      for (int i = 0; i < 12; i++) {
        double xPrime, yPrime;
        double currentRadians = Math.toRadians(30 * i);

        int length = burstY / 2 / steps * currentStep;
        xPrime = (Math.cos(currentRadians)
            - Math.sin(currentRadians)) * length;
        yPrime = (Math.sin(currentRadians)
            + Math.cos(currentRadians)) * length;
        int endX = new Double(xPrime).intValue() + burstX;
        int endY = new Double(yPrime).intValue() + burstY;
```

```
        g.drawLine(burstX, burstY, endX, endY);
      }
    }
    currentStep++;
  }

  // This firework is done, so the panel
  // class can let it be garbage collected.
  public boolean isDone() {
    return currentStep >= steps;
  }
}
```

By the way, you can use similar code to draw a bullet going out and exploding against a target. Ideas are often similar to other ideas, so the same code can often be used for a different purpose with little modification, and this is one of those ideas. I encourage you to create that animation. Try it both with all 12 splines (the lines that radiate from the center) and with just the splines that are not over the target (which might be more realistic, depending on what kind of event you choose to model.)

Sprite Animation

So far, we concentrated on drawing simple objects made of circles and lines. You can use the same technique to create more complex objects, but it's often easier to use a series of images. Those images are called *sprites*. Many animations rely on sprites to create complex images that take a lot of code (and thus time) to create programmatically. Also, using images lets companies hire artists to create the images and programmers to create the animation. Consequently, the quality of both the images and the code improves, making a better program. .Separation of concerns is also a good principle for business, where it's generally called specialization.

In this case, we create a simple four-image sprite that represents an expanding bullseye. Figure 10-4 shows all four sprite images together and zoomed in ten times.

Figure 10-4. *The sprites used by the MouseSprites program*

I zoom it in ten times to reveal something about how things are drawn on a monitor (or TV, your phone, or anything with a digital display)—there are no curves. Any curve you see on a screen is a collection of straight lines (each called a segment of the curve). The more segments, the better the illusion, but there is no curve. Create a circle on the screen (the **drawOval** method in the **Graphics** class will do the job), and then take a close look at it (perhaps by making a screen capture and zooming in on it). You see it's a set of straight lines.

As an aside, I work with a bunch of great digital artists whose favorite quotation is from *The Matrix*, when the little girl says, "There is no spoon." She has realized that the matrix is an illusion, and most digital artists realize (and revel in the fact) that they are making illusions. If you like to make illusions, you can have a lot of fun (and a great career) with digital art and animation.

I'm We no artist, so I created a simple set of sprites. I also set the timer to one quarter of a second, making a relatively slow (a video gamer would probably say it's very slow) animation. If you look closely, you can probably see the individual images as they are drawn. Most animations have a much higher frame rate (at least comparable to a movie), but this one makes a good demonstration.

When you run the program, click repeatedly to see how many animations you can get going at once. Doing so demonstrates that you can have multiple sprite animations going at the same time (and test your ability to click in a hurry—we were able to get four at a time going). Move the mouse a bit between clicks, so that you can see each animation separately.

I also added one more feature: triggered animation. Rather than run through an endless loop (perhaps stopped and started by something like a button click), this animation runs once in response to an event. In this case, the trigger is a mouse click. I added this technique to show you how to create animations that respond to your users' commands. For example, you might have an endless loop draw most of the objects in a game and use triggered animations to draw explosions and other items that appear because of game events.

One other thing to know about sprites is that the individual images can be stored as separate files or as a single file (often called a sprite sheet). Figure 10-4 can be a sprite sheet if used at its normal zoom level. In the case of a single file, the program loads part of the image rather than an entire image. For example, many games that involve maps store the individual terrain symbols together in a single file. The Java graphics API provides a method for reading part of an image: `getSubImage` in the `BufferedImage` class.

Listing 10-6 shows a program class for a sprite animation program (called `MouseSprites` because it's triggered by a mouse click).

Listing 10-6. *The MouseSprites class*

```
package com.bryantcs.examples.animation;

import java.awt.Color;
import java.awt.Dimension;
import java.awt.event.ActionEvent;
import java.awt.event.ActionListener;
import java.awt.event.MouseEvent;
import java.awt.event.MouseListener;

import javax.swing.JFrame;
import javax.swing.JMenu;
import javax.swing.JMenuBar;
import javax.swing.JMenuItem;
import javax.swing.Timer;

public class MouseSprites implements ActionListener, MouseListener {

    private static final long serialVersionUID = 1L;

    private MouseSpritePanel mouseSpritePanel = new MouseSpritePanel();
```

```java
private JFrame frame = new Jframe("MouseSprites");
// Here's our very slow timer. 4 times a second - vroom!
private Timer timer = new Timer(250, this);

private void addMenu(JFrame frame) {
  JMenu file = new JMenu("File");
  file.setMnemonic('F');
  JMenuItem exitItem = new JMenuItem("Exit");
  exitItem.setMnemonic('x');
  exitItem.addActionListener(this);
  file.add(exitItem);
  JMenuBar menuBar = new JMenuBar();
  menuBar.add(file);
  frame.setJMenuBar(menuBar);
}

private void createAndShowGUI() {
  addMenu(frame);
  frame.setDefaultCloseOperation(JFrame.EXIT_ON_CLOSE);
  mouseSpritePanel.setPreferredSize(new Dimension(400, 200));
  mouseSpritePanel.addMouseListener(this);
  mouseSpritePanel.setBackground(Color.WHITE);
  frame.getContentPane().add(mouseSpritePanel);
  frame.pack();
  frame.setVisible(true);
  timer.start();
}

public static void main(String[] args) {
  MouseSprites mouseSprite = new MouseSprites();
  mouseSprite.createAndShowGUI();
}

// This method listens to the timer
public void actionPerformed(ActionEvent e) {
  if (e.getActionCommand() != null) {
    // If the user chooses Exit, we exit
    if (e.getActionCommand().equals("Exit")) {
      timer.stop();
      System.exit(0);
    }
  }
  // otherwise, we redraw the panel
  // (which is how we achieve animation)
  mouseSpritePanel.repaint();
}

@Override
public void mouseClicked(MouseEvent e) {
}
```

```
@Override
public void mouseEntered(MouseEvent e) {
}

@Override
public void mouseExited(MouseEvent e) {
}

@Override
public void mousePressed(MouseEvent e) {
}

// This method adds a new expanding bullseye.
@Override
public void mouseReleased(MouseEvent e) {
    mouseSpritePanel.add(e.getX(), e.getY());
}
}
```

As you can see, this class is similar to the `Fireworks` class, with the addition of implementing the `MouseListener` interface (and all its required methods). We made the `MouseListener` implementation (at the top of the class) and the `MouseListener` methods (at the bottom of the class) bold, to make them easy to find. Like the `Fireworks` class, the `MouseSprites` class has a timer to control how often to draw a new sprite, and it has a panel class to provide a place for drawing the sprites.

▓ **Note** You must create a directory called C:\test\sprites (on Windows) or C:/test/sprites (on Unix or Linux) and put the sprite images in that directory to get the program to show the sprites. Alternatively, you can put the images elsewhere and change the code to point to that directory.

A more complex program might expect the location of the sprite files as an argument to the program. It's generally considered bad form to hard-code paths and file names into a program, but I don't want to introduce the additional complexity of reading them from an argument (I want to focus on animation instead). Adding the location as an argument would be a good exercise, if you want to expand this simple program a bit. If you do, remember that the argument would be handled in the `main` method of the `MouseSprites` class, not in the `MouseSpritePanel` class. Listing 10-7 shows the `MouseSpritePanel` class.

Listing 10-7. The MouseSpritePanel class

```
package com.bryantcs.examples.animation;

import java.awt.Graphics;
import java.awt.Image;
import java.io.File;
```

```java
import java.io.IOException;
import java.util.ArrayList;

import javax.imageio.ImageIO;
import javax.swing.JPanel;

public class MouseSpritePanel extends JPanel {

  private static final long serialVersionUID = 1L;

  private Image[] spriteImages = new Image[4];
  private ArrayList<MouseSprite> currentSprites = new ArrayList<MouseSprite>();

  MouseSpritePanel() {
    try {
      spriteImages[0] = ImageIO.read(new
      File("C:\\test\\sprites\\sprite1.png"));
      spriteImages[1] = ImageIO.read(new
      File("C:\\test\\sprites\\sprite2.png"));
      spriteImages[2] = ImageIO.read(new
      File("C:\\test\\sprites\\sprite3.png"));
      spriteImages[3] = ImageIO.read(new
      File("C:\\test\\sprites\\sprite4.png"));
    } catch (IOException e) {
      System.out.println("Couldn't open a sprite file");
      System.exit(1);
    }
  }

  void add (int x, int y) {
    MouseSprite newSprite = new MouseSprite(x, y, spriteImages, this);
    currentSprites.add(newSprite);
  }

  public void paint (Graphics g) {
    super.paintComponent(g);
    for (int i = 0; i < currentSprites.size(); i++) {
      MouseSprite currentSprite = currentSprites.get(i);
      if (!currentSprite.isDone()) {
        currentSprite.draw(g);
      } else {
        currentSprite = null;
        currentSprites.remove(i);
      }
    }
  }
}
```

The MouseSpritePanel class manages a set of images, which it passes to each new MouseSprite object. When each sprite is done drawing itself, the MouseSpritePanel removes the sprite object, to keep from cluttering the list and let the finished sprite be garbage collected. Otherwise, we'd have a runaway memory leak, which would constitute bad programming.

The the MouseSprite class, shown in Listing 10-8, draws each of the four sprites in turn. Conceptually, it is similar to the Firework class, in that it draws its pieces on the screen and then announces that it's done, so that the class holding a reference to it can let that reference go, which lets the system garbage collect the now useless MouseSprite object.

Listing 10-8. The MouseSprite class

```java
package com.bryantcs.examples.animation;

import java.awt.Graphics;
import java.awt.Image;
import java.awt.image.ImageObserver;

import javax.swing.JPanel;

public class MouseSprite {
  private int spriteX, spriteY, step;
  private boolean done = false;
  Image[] spriteImages= new Image[4];
  JPanel spritePanel;

  MouseSprite(int x, int y, Image[] images, JPanel panel) {
    spriteX = x;
    spriteY = y;
    step = 0;
    spriteImages = images;
    spritePanel = panel;
  }

  void draw(Graphics g) {
    ImageObserver observer = spritePanel;
    if (step < 4) {
      g.drawImage(spriteImages[step], spriteX, spriteY, observer);
      step++;
    } else {
      done = true;
    }
  }

  public boolean isDone() {
    return done;
  }

}
```

Figure 10-5 shows the MouseSprite program.

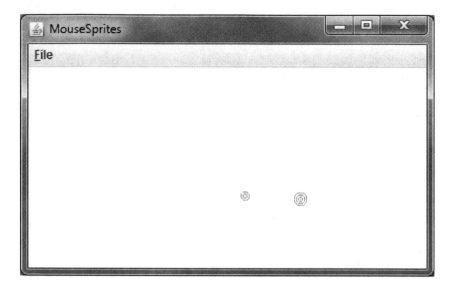

Figure 10-5. *The MouseSprite program*

I can catch only two bullseyes in the screen shot. This problem of trying to catch the animation in motion is one reason why animation programmers often add switches to slow or stop the animation. For non-game animations (such as rotating medical images or animations used in court), slow, pause, and fast forward options are essential. Another good exercise is to add a stop feature to the MouseSprite program (perhaps a right-click can stop and start the animation).

The MouseSprite class draws a different image for each part of its process and then sets a flag to indicate that it's done. As we saw previouslly, the class (MouseSpritePanel) that manages the individual MouseSprite objects can then detect when to remove the MouseSprite object.

Summary

In this chapter, we covered the basics of creating animations with Java. In particular, we discussed the following:

- How to draw on the screen with Java's Graphics package

- How to use a thread to control an animation

- How to use a timer to control an animationHow timers give better control than threads, so we should prefer timers

- How to create a timed animation

- How to create a triggered animation

How to put an image from a file onto the screenIn the first draft of this chapter, I didn't add screen shots. I originally left them out because we hoped you run the code as you read the book. My editor (hi, Ewan) pointed out that readers might want to see them, even if they are running the code, to see how things should look when working correctly. Because Ewan had a good point, I added them, even though the screenshots aren't nearly as good as seeing the animations run on your own computer. I also hope that you "tinker" with the code as you go through the book. Don't just run what you see in the book. Change the book's code to match your own ideas. All the code in the book belongs to you, so change it all you like. Better still, write your own programs to create your own animations. I've tried to provide some ideas, and I imagine you have lots of ideas, too.

As a final thought for this chapter, this chapter was one of my favorite chapters to write. I find animations to be fun to create. If you agree, I encourage you to pursue animation programming as either a hobby or a career (or both—many of the folks I work with go home and do more projects on their own time). It can be rewarding, both in seeing your ideas come to life on a screen and in your pocketbook, because it's a skill valued by many employers.

CHAPTER 11

Debugging with Eclipse

Not every error throws an exception; sometimes, due to poor programming, your code will do something totally wrong without throwing an exception. The computer did exactly what you told it to do, but it didn't do what you meant. When programming, it pays to remember that a computer is just a construction of silicon and various metals, so it is literally as dumb as a box of rocks. It has no conscious ability to adjust for your errors, as another person does when you speak or write.

Software developers love exceptions. Every time Java throws an exception, it provides a stack trace, showing us the classes and methods (and line numbers therein) that led to the exception. That makes finding and fixing the error easy.

In the absence of an exception, though, you have to either puzzle it out by examining the logic of the program or use a debugger. Sometimes, just examining the logic will do the trick. Other times, however, only a debugger will do the job. As my editors could surely tell you, I often miss my own errors. I know what I meant to write and look past what I actually wrote. The same problem applies to programming: we know what we intended to do and often overlook what we actually did. A debugger forces you to look at your code differently, which can help you find the problem. Also, a debugger "steps" through the code one line at a time. That narrow scope (a single line) allows you to really focus to find any error.

Eclipse includes a full-featured debugger, and the rest of this chapter describes how to use that debugger to track down and fix a problem. Other debuggers exist for Java, and Java includes a command-line debugger called JDB (The Java Debugger). However, I think the Eclipse debugger is easier to use and provides all the features one needs. For what it's worth, I generally use it for my own work.

I had a problem with the Fireworks program from Chapter 10, "Animation" that I had to use the debugger to find, so I'll use that program as an example for our debugging exercise. In fact, I'll start by showing you a problem that I used the Eclipse debugger to solve. Figure 11-1 shows the mess I made of the Fireworks program before I got it to work correctly.

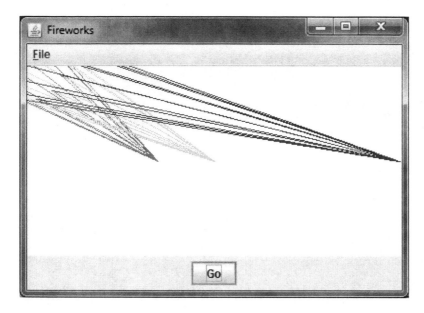

Figure 11-1. *Fireworks problem*

As you can see, I accidentally created searchlights rather than fireworks. The question is: How did I do it? Since the answer didn't just jump out at me when I first read the code, I used the debugger to puzzle out the problem. As always, 99% of the effort went into finding the problem. Once you reach the "Aha!" moment, actually fixing the problem usually takes very little time (except for those times when you discover that you need to rewrite the whole program—those are bad days.)

Before we can analyze what went wrong, though, you need to learn more about debugging in general and how to use the Eclipse debugger in particular, so we'll return to this busted Fireworks program near the end of the chapter.

The Flow of Debugging

Before we dive into the Eclipse debugger, I think it would be a good idea to present a walkthrough of the overall debugging process.

1. Identify the problem. That sounds trivial, but it's often not. In complex systems (and sometimes even in simple ones), just stating the trouble can be tricky. Ask yourself: Exactly which behavior is wrong?

2. Set a breakpoint at a line you think (you often can't be entirely sure) will be executed before your problem occurs. As you gain skill with debugging, you'll get better at setting your initial entry point.

3. Step over the lines until you hit the error. The line you just stepped over is the problem line (or possibly one of multiple problem lines, if you have nested issues). If it's helpful, examine the values of the variables as you go. That can be especially useful in loops.

4. Set a breakpoint on that line and restart your application. When you get to that line, step into it.

5. Alternate between stepping over and stepping into lines until you finally have the defective code at its lowest level. Again, examine the values of any variables related to the problem as you go.

By following that the preceding general flow, you can use a debugger to identify exactly where your program did what you didn't want it to do, even though it didn't throw an exception.

Debugging without a Debugger

In Java's early days (circa 1995), there was no debugger, either at the command line or in a nice program such as Eclipse. Yet those of us using Java still had to find and fix our bugs. So, we fell back on the old practice of writing values to the console. The `System.out.println()` method was our friend (though we certainly got tired of writing it). We would add print statements to show the values of all the relevant variables wherever we suspected a bug existed. In that fashion, we could inspect the values as the code ran. It was a poor substitute for being able to step over and into lines with an actual debugger, but it worked.

Programmers sometimes still use that technique, even when a debugger is available. For example, if I think I can figure out a problem quickly with just a print statement or two, I'll try that first. If you use print statements this way, remember to remove them when you solve the issue. I've been embarrassed in more than one code review by a lingering print statement.

Fortunately for you, you get to learn Java at a time when mature tools have already been created, so you don't have to rely on print statements. To that end, let's fire up the Eclipse debugger and see how it works.

Starting the Eclipse Debugger

To start the Eclipse debugger:

1. Open Eclipse.

2. From the **Window** menu, choose **Open Perspective**, and then choose **Debug**. The Debug perspective appears.

■ **Tip**   After the first time you open the Debug perspective, a shortcut button appears on the right side of the Eclipse toolbar. In the future, you can switch to the Debug perspective by clicking that button and back to the regular perspective by clicking the **Java** button.

Let's start by opening the Firework class (the object that controls drawing a single firework). When you first open the Firework class in the Debug perspective, you'll see a screen very similar to the one in Figure 11-2.

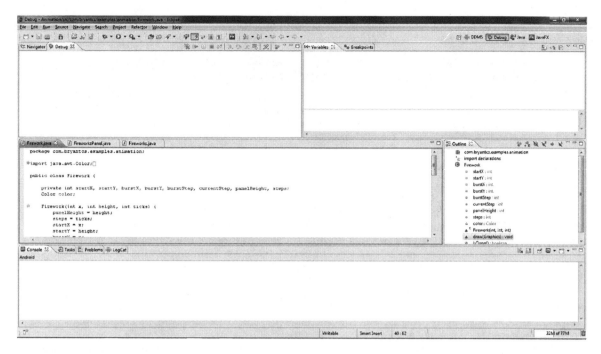

Figure 11-2. *Eclipse Debug perspective*

Let's look at this screen in more detail. You can see the code in the middle left panel of the application. The middle right panel displays an outline of the class. So far, it's the same as the Java perspective, but with a lot less space. The top left area shows the Debug panel and a tab to switch back to the Navigator panel. When you run the debugger, the Debug panel shows the call stack (all the objects the program went through to get to its current point). The top right area shows the breakpoints and variables. We'll talk about breakpoints and variables shortly. Finally, the bottom panel shows a number of possible views. You generally want the console view when debugging.

Don't worry if your debugger doesn't look exactly like mine. Like every software developer, I've customized my environment a bit, and we may be on different versions. The general layout is still the same, though, and that's enough to show you the relevant parts.

Breakpoints and Variables

A breakpoint is a place in the code where you want to stop the execution of a program. Computers run programs one instruction at a time. As a result, you can interrupt the flow of instructions and make the computer wait while you look at the values that are produced by your code at a particular spot. Fortunately, computers don't get bored, so you can make them wait as long as you like.

When you debug an application, you create temporary breakpoints, which appear in the Breakpoints view, wherever you want the debugger to stop. The debugger lets your application run until it reaches one of those points in the code; it then suspends your program, and shows you the values of the various objects and primitives in the Variables view.

Eclipse lets you set a number of different kinds of breakpoints:

- Line breakpoints

- Exception breakpoints

- Classloading breakpoints

- Watchpoints

- Method breakpoints

- Printpoints

I'm going to cover only line breakpoints, as they will solve nearly all the problems you are likely to encounter—I made it a long way into my career before I ever needed anything other than a line breakpoint. However, I encourage you to investigate the other kinds of breakpoints on your own. Start by reading the Eclipse help file's content about breakpoints.

Setting a Line Breakpoint

To set a line breakpoint:

1. Right-click in the thin area to the left of the line of code where you want to set a breakpoint.

2. Choose **Toggle Breakpoint**. A breakpoint appears at the line where you right-clicked, as shown in Figure 11-3. The blue dot to the far left of the first line in the draw method is the breakpoint indicator. When your program runs, it stops at that point and shows you the values of all the objects and primitives that are in scope at the time.

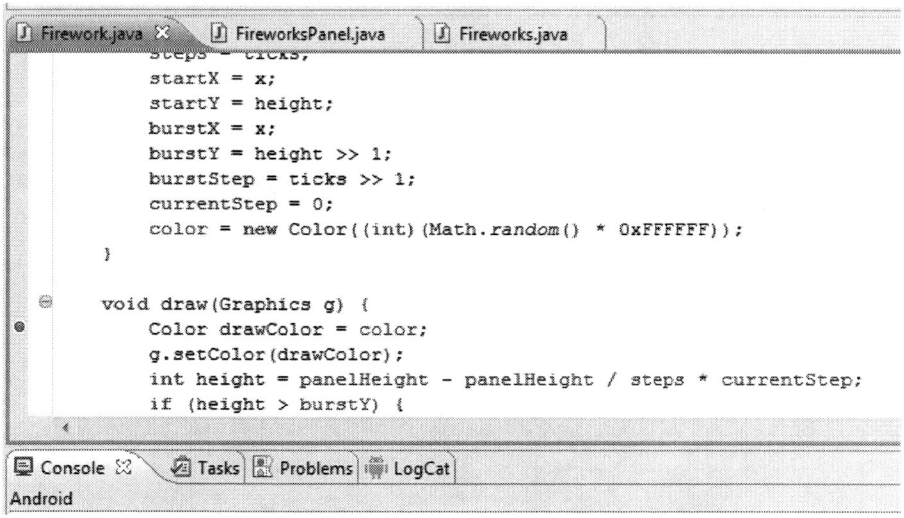

```
 Firework.java       FireworksPanel.java       Fireworks.java
                steps = ticks;
                startX = x;
                startY = height;
                burstX = x;
                burstY = height >> 1;
                burstStep = ticks >> 1;
                currentStep = 0;
                color = new Color((int)(Math.random() * 0xFFFFFF));
            }

        void draw(Graphics g) {
            Color drawColor = color;
            g.setColor(drawColor);
            int height = panelHeight - panelHeight / steps * currentStep;
            if (height > burstY) {
```

Figure 11-3. Breakpoint in code:

209

Let's see what happens when we run the program (Figure 11-4).

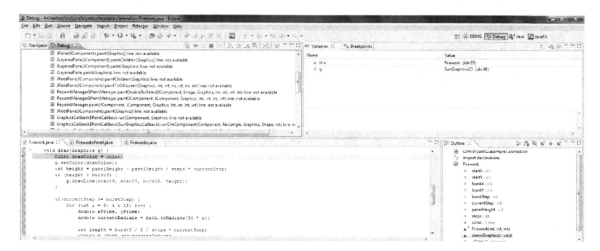

Figure 11-4. *Execution suspended at breakpoint:*

Notice the line highlighted in green. That green line indicates the current execution point (that is, the line that was being processed before the program was suspended). When the debugger stops at a line, it shows you the values in scope for that line in the Variables list, the method containing the line in the Outline panel, and the call stack in the Debug panel. From there, you can step through the code, either one line at a time or even within a line. We'll get to stepping shortly. First, though, let's be sure you understand the concept of scope.

About Scope

What does "in scope" mean? The objects and primitives (that is, the variables) that are in scope are those that are capable of being used at a particular point in the program. In the case of the breakpoint above, the only local value we can see is g, the instance of the Graphics class that will be used for the drawing. However, we can also see a value called this, which is the containing class. By expanding the this entry in the variable list, we can see all the class variables declared within it (rather than in a method). Figure 11-5 displays what an expanded view of the this value looks like.

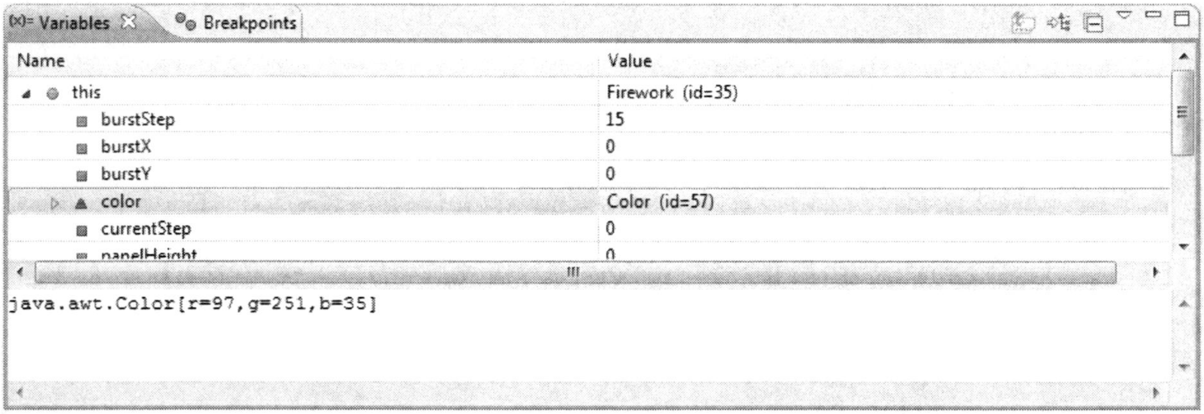

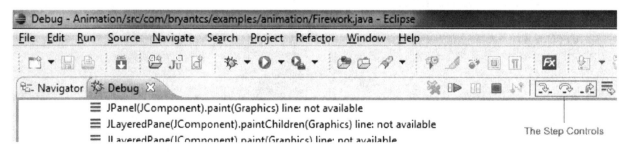

Figure 11-5. *Expanded containing class value* this

As you can see, the expanded this listing shows the values of all the class variables (the arrow to the left of an entry indicates that that entry can be expanded). Clicking on one of them causes details about it to appear at the bottom of the Variables view. In this case, we can see the RGB values (values for red, green, and blue) that constitute the color for this particular firework. You can also right-click the entry and get even more information, but we'll skip that for now. Once you've mastered the basics of debugging, you can try out those more advanced features.

Stepping:

"Stepping" in debuggers refers to the ability to move to the next execution point in the program. For convenience, Eclipse offers three kinds of stepping commands: Step Into, Step Over, and Step Return. Figure 11-6 shows the step buttons on the debug toolbar.

Figure 11-6. *Callout of step controls on debug toolbar*

You can also use function keys to step. **F5** corresponds to Step Into, **F6** corresponds to Step Over, and **F7** corresponds to Step Return.

Stepping Into

When you step into a line, you advance to the first of whatever methods may be in the line. Consider the second line in the draw method:

```
g.setColor(drawColor);
```

When you step into that line, you step to the top of the `setColor` method in the Graphics class. That's probably not very useful; you only want to use this command to step into your own code.

For some lines, stepping into is the same as stepping over, because nothing in the line changes the execution point. For example, stepping into the first line of the draw method has the same effect as stepping over it, because that line just assigns one value to another value.

Stepping Over

When you step over a line, you let the debugger run through whatever methods may be called by that line. That includes any classes and methods that may be called by those methods, and so on. Sometimes, that amounts to very little code; other times, it's a large chunk of a Java library.

Stepping over lines is a good way to find the place in your program where you have a problem. Step over until the problem behavior presents itself. Then you know which line is bad. From that point, you can step into the methods under that line, and then step over the lines in those methods until you hit the problem spot again. Thus, by swapping back and forth between stepping over and stepping into code, you can narrow down and finally locate the failure in your code.

Stepping to Return

Step Return lets the program run until the current method returns. Step Return is really just a convenience feature so that you don't have to step through all the lines in a method. If you step into a method and realize that it can't possibly be the source of your problem, Step Return offers a handy way to move along.

Removing a Line Breakpoint

You may have noticed that the command for creating a breakpoint is **Toggle Breakpoint**. Toggling an existing breakpoint removes it.

Disabling a Line Breakpoint

Sometimes, it's handy to leave a breakpoint in place but not use it for a while. For example, you might disable a breakpoint while you track down some other bug that you have to fix sbefore you can deal with the one you originally started to fix. You'll sometimes find that a bug is really a nested set of bugs, and you have to fix one before you can fix another. The good news is that identifying one bug often gives you insight into the larger problem, and fixing the remaining issues then becomes largely mechanical. There are times, though, when you hit a series of hard-to-solve problems, and then you'll be happy to have a good debugger. To disable a breakpoint:

1. Right-click the breakpoint you want to disable.

2. Choose Disable Breakpoint.

Making a Conditional Breakpoint

Another common need is to make a breakpoint conditional:, such that it only triggers when a variable has a particular value. You can check the values of multiple variables, too.

To set a conditional breakpoint

1. Right-click the breakpoint you want to be conditional.

2. Choose **Breakpoint Properties**. The Properties window for your breakpoint appears (Figure 11-7).

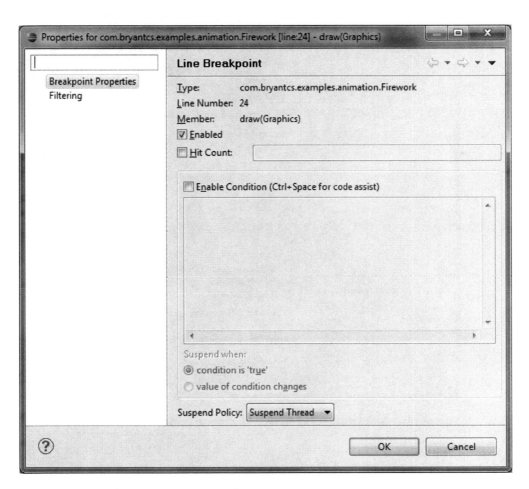

Figure 11-7. Breakpoint Properties window:

3. Set the **Enable Condition** checkbox.

4. In the text field below the checkbox, type the code for your condition. This is generally a single line of normal Java code, without the semicolon. For example, if you want to hit this breakpoint only when the value of `currentStep` is 15 or higher, set a condition as shown in Figure 11-8.

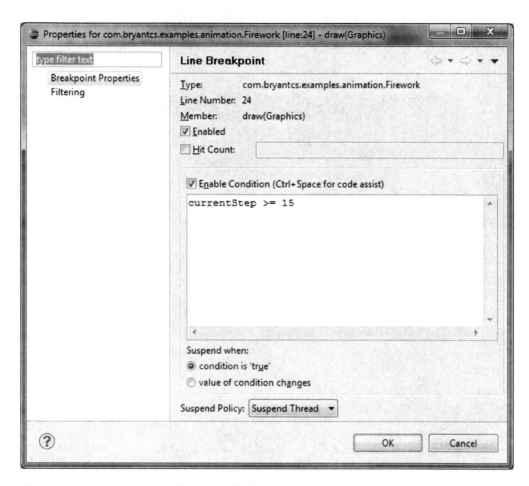

Figure 11-8. Breakpoint condition enabled and specified:

5. Click **OK**.

When you let the code run (and click the **Go** button in the application to get the drawing started), you get the set of variables shown in Figure 11-9 after a very short wait:

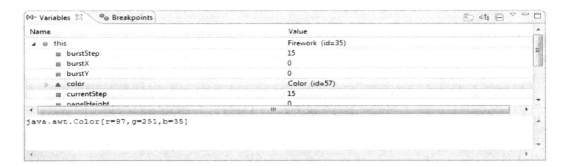

Figure 11-9. *Variables at conditional breakpoint:*

As you can see, it stopped when currentStep got to 15.

Debugging Tips and Tricks

Now that you know the basics of using the Eclipse debugger, here are a few tips and tricks to help you along when you use any debugger:

- Be especially watchful in loops. By nature, loops repeatedly check and define a small set of values. So, examine those variables as you work through a loop. I can't tell you how often a badly set looping variable has been the source of my troubles, but it's a large percentage of the time.

- Use conditional breakpoints in loops. Often, a problem doesn't surface until a particular value is reached. It's not much fun to watch the same set of values, and boredom can dull your focus and make you miss the actual problem, so use conditional breakpoints to skip over the things you know aren't problems.

- Watch for "copy and paste" errors. If you're using code you got from somewhere else (including this book), it's very easy to neglect to change a variable to the value you need from whatever was in the example you borrowed. It may look right, because it's what you read when you went looking for an example, but it's wrong because it's not what your program needs.

- Take the time to understand the code. I'm a great one for rushing through things I think are simple, only to discover they're not so simple. Painful experience has taught me to take the time to fully understand the code I'm using (whether from a library or a sample or my own code). Only by understanding the code in all its detail can you understand the results the debugger is giving you.

That last one is actually the hardest things developers do, by the way. Getting all the relationships within a codebase into your head so that you have a clear idea of how it works, usually called visualization, is a tough task. Good developers are good at visualization. It's also why so many developers are good musicians, master video game players, or both. All three pursuits require good visualization skills, and all good developers are good puzzle solvers for the same reason. More so than formal education or even experience, visualization is the key to being a good developer. Of course, education and experience help you develop and refine your visualization skill.

Fixing the Fireworks Program

Now that you know enough to be able to understand how I used the debugger to find and fix the issue, we can return to my problem of making searchlights when I wanted fireworks.

The first thing I had to do was figure out where the problem was happening. Fortunately, I had isolated all of the code for drawing an individual firework into the draw() method of the Firework class. Remember, each method should do one easily identified task. Making debugging easier is one of the biggest reasons Java developers follow that practice.

Fireworks programListing 11-1 shows the version of the method that was causing the problem.

Listing 11-1. The flawed Firework.draw() method

```java
void draw(Graphics g) {
  Color drawColor = color;
  g.setColor(drawColor);
  int height = panelHeight - panelHeight / steps * currentStep;
  if (height > burstY) {
    g.drawLine(startX, startY, burstX, height);
  }
  if(currentStep >= burstStep) {
    for (int i = 0; i < 12; i++) {
      double xPrime, yPrime;
      double currentRadians = Math.toRadians(30 * i);

      int length = burstY / 2 / steps * currentStep;
      xPrime = (Math.cos(currentRadians)
          - Math.sin(currentRadians)) * length;
      yPrime = (Math.sin(currentRadians)
          + Math.cos(currentRadians)) * length;
      int endX = new Double(xPrime).intValue();
      int endY = new Double(yPrime).intValue();

      g.drawLine(burstX, burstY, endX, endY);
    }
  }
  currentStep++;
}
```

Within the draw method, I knew that the problem had to be inside the loop that drew the twelve splines (the lines from the center to the edge of the firework). So, I was able to determine that a good starting point for stepping through the code would be at the first line inside the for loop.

From that breakpoint, I stepped over each line to the last line inside the for loop (that is, until I got to the drawLine method). At that point, I could see that endX and endY had values I didn't expect, and I had my first clue. (Debugging often makes me feel like a detective—maybe that's why I like Sherlock Holmes so much.) Figure 11-10 shows the values in the debugger.

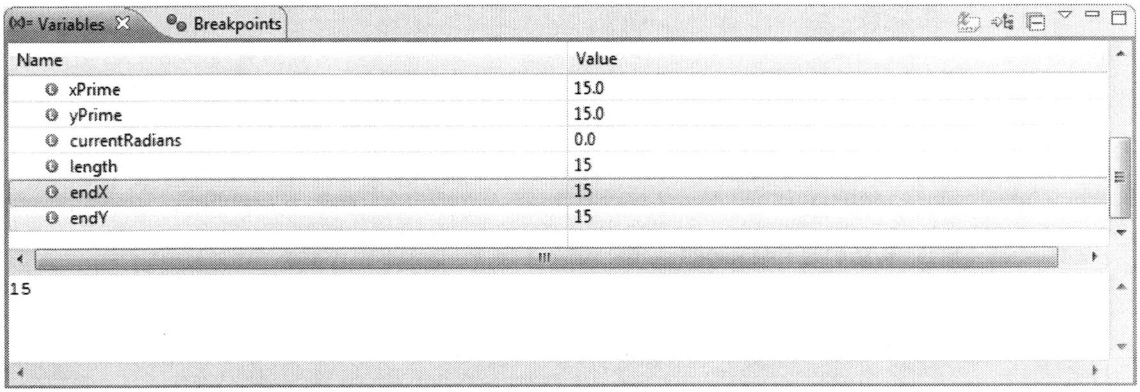

Figure 11-10. Incorrect values in the debugger

The thing that tipped me off was that the endX and endY values were the same as the value for the length of the line. Those two values should be somewhere near the middle of the width and height of the panel, which would be 200 for endX and 100 for endY (though endX could vary a great deal more than endY because of the random starting X location).

So, on my second debug run, I paid special attention to where endX and endY got defined: in the two lines just before the drawLine method call. That's when I realized that I had forgotten to account for the offset from the edges of the screen (one of those palm-to-forehead moments wherein I call myself an idiot, but at least I found the problem).

Finally, I corrected the code to the version you saw in Chapter 10, which I'll give you again in Listing 11-2.

Listing 11-2. The corrected Firework.draw() method

```
void draw(Graphics g) {
  Color drawColor = color;
  g.setColor(drawColor);
  int height = panelHeight - panelHeight / steps * currentStep;
  if (height > burstY) {
    g.drawLine(startX, startY, burstX, height);
  }
  if(currentStep >= burstStep) {
    for (int i = 0; i < 12; i++) {
      double xPrime, yPrime;
      double currentRadians = Math.toRadians(30 * i);

      int length = burstY / 2 / steps * currentStep;
      xPrime = (Math.cos(currentRadians)
          - Math.sin(currentRadians)) * length;
      yPrime = (Math.sin(currentRadians)
          + Math.cos(currentRadians)) * length;
      int endX = new Double(xPrime).intValue() + burstX;
      int endY = new Double(yPrime).intValue() + burstY;
```

```
            g.drawLine(burstX, burstY, endX, endY);
        }
    }
    currentStep++;
}
```

The parts I added are in bold. Simple little oversights such as this one are a common source of bugs. So, remember to fully understand what your code is doing and to proofread very carefully. And you'll still miss things, which is why you should get to know at least one good debugger.

Figure 11-11 shows the values yielded by the correct code.

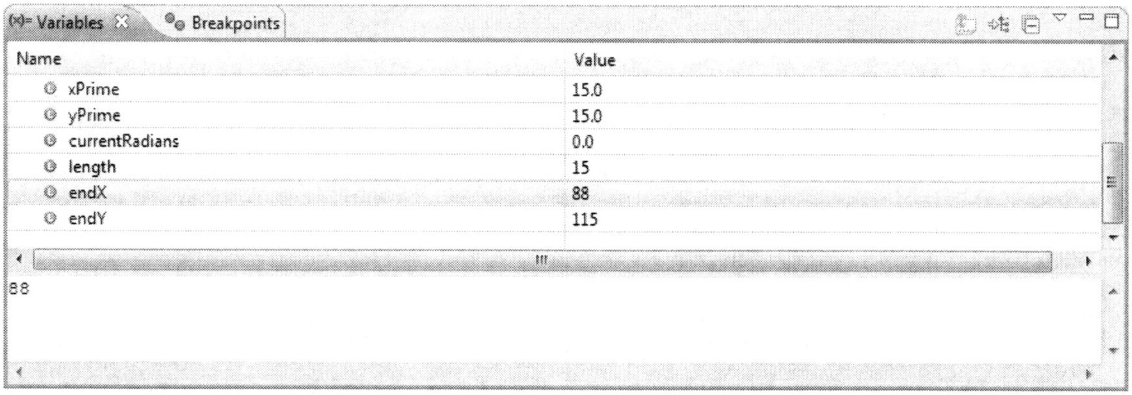

Name	Value
⊙ xPrime	15.0
⊙ yPrime	15.0
⊙ currentRadians	0.0
⊙ length	15
⊙ endX	88
⊙ endY	115

88

Figure 11-11. *Correct values in the debugger*

As you can see, the values for endX and endY are closer to the values I expected, which brings us to one more thing that you need to do when writing software: figure out what values to expect. If you don't know what values should appear in the debugger, you can't be sure your code is doing the right (or wrong) thing.

Summary

We covered a lot of ground in this chapter. You learned:

- The general flow of debugging.

- How to debug without a debugger (and why it's better to have one).

- How to set a line breakpoint.

- That other kinds of breakpoints are available to expand with your debugging needs.

- How to step over code and how to step into code.

- How to examine the values of the variables as they are affected by the code.

- That you need to know what to expect before you can know what's wrong.

- How to use those expectations to find and fix a problem.

As you do more with programming, you'll go through this basic process many, many times. With practice, you'll gradually develop your own feel for where problems lie and how to find them. Honestly, debugging is an art form, and it's the sense of what's wrong that comes with experience that will let you do more, rather than any formal understanding of debuggers. So, use the Eclipse debugger and any other debuggers you may encounter in the future to develop your own debugging skill. Having a knack for debugging is one of the things that separate senior developers from junior developers, and experience is the only way to create that knack for yourself.

Now, go point the Eclipse debugger at the code you've developed while reading this book, set a few breakpoints, and see what you can learn. I bet you'll be surprised.

CHAPTER 12

Video Games

By "video games," I mean games which have very limited controls and a primary interface that is somehow animated. Other computer games still use animation but aren't video games in classic parlance. For example, an old game called BattleZone (which I used to play in college) is a video game. Civilization, in all of its incarnations, is a computer game but not a video game. What's the difference? Complexity and the skill used to play the game. Video games tend to be simple and require dexterity. Other games tend to be more complex and rely on intelligence. As an avid gamer, I enjoy both, depending on my mood.

I bet a lot of the people who read this book want to learn to write video games. Fair enough. I probably would do that, too. If you love games so much that you jumped to this chapter first, I suggest you at least read the chapter on animation as those concepts very much apply to programming video games.

The Mechanics of a Video Game

Before we plunge into the game, let's first consider the core components of a video game in terms that aren't specific to any programming language, including Java. Then, as we go through a couple of examples, we can talk about how the examples implement these mechanics. Video games consist of three main pieces:

- The user interface
- The game logic
- The game loop

The User Interface

As we have seen in the previous chapters, any program with a graphical user interface devotes much of its code to creating and responding to that user interface. Unfortunately, that can mean losing sight of the game logic in the user interface code. Complex games (such as most modern video games) separate the logic from the presentation (another name for the user interface) by having the logic in one set of classes and having the presentation in another set of classes. Simple games may blend logic and presentation in the same classes (though probably in different methods). The sample games in this chapter use the latter organization as they are very simple games. We've already discussed the idea of blending logic and presentation in Chapter 6, "Object-oriented Programming."

However, there's always some point in the user interface code that triggers behavior in the logic code. These points are usually where the code handles input from the user. If you click a button on a mouse, the input does go through the user interface layer (via the mouse handler), but that click almost certainly triggers some kind of game logic as well. When you read the code for video games (you can find code for lots of games on the web, by the way), watch for those entry points to the game logic. They are key spots in any computer game.

The Game Logic

"Game logic" refers to the way the game responds to the user's input and possibly to other conditions (such as timers or network events). Here are some examples of game logic that you may have seen in various games:

- The player scores points after hitting a target.

- The game is over when the timer runs down.

- Jumping on a particular spot opens a secret door.

All games have at least a little game logic. The game (usually) needs some kind of ending condition (the game-over condition), and most games have some way of keeping score. Not all games need these things, but most do. For instance, the second example (a very simple shooting gallery game) in this chapter has no ending condition. You can keep shooting things as long as you like.

The Game Loop

As you may recall from Chapter 10, "Animation," the number of times a program redraws the screen is its frame rate, and the number of times a program processes all of its inputs and produces all of its outputs is its hertz. The game loop dictates both of those measures of speed. The second sample in this chapter (the shooting gallery game) runs through its game loop 50 times a second, so both its frame rate and its hertz are 50.

So what does a game loop do? That can vary from game to game, but there are some basics that any game loop has to do:

- Process the user input and all other inputs

- Process the game logic

- Redraw the playing field

The TargetClick Game

TargetClick is very much a video game version of the mechanical classic, Whac-a-Mole. A spot shows up, and you have to click it before it disappears. The more spots you click, the bigger your score. You can (indirectly) control the length of the game by setting the number of successful clicks needed to win. If you want a more difficult game, expand the game's window (making the spots farther apart). Figure 12-1 shows the TargetClick game in progress.

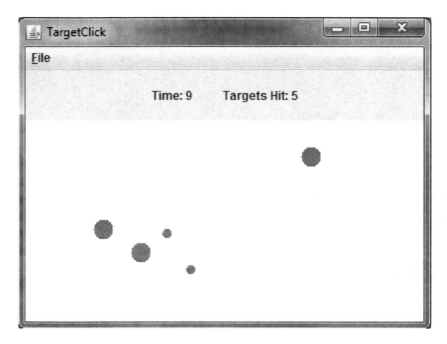

Figure 12-1. *The TargetClick game*

Wondering why the spots are different sizes? We'll see why that happens as we study the game's code.

The TargetClick game consists of three classes:

- **TargetClick** manages the user interface, the game logic, and the game loop
- **TargetClickPanel** creates the playing field and manages the targets
- **Target** draws the targets

As you can tell from that description, the **TargetClick** class contains most of the game's complexity.

Listing 12-1. *The TargetClick class*

```
package com.bryantcs.examples.videogames;

import java.awt.Color;
import java.awt.Dimension;
import java.awt.event.ActionEvent;
import java.awt.event.ActionListener;
import java.util.Random;

import javax.swing.BoxLayout;
import javax.swing.JFrame;
import javax.swing.JLabel;
```

```
import javax.swing.JMenu;
import javax.swing.JMenuBar;
import javax.swing.JMenuItem;
import javax.swing.JOptionPane;
import javax.swing.JPanel;
import javax.swing.Timer;

public class TargetClick implements ActionListener {

  // Create the user interface components
  private TargetClickPanel targetClickPanel = new TargetClickPanel();
  private JPanel scorePanel = new JPanel();
  private JLabel timeLabel = new JLabel("Time: ");
  private JLabel scoreLabel = new JLabel("          Targets Hit: ");
  private JLabel timeDisplayLabel = new JLabel("0");
  private JLabel scoreDisplayLabel = new JLabel("0");
  private JFrame frame = new JFrame("TargetClick");

  // Create the timer, which will manage the game loop
  private Timer timer = new Timer(400, this);

  // Create some other bits needed by the game logic
  static Random random = new Random();
  static int score;
  private long startTime;
  long elapsedTime = 0;
  private int gameLength = 50;

  // Add a menu, as we've seen before  private void addMenu(JFrame frame) {
    JMenu file = new JMenu("File");
    file.setMnemonic('F');
    JMenuItem exitItem = new JMenuItem("Exit");
    JMenuItem newGameItem = new JMenuItem("New Game");
    JMenuItem gameLengthItem = new JMenuItem("Set Game Length");
    exitItem.setMnemonic('x');
    exitItem.addActionListener(this);
    newGameItem.setMnemonic('n');
    newGameItem.addActionListener(this);
    gameLengthItem.setMnemonic('s');
    gameLengthItem.addActionListener(this);
    file.add(exitItem);
    file.add(newGameItem);
    file.add(gameLengthItem);
    JMenuBar menuBar = new JMenuBar();
    menuBar.add(file);
    frame.setJMenuBar(menuBar);
  }

  // Display the user interface, as we've seen before
  private void createAndShowGUI() {
    addMenu(frame);
    frame.setDefaultCloseOperation(JFrame.EXIT_ON_CLOSE);
```

```java
      targetClickPanel.setPreferredSize(new Dimension(400, 200));
      targetClickPanel.setBackground(Color.WHITE);
      scorePanel.setPreferredSize(new Dimension(400, 50));
      scorePanel.setLayout(new BoxLayout(scorePanel, BoxLayout.X_AXIS));
      scorePanel.add(timeLabel);
      scorePanel.add(timeDisplayLabel);
      scorePanel.add(scoreLabel);
      scorePanel.add(scoreDisplayLabel);
      frame.getContentPane().add(scorePanel);
      frame.getContentPane().add(targetClickPanel);
      frame.getContentPane().setLayout(new
        BoxLayout(frame.getContentPane(), BoxLayout.Y_AXIS));
      frame.pack();
      frame.setVisible(true);
    }

    // start or restart the game
    private void init() {
      timer.start();
      startTime = System.currentTimeMillis();
    }

    // The main method
    public static void main(String[] args) {
      TargetClick targetClick = new TargetClick();
      targetClick.createAndShowGUI();
      targetClick.init();
    }

    // The game loop (which isn't a loop)
    // Also contains the game logic
    public void actionPerformed(ActionEvent e) {
      // check for user input (step 1 in a game loop)
      if (e.getActionCommand() != null) {
        if (e.getActionCommand().equals("Exit")) {
          timer.stop();
          System.exit(0);
        }
        if (e.getActionCommand().equals("New Game")){
          newGame();
        }
        if (e.getActionCommand().equals("Set Game Length")) {
          String option = JOptionPane.showInputDialog(frame,
            "Number of Targets:");
          if (option != null) {
            gameLength = Integer.parseInt(option);
          }
          newGame();
        }
      }
      // update the score
      updateScorePanel();
```

```
      // game over? (part of step 2 in a game loop)
      // the rest of step 2 (processing the game logic)
      // is in the TargetClickPanel and Target classes
      if (score == gameLength) {
        endGame();
      }
      // redraw the playing field (step 3 in a game loop)
      targetClickPanel.repaint();
    }

    // A convenience method for showing the time and score
    private void updateScorePanel() {
      elapsedTime = System.currentTimeMillis() - startTime;
      timeDisplayLabel.setText(Long.toString(elapsedTime / 1000));
      scoreDisplayLabel.setText(Integer.toString(score));
    }

    // What to do when the game ends - part of the game logic
    private void endGame() {
        timer.stop();
      String scoreString = "You clicked " + gameLength +
          " targets in " + (elapsedTime / 1000) + " seconds";
      int option;
      option = JOptionPane.showConfirmDialog(frame, scoreString
          + " Play again?", "Game Over",
             JOptionPane.YES_NO_OPTION);
      if (option == 1) {
        System.exit(0);
      } else {
        newGame();
      }
    }

// What to do when the user starts a new game
  private void newGame() {
    score = 0;
    scoreDisplayLabel.setText("0");
    startTime = System.currentTimeMillis();
    timeDisplayLabel.setText("0");
    if (!timer.isRunning()) {
      timer.start();
    }
  }
}
```

Nearly all of the TargetClick class creates and manages the user interface. The actionPerformed method contains part of the game logic (with the rest in the TargetClickPanel and Target classes, which we'll soon see). The endGame and startGame methods show those places where user interface code meshes with game logic. The endGame method has just enough logic to stop the timer. The rest of the endGame method provides the user with a way to either start a new game or exit. The newGame method resets everything (including the user interface) and starts a new game.

The `actionPerformed` method also contains the game loop. That's not obvious because there's no actual loop present. Instead, the `Timer` object calls the `actionPerformed` method each time the timer ticks. As a result, we get a continuous loop so long as the timer runs. When you examine the `actionPerformed` method, you can see that it does all three tasks that go in a game loop; it handles user input (through the `getActionCommand` method), handles the game logic (by checking to see if the user has clicked enough targets to end the game), and redraws the game area (by calling the `repaint` method of the `TargetClickPanel` object).

The `TargetPanel` class provides the game field and keeps five targets in play. As part of keeping five targets in play, it also checks to see if a mouse click in its area hits a target. Those functions are part of the game logic. In this case, it's acceptable for the game logic to be distributed over more than one class. The guiding principle is that each class has a clear, well-defined task. Keeping the right number of targets in play and checking for targets being hit is part of managing the field of play, and that's the job of the `TargetClickPanel` class. There's a lesson here: where possible, separate logic from user interface. However, favor the principle of each class having a clear purpose over separating logic from presentation. Ideally, you can achieve both goals, but that's not always practical (as here).

Listing 12-2. The TargetClickPanel class

```
package com.bryantcs.examples.videogames;

import java.awt.Graphics;
import java.awt.event.MouseEvent;
import java.awt.event.MouseListener;

import javax.swing.JPanel;

public class TargetClickPanel extends JPanel implements MouseListener{

  private static final long serialVersionUID = 1L;

  // Keep track of the targets
  private Target targets[] = new Target[5];

  // The constructor, which populates the array with nulls
  public TargetClickPanel() {
    addMouseListener(this);
    for (int i = 0; i < targets.length; i++) {
      targets[i] = null;
    }
  }

  // Here's where we update the game field
  public void paint (Graphics g) {
    super.paintComponent(g);
    for (int i = 0; i < targets.length; i++) {
      // here's where we make the initial targets
      // on the first time through the loop
      if (targets[i] == null) {
        targets[i] = new Target(this);
      }
      // Is the target done (either fully drawn or has been clicked?)
```

```
      if (!targets[i].isDone()) {
        // if not done, draw it in the game area
        targets[i].draw(g);
      } else {
        // if it is done, make a new one and put it in the array;
        // the old one can then be garbage collected
        // as no reference to it now exists
        targets[i] = new Target(this);
      }
    }
  }

  // We have to have this method to fulfill the MouseListener contract
  @Override
  public void mouseClicked(MouseEvent e) {
  }

  // We have to have this method to fulfill the MouseListener contract
  @Override
  public void mouseEntered(MouseEvent e) {
  }

  // We have to have this method to fulfill the MouseListener contract
  @Override
  public void mouseExited(MouseEvent e) {
  }

  // We have to have this method to fulfill the MouseListener contract
  @Override
  public void mousePressed(MouseEvent e) {
  }

  // Here's where we check for user input within the game field
  // and check to see if the input changes the game
  // (because the user hit a target)
  @Override
  public void mouseReleased(MouseEvent e) {
    for (int i = 0; i < targets.length; i++) {
      targets[i].pointInTarget(e.getX(), e.getY());
    }
  }
}
```

As we've just seen, the TargetClickPanel class only provides a place for targets to appear, handles mouse clicks in the play area (the TargetClick class handles mouse clicks in the menu and the frame), and keeps the five targets in play.

The Target class has the simplest mission of the three classes that comprise the TargetClick game: It draws a target and figures out whether a target has been hit. That may seem like too much to do, and your first instinct may be to move the hit logic out of this class. However, an instance of the Target class has to stop drawing its target if the player hits the target. Consequently, it makes sense to put the hit logic in the Target class. Again, giving each class a clear purpose trumps separating logic from presentation. When deciding whether to separate code, ask yourself two useful questions: Can I separate further? Does further separation make the code easier to understand or maintain? In this case, the code could have been separated further. However, further separation would just clutter this simple program.

Listing 12-3. *The Target class*

```java
package com.bryantcs.examples.videogames;

import java.awt.Color;
import java.awt.Graphics;

import javax.swing.JPanel;

public class Target {
  // The essential information drawing a target:
  // where is it and how big is it right now?
  private int drawX, drawY, step;

  // Are we done yet? By default, no
  private boolean done = false;

  // a reference to the game area, which we use
  // to find a spot for this target
  JPanel panel;

  // The constructor
  Target(JPanel panel) {
    this.panel = panel;
    // -30 + 15 creates a 15-pixel border

    // Find a random spot in the game field
    drawX = TargetClick.random.nextInt(panel.getWidth() - 30) + 15;
    drawY = TargetClick.random.nextInt(panel.getHeight() - 30) + 15;

    // Start the step counter
    step = 0;
  }

  // Here's where we draw the target
  void draw(Graphics g) {
    if (!done) {
      // if not done, draw a circle that varies in size by the current step
      if (step == 0) {
        g.setColor(Color.RED);
        g.fillOval(drawX - 15, drawY - 15, 10, 10);
      }
      if (step == 1) {
        g.setColor(Color.RED);
        g.fillOval(drawX - 15, drawY - 15, 20, 20);
      }
```

```
    if (step == 2) {
      g.setColor(Color.RED);
      g.fillOval(drawX - 15, drawY - 15, 30, 30);
    }
    if (step == 3) {
      g.setColor(Color.RED);
      g.fillOval(drawX - 15, drawY - 15, 20, 20);
    }
    if (step == 4) {
      g.setColor(Color.RED);
      g.fillOval(drawX - 15, drawY - 15, 10, 10);
      done = true;
    }
  } else {
    // if we are done, erase the remaining circle
    g.setColor(Color.WHITE);
    g.fillOval(drawX + 1, drawY + 1, 30, 30);
  }
  step++;
}

// This is how we let the playing field
// know whether this target is done
public boolean isDone() {
  return done;
}

// Did this target get hit?
public void pointInTarget(int x, int y) {
  if (x > drawX -15 && x < drawX + 15 && y > drawY - 15 && y < drawY + 15) {
    // A hit! So add 1 to the sore and indicate that this target is done
    TargetClick.score++;
    done = true;
  }
  // no need to do anything if not a hit
}
}
```

The Target class contains the logic for drawing a target and for figuring out whether a target has been clicked. As a simplification, I determined whether the click was within a square that contains the target spot. For a more certain method, you could check the color of the pixel the player clicked on and award a hit if it is not white. My simplification makes the game a bit easier.

TargetClick is about as simple as a game gets. Let's move on to a more complex game.

The Shooting Gallery Game

As the title indicates, Shooting Gallery is a very simple shooting gallery game. I created it mostly to show the concept of controlling multiple items with a single timer, to show similar objects moving at different speeds, and to show one simple way to resolve collision detection (which means detecting when one object interacts with another – usually by running into one another). I'll also show one way to achieve double buffering, which makes games have less of that irritating flicker. When you write your own (no doubt far more interesting and entertaining) games, you'll need to know how to do those things.

Before we dive into the code, let's see what the game looks like. Figure 12-2 shows the ShootingGallery game during play.

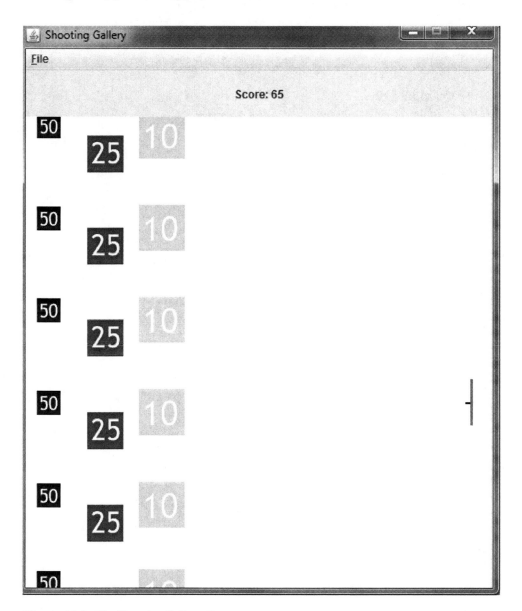

Figure 12-2. *The ShootingGallery Game*

As you can tell from the score, I hit four 10-point targets and one 25-point target before I took the screen shot. I find the back row to be hard to hit, but it's supposed to be that way, so I guess that's a good sign.

The ShootingGallery game consists of six classes:

- ShootingGallery defines and manages the user interface.

- ShootingGalleryPanel manages the playing area and contains the game loop.

- ShootingGalleryShooter manages the cursor.

- ShootingGalleryTargetRow manages an individual row of targets.

- ShootingGalleryTarget manages an individual target.

- ShootingGallerySprites manages the sprites used by the game.

Listing 12-4. The ShootingGallery class

```java
package com.bryantcs.examples.videogames;

import java.awt.Dimension;
import java.awt.event.ActionEvent;
import java.awt.event.ActionListener;

import javax.swing.BoxLayout;
import javax.swing.JFrame;
import javax.swing.JLabel;
import javax.swing.JMenu;
import javax.swing.JMenuBar;
import javax.swing.JMenuItem;
import javax.swing.JPanel;

public class ShootingGallery implements ActionListener {

  // Define the components
  private ShootingGalleryPanel shootingGalleryPanel;
  private JPanel scorePanel = new JPanel();
  private JLabel scoreLabel = new JLabel("Score: ");
  static JLabel scoreDisplayLabel = new JLabel("0");
  private JFrame frame = new Jframe("Shooting Gallery");
  // Set up a place to keep score (default is 0)
  static int score;
  // Set the game size
  static Dimension gameDimension = new Dimension(500, 500);

  // Add a menu (just one option, Exit)
  private void addMenu(JFrame frame) {
    JMenu file = new JMenu("File");
    file.setMnemonic('F');
    JMenuItem exitItem = new JMenuItem("Exit");
    exitItem.setMnemonic('x');
    exitItem.addActionListener(this);
```

```
    JMenuBar menuBar = new JMenuBar();
    menuBar.add(file);
    frame.setJMenuBar(menuBar);
  }

  // Setup and display the user interface
  private void createAndShowGUI() {
    shootingGalleryPanel = new ShootingGalleryPanel();
    addMenu(frame);
    frame.setDefaultCloseOperation(JFrame.EXIT_ON_CLOSE);
    frame.setExtendedState(frame.getExtendedState()|JFrame.MAXIMIZED_BOTH);
    shootingGalleryPanel.setPreferredSize(gameDimension);
    scorePanel.setPreferredSize(new Dimension(400, 50));
    scorePanel.setLayout(new BoxLayout(scorePanel, BoxLayout.X_AXIS));
    scorePanel.add(scoreLabel);
    scorePanel.add(scoreDisplayLabel);
    frame.getContentPane().add(scorePanel);
    frame.getContentPane().add(shootingGalleryPanel);
    frame.getContentPane().setLayout(new
      BoxLayout(frame.getContentPane(), BoxLayout.Y_AXIS));
    frame.pack();
    frame.setVisible(true);
    frame.setResizable(false);
  }

  // The main method
  public static void main(String[] args) {
    ShootingGallery shootingGallery = new ShootingGallery();
    shootingGallery.createAndShowGUI();
  }

  // Listen for the user choosing Exit from the menu
  //
  public void actionPerformed(ActionEvent e) {
    if (e.getActionCommand() != null) {
      if (e.getActionCommand().equals("Exit")) {
        System.exit(0);
      }
    }
  }
}
```

As usual, the ShootingGallery class just sets up the window and handles clicks to the menu and the window's controls (minimize and close, in this case). I disabled the resize control on the window, both because it simplified the math in the game and because it's something you might want to know how to do someday. The following line removes the ability to resize the window:

Listing 12-5. Preventing Resizing

```
    frame.setResizable(false);
```

I try to not restrict the user's actions unless I have a good, user-friendly reason to do so. So I would not normally have removed the ability to resize the window. Again, though, I thought it would make a good example, and it simplified the programming a bit. Restricting the user's actions to make your own life easier is poor practice though (it's a form of intellectual laziness) – don't do it unless you're doing it just to show how it's done.

One last thing to note about the ShootingGallery class (and the game) is that it has no start or stop control. It just runs continuously without end. I left out a number of common features that you might expect in a game so that you can implement them yourself. I've added a list of those ideas near the end of the chapter.

Listing 12-6. The ShootingGalleryPanel class

```java
package com.bryantcs.examples.videogames;

import java.awt.Dimension;
import java.awt.Graphics;
import java.awt.event.ActionEvent;
import java.awt.event.ActionListener;

import javax.swing.BoxLayout;
import javax.swing.JPanel;
import javax.swing.Timer;

public class ShootingGalleryPanel extends JPanel implements ActionListener{

    private static final long serialVersionUID = 1L;

    // The cursor, controlled by the player
    private ShootingGalleryShooter shooter;

    // The sprites that march down the game area
    private ShootingGalleryTargetSprites sprites;

    // The width of the widest target
    public final static int TARGET_SPACE = 50;

    // A tick counter to control the animation
    private int ticks;

    // Three rows of targets
    static ShootingGalleryTargetRow row1, row2, row3;

    // The timer, to control the game loop
    private Timer timer = new Timer(20, this);

    // The constructor
    public ShootingGalleryPanel() {
```

```
  // Set up the sprites
  sprites = new ShootingGalleryTargetSprites();
  sprites.init();

  // Set a horizontal layout, because we'll
  // add three vertical rows to the left side
  setLayout(new BoxLayout(this, BoxLayout.X_AXIS));

  // Set up and add the left-most row (the smallest and most valuable targets)
  row1 = new ShootingGalleryTargetRow(sprites.getSpriteBySize(25), 50);
  row1.setPreferredSize(new Dimension(TARGET_SPACE + 10, getHeight()));
  add(row1);

  // Set up and add the middle row (slower and worth less)
  row2 = new ShootingGalleryTargetRow(sprites.getSpriteBySize(40), 25);
  row2.setPreferredSize(new Dimension(TARGET_SPACE + 10, getHeight()));
  add(row2);

  // Set up and add the right-most row (slowest and least valuable targets)
  row3 = new ShootingGalleryTargetRow(sprites.getSpriteBySize(50), 10);
  row3.setPreferredSize(new Dimension(TARGET_SPACE + 10, getHeight()));
  add(row3);

  // Figure out how far to indent the player's cursor and add it
  int shooterOffset = (3 * (TARGET_SPACE + 10));
  int gameWidth = ShootingGallery.gameDimension.width;

  // Set up and add the player's cursor
  shooter = new ShootingGalleryShooter(gameWidth - shooterOffset);
  shooter.setPreferredSize(new Dimension(gameWidth - shooterOffset, getHeight()));
  add(shooter);

  // Start the timer
  timer.start();
}

// Let the parent component paint itself
@Override
public void paintComponent(Graphics g) {
  super.paintComponent(g);
}

// The game loop
@Override
public void actionPerformed(ActionEvent e) {

  // increment the tick counter
  ticks++;
```

```
    // Once a second, reset the tick counter
    // to keep it from overflowing the value of an int
    if (ticks == 50) {
      ticks = 0;
    }

    // Move the left-most row every tick
    row1.tick();

    / Move the center row every second tick
    if (ticks == 0 || ticks % 2 == 0) {
      row2.tick();
    }

    // Move the right-most row every third tick
    if (ticks == 0 || ticks % 3 == 0) {
      row3.tick();
    }

    // Update the location of the player's cursor every tick
    shooter.tick();
  }
}
```

As with the `TargetClickPanel` class, most of the ShootingGalleryPanel class sets up and manages the playing area (the user interface). The `actionPerformed` method, however, consists entirely of game logic and contains the game loop. It works by moving the rows every so many ticks. The left-most row (which contains the smallest and most valuable targets) updates on every tick, making it very fast (I have a hard time hitting those, but that's how it should be). The middle row updates on every second tick, and the right-most row (containing the largest and least valuable targets) updates every third tick. Consequently, the big and slow targets are in the way of the speedy and valuable targets, as is typical of shooting gallery games.

Finally, the `actionPerformed` method updates the location and status of the cursor. The cursor is the only thing the user controls, so we have to update its location and status as often as possible. Fifty times a second is enough to keep up with the actions of any player I've ever met.

Once the timer has run for a full second, the `actionPerformed` method resets it. Otherwise, a long game might see the number of ticks exceed the maximum possible value of the ticks' variable. That's unlikely, but why not head off a potential problem before it starts? We could just as easily reset every thousand or every million ticks, but setting an `int` to 0 is a very cheap operation, so I chose to reset every second.

The `actionPerformed` method handles all three of the tasks a game loop needs to do, but not in the same order or in the same way as we saw in the TargetClick game. This time, the updating of the interface is pushed off to other classes (ShootingGalleryTargetRow and ShootingGalleryShooter), and the handling of the user input comes last rather than first. In this case, whether the user input gets handled first or last makes no difference. I did it this way to demonstrate that the order of the tasks doesn't usually matter. There are exceptions, but you'll be able to identify those when you encounter them, as they will be part of how your game works.

Since one of the three main functions of the `ShootingGalleryPanel.actionPerformed` method is to update the rows, let's look at how the rows work (the other main functions are updating the cursor and managing the ticks). As you read the code for the ShootingGalleryTargetRow class, pay particular attention to the tick method (which removes objects as they go off the bottom and replaces them with new objects at the top, assuming the player doesn't shoot that particular target).

Listing 12-7. The ShootingGalleryTargetRow class

```java
package com.bryantcs.examples.videogames;

import java.awt.Color;
import java.awt.Graphics;
import java.awt.image.BufferedImage;
import java.util.LinkedList;

import javax.swing.JPanel;

public class ShootingGalleryTargetRow extends JPanel {

  private static final long serialVersionUID = 1L;

  // We need a list of targets
  private LinkedList<ShootingGalleryTarget> targets =
      new LinkedList<ShootingGalleryTarget>();

  // We need to know how many points this target is worth
  private int targetValue;

  // We need to know when to remove a target
  // off the bottom and add a new one at the top
  private int newTargetTicker;

  // We need a sprite for the player to shoot
  // Using a buffered image to reduce flicker
  private BufferedImage sprite;

  // The constructor, in which we set the values of the things we need to know
  public ShootingGalleryTargetRow(BufferedImage sprite, int value, int delay) {
    targetValue = value;
    newTargetTicker = 0;
    this.sprite = sprite;
  }

  public LinkedList<ShootingGalleryTarget> getTargets() {
    return targets;
  }

  @Override
  public void paintComponent(Graphics g) {
    super.paintComponent(g);
    this.setBackground(Color.WHITE);
    for (int targetCounter = 0; targetCounter < targets.size(); targetCounter ++) {
      ShootingGalleryTarget currentTarget = targets.get(targetCounter);
      if (currentTarget.getY() > getHeight() + ShootingGalleryPanel.TARGET_SPACE) {
```

```
            targets.remove(currentTarget);
        } else {
            currentTarget.setY(currentTarget.getY() + ShootingGalleryPanel.TARGET_SPACE / 10);
            currentTarget.draw(g);
        }
    }
}

public void tick() {
    for (int targetCounter = 0; targetCounter < targets.size(); targetCounter ++) {
        ShootingGalleryTarget currentTarget = targets.get(targetCounter);
        currentTarget.setY(currentTarget.getY() + ShootingGalleryPanel.TARGET_SPACE / 10);
    }
    newTargetTicker++;
    if (newTargetTicker > 9) {
        newTargetTicker = 0;
        ShootingGalleryTarget newTarget =
            new ShootingGalleryTarget(targetValue, sprite, 0,
                -ShootingGalleryPanel.TARGET_SPACE, this);
        targets.add(newTarget);
    }
    repaint();
}
}
```

The `ShootingGalleryTargetRow` class handles the targets in a given row. The `paintComponent` method removes targets that move off the bottom and draws all the remaining targets in the row (the `ShootingGalleryShooter` class, which handles the player's cursor, removes targets that get shot). The `tick` method handles updating the information about the collection of targets. In particular, the `tick` method adds a new target to the top of the row every tenth tick, which has the effect of constantly replenishing the row (one possible way to limit the time the game runs is to limit the total number of targets in each row – run out of targets and the game is over. Feel free to implement that idea if it interests you).

Using a `LinkedList` object to hold the targets allows for adding and removing targets without having to have a fixed number of targets. Given that targets get shot, the number of targets fluctuates, so we need a data structure that accommodates the fluctuation.

Now that we've seen how rows of targets work, let's move on to the actual `Target` objects.

Listing 12-8. The ShootingGalleryTarget class

```
package com.bryantcs.examples.videogames;

import java.awt.Graphics;
import java.awt.Polygon;
import java.awt.Image;

public class ShootingGalleryTarget {

    // The integer things we need to know: value, size, position,
    // and offset from the edge of the row (for centering)
    private int value, size, xPosition, yPosition, offset;
```

```
// A reference to the row that holds the target (which
// we need to use as the ImageObserver for the sprite)
private ShootingGalleryTargetRow row;

// The sprite
private Image sprite;

// A polygon object that we use for collision detection
Polygon polygon;

// The constructor, wherein we set the values of all the things we need
 public ShootingGalleryTarget(int value, Image sprite, int x, int y, ShootingGalleryTargetRow
row) {
   size = sprite.getWidth(row);
   this.value = value;
   this.sprite = sprite;
   xPosition = x;
   yPosition = y;
   this.row = row;
   offset = (ShootingGalleryPanel.TARGET_SPACE - size) / 2;
 }

// The draw method
 public void draw(Graphics g) {

   // Set the target's position
   int x = xPosition + offset;
   int y = yPosition + offset;

   // Draw the sprite
   g.drawImage(sprite, x, y, size, size, row);

   // Create a polygon that matches the sprite
   // We'll use the polygon to see if the sprite gets hit
   polygon = new Polygon();
   polygon.addPoint(x, y);
   polygon.addPoint(x, y + size);
   polygon.addPoint(x + size, y + size);
   polygon.addPoint(x + size, y);
 }

// Provide a way to update the vertical position
 public void setY(int y) {
   yPosition = y;
 }

// Provide a way to get the vertical position
 public int getY() {
   return yPosition;
 }
```

```
    // Provide a way to get the value
    // (used when the target is hit)
    public int getValue() {
      return value;
    }
}
```

The `ShootingGalleryTarget` class is a very simple object that keeps track of a target's position, its value (if it gets hit), and the way in which it draw itself within its row. To make collision detection easier, I implemented the target as a `Polygon` object, because the `Polygon` class has a handy method called `contains` that lets us know whether a point is in the polygon. I could have used the properties of the image itself, but doing so would require more code and more math, which would neither perform better nor be more readable.

Collision detection usually means two objects end up in the same space and the game has to figure out what to do about it (such as draw an explosion, or open a door, or any other number of possibilities that are determined by the nature of the game). In this case, I elected to simplify the game by not drawing a bullet (or laser beam or whatever) going from the cursor to the target area. However, we still have to determine whether a target has been hit when the player shoots. So I make the shooter class see whether a target has the same vertical position as the center of the player's cursor and (working from the right-most row to the left-most row) remove the first target that matches the vertical location.

An excellent exercise would be to add an animation for the shot. You could either add a bullet object (use another class) and move it across the screen or just draw a line from the cursor to the first target it touches (an expansion of the `ShootingGalleryShooter` class will do this trick).

Speaking of the shooter class, let's look at it a little more closely. As you read the class, notice that it implements both the `MouseListener` and the `MouseMotionListener` interfaces. No other object in the game needs to listen for mouse clicks and mouse motion, so only the `ShootingGalleryShooter` class implements those interfaces. You might also want to study the `paintComponent` method to see how it changes the color of the bar after a player shoots and enforces a one-second delay between shots. Finally, take a close look at the `analyzeShot` and `analyzeShotForRow` methods. Those two contain the logic for determining whether a shot hit a target.

Listing 12-9. The ShootingGalleryShooter class

```
package com.bryantcs.examples.videogames;

import java.awt.Color;
import java.awt.Graphics;
import java.awt.event.MouseEvent;
import java.awt.event.MouseListener;
import java.awt.event.MouseMotionListener;

import javax.swing.JPanel;

public class ShootingGalleryShooter extends JPanel implements MouseListener,
MouseMotionListener {

  private static final long serialVersionUID = 1L;

  // We need to know where the cursor is
  private int xPosition, yPosition;
```

```
    // We need to know whether the player can shoot
    private boolean readyToShoot;

    // We need to know the current step
    // when drawing the cursor after a shot
    private int currentStep;

    // We need to know the maximum steps
    // (Changing this value would change
    // the timeout between shots, by the way.)
    private int maxSteps = 50;

    // The constructor
    public ShootingGalleryShooter(int width) {

        // Add the listeners for mouse clicks and motion
        addMouseListener(this);
        addMouseMotionListener(this);

        // Let the player shoot right away
        readyToShoot = true;
        currentStep = maxSteps;

        // Draw the cursor 20 pixels from the right edge
        xPosition = width - 20;
    }

    public void paintComponent(Graphics g) {
        // Let the parent draw itself
        // (sets the panel's background color)
        super.paintComponent(g);

        // Set the cursor's background color
        this.setBackground(Color.WHITE);

        // Figure out whether the player can shoot
        if (currentStep < maxSteps) {
            // If not, increment the current step
            currentStep++;
            readyToShoot = false;
        } else {
            readyToShoot = true;
        }

        // Fill two rectangles to show how long
        // the player has to wait to shoot again
        g.setColor(Color.RED);
        g.fillRect(xPosition, yPosition - (maxSteps / 2), 3, currentStep);
        g.setColor(Color.YELLOW);
        g.fillRect(xPosition, yPosition - (maxSteps / 2) + currentStep, 3, maxSteps -
currentStep);
```

```
    // Draw the actual position from which a shot comes
    g.setColor(Color.BLACK);
    g.fillRect(xPosition - 5, yPosition, 5, 2);
  }

  // Provide a way to set the Y location
  public void setY(int newY) {
    yPosition = newY;
  }

  // Convenience method for indicating that the player can shoot
  private void setReadyToShoot(boolean ready) {
    readyToShoot = ready;
    if (ready == false) {
      currentStep = 0;
    }
  }

  // Work through the rows from right to left to see if a shot hit a target
  private void analyzeShot(int shotY) {
    if (!analyzeShotForRow(ShootingGalleryPanel.row3, shotY)) {
      if(!analyzeShotForRow(ShootingGalleryPanel.row2, shotY)) {
        analyzeShotForRow(ShootingGalleryPanel.row1, shotY);
      }
    }
  }

  // Work through the targets in a row to see if we hit one
  private boolean analyzeShotForRow(ShootingGalleryTargetRow row, int shotY) {
    boolean hit = false;
    int count = row.getTargets().size();

    while(!hit && count > 0) {
      ShootingGalleryTarget currentTarget = row.getTargets().get(count - 1);

      // Here's where we check the target's polygon for a hit
      if (currentTarget.polygon.contains(ShootingGalleryPanel.TARGET_SPACE / 2, shotY)) {
        // If we get a hit, stop checking
        hit = true;

        // Update the score
        ShootingGallery.score += currentTarget.getValue();
        ShootingGallery.scoreDisplayLabel.setText(new
Integer(ShootingGallery.score).toString());

        Remove the target that got hit
        row.getTargets().remove(currentTarget);
      } else {
        // We're working backwards because doing so makes
        // it easy to detect when we've run out of targets to check
        count--;
      }
```

```
  }
  return hit;
}

// We have to have this method to fulfill the MouseListener contract
@Override
public void mouseClicked(MouseEvent e) {
}

// We have to have this method to fulfill the MouseListener contract
@Override
public void mouseEntered(MouseEvent e) {
}

// We have to have this method to fulfill the MouseListener contract
@Override
public void mouseExited(MouseEvent e) {
}

// We have to have this method to fulfill the MouseListener contract
@Override
public void mousePressed(MouseEvent e) {
}

// Here's where we check for mouse clicks
@Override
public void mouseReleased(MouseEvent e) {
  if(readyToShoot){
    // If ready to shoot, process the shot
    setReadyToShoot(false);
    analyzeShot(e.getY());
  }
  // If not ready to shoot, do nothing
}

// We have to have this method to fulfill the MouseMotionListener contract
@Override
public void mouseDragged(MouseEvent e) {
}

// Here's where we listen for mouse movement and use
// the setY method to update the cursor's position
@Override
public void mouseMoved(MouseEvent e) {
  setY(e.getY());
}

// process a tick from the timer (in ShootingGalleryPanel)
public void tick() {
  if (currentStep < maxSteps) {
    // If we're still drawing the cursor after a shot, then increment
    // the step counter and ensure that the player can't shoot yet
```

```
            currentStep++;
            readyToShoot = false;
        } else {
            // Otherwise, let the player shoot
            readyToShoot = true;
        }

        // repaint the cursor (otherwise, the cursor won't move)
        repaint();
    }
}
```

The ShootingGalleryShooter class handles the only object the player controls: the cursor that indicates both where a shot will go and whether the player can shoot. Remember that the timer in the ShootingGalleryPanel class ticks fifty times a second. For that reason, the ShootingGalleryShooter class keeps track of fifty steps, so that it can impose a one-second delay between shots. Then it uses those 50 steps to draw the cursor's vertical bar, setting it to yellow when a player shoots and, over the course of a second, setting it back to red as the second passes. When it's all red, the player can shoot again.

There's one last class that we need to examine in order to fully understand the ShootingGallery game (as we learned in Chapter 11, "Debugging with Eclipse," fully understanding a program's code is a key part of software development). The ShootingGalleryTargetSprites class loads the three different target images and makes them available to the rest of the program. Listing 12-10 shows the ShootingGalleryTargetSprites class.

Listing 12-10. The ShootingGalleryTargetSprites class

```java
package com.bryantcs.examples.videogames;

import java.awt.Image;
import java.io.File;
import java.io.IOException;

import javax.imageio.ImageIO;

public class ShootingGalleryTargetSprites {

    // Variables for the images
    // Static so that each one exists in memory only once
    private static Image smallTarget = null;
    private static Image mediumTarget = null;
    private static Image largeTarget = null;

    // Load the images into the variables
    public void init() {
        try {
            smallTarget = ImageIO.read(new File("C:\\test\\sprites\\target_small.png"));
            mediumTarget = ImageIO.read(new File("C:\\test\\sprites\\target_medium.png"));
            largeTarget = ImageIO.read(new File("C:\\test\\sprites\\target_large.png"));
        } catch (IOException e) {
```

```
      System.err.println("Couldn't load one or more sprite images");
      System.exit(1);
    }
  }

  // Get the sprite that corresponds to the size of the target
  public Image getSpriteBySize(int size) {
    // Set up an object to return
    Image imageToReturn = null;

    if (size == 25) { // Get the little black target
      imageToReturn = smallTarget;
    } else if (size == 40) { // Get the medium-sized blue target
      imageToReturn = mediumTarget;
    } else if (size == 50) { // Get the large green target
      imageToReturn = largeTarget;
    } else { // oops - no such target, so tell the player and stop
      throw new IllegalArgumentException("Unknown Sprite Size: " + size);
      System.exit(1);
    }

    return imageToReturn;
  }
}
```

If you didn't skip straight to this chapter, then you've seen a very similar class in Chapter 7, "Writing a User Interface," when we examined the MineIcon class. That class creates a set of ImageIcon objects rather than a set of Image objects and doesn't have an init method, but the idea is the same. We load a set of images into a set of static variables.

An important implementation detail is that those variables being static: being static ensures that each memory gets loaded into the memory only once. Imagine the memory consumption if every target loaded its own separate image. We'd quickly have a problem, either with a crash because we ran out of memory or with horrible performance because images are constantly loading. As it happens, the init method gets called only once, so the images would get loaded into memory only once. However, the static loading technique is still a good idea to keep around, just in case. There's an old joke (familiar to members of the United States Navy) that goes: "I know I'm being paranoid, but am I being paranoid enough?" It's often a good question for software developers, too.

Expanding the ShootingGallery Game

As I promised earlier, here's a collection of ideas for making the ShootingGallery game more complex (and more like a game you'd actually want to play):

- A button or menu item or keyboard command (use the KeyListener interface, which works much like the MouseListener interface) that toggles between Start and Stop

- A Pause button or menu item or keyboard command

- A New Game menu item or keyboard command

- A timer that ends the game after some amount of time – perhaps settable by the player

- A target score (the game ends when the player reaches a certain score – don't forget to show the elapsed time) – perhaps settable by the player

- A fixed number of targets (either total or for each row – the game ends when the targets run out) – perhaps settable by the player

- A fixed number of bullets (which makes the game a bit more of a thinking game, since unaimed shots get punished) – perhaps settable by the player

- Bullet or laser beam animation

A Note about Limitations

Larry Niven, a great science fiction author, in a collection of short stories entitled *Limits*, wrote that "Often enough, it's the limits that *make* [emphasis in original] the story."

That excellent observation very much applies to software development as well. No program can do everything, so we have to choose what each program will and won't do. In addition to design considerations, we often also have to battle performance and hardware constraints. For example, I am currently working as a member of a team attempting to re-engineer content delivery for a major web site (it's a household name and one that you'd recognize instantly). The site gets 80 million visits a month (on average – during the holiday shopping season, that number goes up substantially). We have to ensure that each page request (each click a user makes on the web site, in other words) gets a response in less than two seconds. Otherwise, the user might take their business elsewhere, and our company wouldn't make all the money it can. That two-second limit is a huge factor in every decision we make. And we can't just throw hardware (more and bigger servers) at the problem, even though the company makes computers, including extremely high-end web servers. At some point, we run out of address space for servers (each computer on the Internet has to have a unique address, known as its IP address). So there's yet another limitation.

So why tell you all this here? Because games, even more than software, rely on limitations. In a very real sense, a game is a collection of limitations. Each rule in a game is a limitation, and a game is nothing without its rules. If you could put a card wherever you want when you play solitaire, would it still be a game? If you could shoot multiple times a second, wouldn't ShootingGallery be less challenging (and so less fun)?

In that same essay (the introduction to *Limits*), Mr. Niven also states that "puzzles *require* [emphasis in original] rules." All games are puzzles. The player always asks, even if only subconsciously, "What is the proper set of steps that I need to follow in order to beat this game?" Thus, all games require rules, and all rules are limitations. As you design your own games, remember to make a set of limitations that make the game fun. If the limitations are too many or too severe, they will make the game frustrating. If the limitations are too few or too loose, the game is such a poor challenge that it's not worth playing.

Game Design Resources

I anticipate that many of the people who read this book are doing so because they want to create their own games. To that end, here's a short list of resources that I've found useful when thinking about games and how to design good ones. Note that these resources apply to designing games in general, not just computer games.

- *Game Design (Volume 1: Theory and Practice)* by Nick Schuessler and Steve Jackson (1981). You can get it from http://e23.sjgames.com. Steve Jackson is the fellow who made Ogre (one of my favorite board games), GURPS (the role-playing system I use), and Munchkin (a commercial hit that spoofs role-playing games). He does not make computer games, but the wisdom in this small book applies to all games, computer or otherwise.

- *A Theory of Fun for Game Design* by Raph Koster (Foreword by Will Wright) (2004). Raph Koster is a veteran of many large computer game efforts, including MMOGs (Massively Multiplayer Online Games). His book combines thoughts on learning theory with thoughts on game design, bringing good ideas to both fields.

- "I Have No Words & I Must Design: Toward a Critical Vocabulary for Games" by Greg Costikyan (online essay). You can find this excellent exploration of what a game is and how a game works at http://www.costik.com/nowords2002.pdf You can find his blog, which contains other content of interest to game developers, at http://www.costik.com

Summary

In this chapter, I hope you learned the basics of making a computer game with Java. In particular, I hope you learned:

- The three basic components of a computer game:
  - The user interface
  - The game logic
  - The game loop
- The essential tasks of a game loop:
  - Processing the user input and all other inputs
  - Processing the game logic
  - Redrawing the playing field
- How to animate multiple objects at once
- How to make multiple objects move at different speeds
- How to test for conditions to see if a game should end or something else should happen
- How to update a score display in response to game events

As I have mentioned several times, there's nearly always more than one way to do any given thing in software (that's part of both the fun and the frustration of writing software). So, when I say that I've shown you how to do something, I really mean that I've shown you one way to do something. I hope you'll experiment with other ideas and find your own ways to meet your software goals. Writing a game of your own would be a great way to do just that, so go write a game.

CHAPTER 13

Garbage Collection

Java relies on garbage collection. A garbage collector removes unused objects from memory and lets your programs re-use memory rather than constantly grow. For very small programs, this constant growth doesn't matter much. However, even a program of fairly low complexity and scale can quickly chew through a lot of memory. Therefore, most programs really need some kind of garbage collection mechanism.

When they use many other languages, including C++, programmers have to manage memory themselves, writing code to remove objects from memory at the right time. Java frees developers from this problem. That's not to say that Java is better than C++. Both languages have their strengths and weaknesses. Many developers who prefer Java would tell you that having to manage memory yourself is a weakness in C++ and that garbage collection is a strength of Java. Conversely, many C++ developers would tell you the opposite. Both are true: Garbage collection can be a problem in Java, yet is also an inherent feature and very powerful if managed correctly.

So how do we turn garbage collection into an advantage rather than a burden?

Understanding Memory Allocation

Before we can really talk about garbage collection, we need a basic understanding of how the Java Virtual Machine (JVM) allocates memory in the first place. Every time you create a new object or primitive, the heap grows by the size of that object or primitive. In addition, if you create a complex object (an object that itself contains other objects, as many objects do), the heap grows by the size of all those objects as well. For example, consider a class we've seen before (in the previous chapter), the `TargetClickPanel` class:

Listing 13-1. Memory Allocation in the TargetClickPanel Class

```
package com.bryantcs.examples.videogames;

import java.awt.Graphics;
import java.awt.event.MouseEvent;
import java.awt.event.MouseListener;

import javax.swing.JPanel;
```

```java
public class TargetClickPanel extends JPanel implements MouseListener{

  private static final long serialVersionUID = 1L;

  private Target targets[] = new Target[5];

  public TargetClickPanel() {
    addMouseListener(this);
    for (int i = 0; i < targets.length; i++) {
      targets[i] = null;
    }
  }

  public void paint (Graphics g) {
    super.paintComponent(g);
    for (int i = 0; i < targets.length; i++) {
      if (targets[i] == null) {
        targets[i] = new Target(this);
      }
      if (!targets[i].isDone()) {
        targets[i].draw(g);
      } else {
        targets[i] = new Target(this);
      }
    }
  }

  @Override
  public void mouseClicked(MouseEvent e) {
  }

  @Override
  public void mouseEntered(MouseEvent e) {
  }

  @Override
  public void mouseExited(MouseEvent e) {
  }

  @Override
  public void mousePressed(MouseEvent e) {
  }

  @Override
  public void mouseReleased(MouseEvent e) {
    for (int i = 0; i < targets.length; i++) {
      targets[i].pointInTarget(e.getX(), e.getY());
    }
  }
}
```

Consider the lines in bold (the `targets` array and the lines within the paint method that create new instances of the `Target` object). If you visualize the values of all of the objects and primitives as the program runs, you can see that the paint method first creates five instances of the Target class and then keeps five of the instances going as the existing instances declare themselves to be finished. Consequently, the result of creating an instance of the `TargetClickPanel` also creates five instances of the `Target` class.

However, creating an instance of the `TargetClickPanel` class actually creates many more than just five instances of the `Target` class. The instances of the Target class that have marked themselves as finished still exist, even though the instance of the `TargetClickPanel` no longer has references to them. That's the key to garbage collection: references. We'll get to that shortly. First, let's consider the state of the Target objects that have been created after the `TargetClick` game has run for a few seconds:

Target 1: Created because targets[0] was null. Now finished.

Target 2: Created because targets[1] was null. Now finished.

Target 3: Created because targets[2] was null. Now finished.

Target 4: Created because targets[3] was null. Now finished.

Target 5: Created because targets[4] was null. Now finished.

Target 6: Created because targets[0] was finished. Now finished.

Target 7: Created because targets[1] was finished. Now finished.

Target 8: Created because targets[2] was finished. Still in play.

Target 9: Created because targets[3] was finished. Still in play.

Target 10: Created because targets[4] was finished. Still in play.

Target 11: Created because targets[0] was finished. Still in play.

Target 12: Created because targets[1] was finished. Still in play.

And so on...

At any given moment, the instance of the `TargetClickPanel` class has references to five instances of the Target class. But what happens to all the finished instances? As it happens, they get garbage collected. And there's the primary rule of garbage collection: If an object no longer has references held on it by other objects, that object gets garbage collected. In other words, once an object no longer has any other objects using it, that object is ready to be removed from memory. Yet another way to say this is that the object is now unreachable, meaning that no other bit of code can reach that object.

The Java Garbage Collection Algorithm: Marking and Sweeping

The algorithm that Java uses for garbage collection is called marking and sweeping. Conceptually, it's a simple idea. First, make an initial pass of the memory and mark any memory that can be collected. Then make another pass and free the memory that was marked in the first pass.

In practice, though, the process becomes much more complex. The basic algorithm (often called naïve mark and sweep) works fine, so long as the whole program stops while the garbage collector runs. The program has to stop so that the garbage collector can be sure that no new objects are being created and that no existing objects have gotten into a state such that they can be garbage collected while the collector runs. Java's earliest versions used just such an algorithm. Consequently, Java earned a reputation for being unsuitable for applications that required high performance, from video games to real-time monitoring of things like valves in a refinery. Later versions fixed that problem, but the reputation lingered for several more versions (and still pops up in some circles).

So how does one collect objects and still let the program run? In particular, how does one allow creation of new objects and send existing objects to collection while letting the garbage collector run? Two more advanced algorithms have been developed: Incremental garbage collection and concurrent garbage collection.

Incremental garbage collection relies on intermittently stopping and starting both the program and the garbage collector (which is really just another program being run in parallel by the JVM). Essentially, the program gets to do a bit of work, and then the garbage collector gets to do a bit, and so on. In this fashion, the program gets to do some work while the garbage collector runs. As you can imagine, though, the program's performance is still slower than when the garbage collector is not running. In fact, versions of Java had noticeably slower performance when the garbage collector ran. I recall playing a video game written in Java and being able to tell when the garbage collector started and stopped.

Concurrent garbage collection lets the program run at full speed, with one exception: The program must be halted while the stack (the list of objects in memory) is scanned. Fortunately, scanning the stack takes very little time. Scanning the stack (which is really just a list) takes much less time than does scanning the heap (which is all of the objects in memory). Imagine reading a book's table of contents versus reading the whole book, and you'll have an idea of the difference.

So how does a concurrent garbage collector let the program run at (almost) full speed? The garbage collector doesn't concern itself with finding everything that can be collected. Instead, it finds what it can be sure of and frees those objects. On its next pass, it can catch anything it missed, as well as anything that has become removable in the meantime. Thus, the concurrent garbage collection rarely gets a perfect sweep, but it lets the program run much more smoothly.

Java 1.4.2 (which was a "red letter" release in the Java community, partly because of garbage collection) introduced a garbage collector that can be switched between incremental garbage collection and concurrent garbage collection. (It actually supports 4 kinds of garbage collection: two variants of naïve garbage collection, incremental garbage collection, and concurrent garbage collection.) Software developers could then decide (preferably through testing) which kind of collection worked best for their programs. Suddenly, the performance of many Java programs got a big boost. At that point, Java could finally compete with non-garbage-collecting languages (notably C++) in the arena of high performance applications. Java 5 (also known as Java 1.5) and Java 6 (or Java 1.6) continued to add fine tuning to the garbage collector, through various switches that could be set on the collector. We'll cover the most helpful of these switches near the end of this chapter.

Enter Java 7. Java 7 provides a new collector, called G1 (for "garbage first"). The G1 collector offers a step up from the previous garbage collectors by dividing the heap into regions (or sectors) and then garbage collecting each sector beginning with the sector that has the most the most garbage to collect. As a result of this "garbage-first" collection scheme, the G1 collector ensures that it gets as much garbage as possible on any given sweep. If the G1 collector was unable to sweep the whole thing because the program needed to run, at least it got to the worst sectors while it had a chance. Over subsequent sweeps, the other regions gradually fill up and come to contain the most garbage. Those sectors then get swept in their turn. Thus, the collector eventually gets to all regions in memory but doesn't try to get them all at once. It's a nice bit of optimization that is made all the better by not needing any new settings to control it. It's just how the G1 collector works. Also, there's no need to enable the G1 collector. If you're using Java 7, you're using the G1 collector, unless you specify an older collector.

Understanding Memory Settings

Some programs must keep large numbers of objects in memory to work correctly. In those cases, the only way to make them work is to expand the amount of memory available to the programs.

As a case in point, consider an XML parser. It must have a reference to each node in the document tree from the top to its current location. In addition, processing each node creates a reference to each child node. Consequently, by the time an XML parser has gotten very far into a document tree, it probably has references to a lot of nodes, each represented by an object, and each object having a reference from the object that represents its parent node. Parsers are one common example of the types of programs that don't benefit much from garbage collection. Of course, a program that parses a document and then does something else could free the memory used by the parser when the parsing is done. That memory could then be for another purpose, such that the program's footprint would be just the larger of the parsing or whatever else it does, rather than the total of both parsing and other work. Conversely, a program that runs other processes in the background must have enough memory to enable all of its concurrent processes.

So how do Java programmers give their programs more memory? They do it through switches on the JVM when they start the program. Here are the basic memory settings:

Table 13-1. *Basic Java Memory Settings*

Switch	Effect
-Xms\<size>	Sets the starting heap size. For example: -Xms64M sets the starting heap size to 64 megabytes (64MB is the default memory allocation, by the way)
-Xmx\<size>	Sets the maximum heap size. For example: -Xmx1024M sets the maximum heap size to 1024 megabytes (that is, 1 gigabyte)

You can increase a program's performance by setting the starting heap size properly. If you set the number too low, the JVM starts at that amount and then has to adjust upward (perhaps several times) until it has enough memory for your program's initial set of objects. Then, as soon as the program does something (perhaps because a user did something with the program), the JVM has to allocate yet more memory. Rather than force your users to put up with the slow performance that a low starting memory value creates, you should instead allocate enough initial memory to handle all the objects your program needs at start-up time and to handle the first several operations it might need to perform.

The maximum memory setting is both more obvious and more critical. If you don't allocate enough memory, your program crashes. Usually, finding the right amount of maximum memory is a matter of experimentation. You have to start the program, let it run for a while, and see how much memory it uses. On Windows, the Task Manager shows how much memory each process, including a Java program, uses. Other operating systems reveal that information in other ways, but it should be there somewhere.

Here's an example of using the memory switches when you start a Java program:

Listing 13-2. *Example of Java Memory Switches*

```
java -Xms1024M -Xmx8192M ExampleProgram
```

Understanding Garbage Collection

The first thing to understand about the Java garbage collector is that you can't directly control it. You can give it hints that certain objects are now ready for collection. You can also set a number of garbage collection options when you start your program, and those settings will control the garbage collector's behavior. However, you cannot explicitly tell the garbage collector to remove an object from memory right now. That is, no method or class exists to let you specifically collect an existing object. You may be sure that the object can safely be removed, but you can't force the garbage collector to remove it.

This lack of control drives plenty of software developers a little nuts. As a group, software developers tend to want to control the computers they program, so a system that offers only indirect control is often not welcomed. For programmers accustomed to other languages (especially C++), that's often a primary complaint when they start using Java. Rather than have direct control, Java developers must instead be careful not to allow unnecessary references to exist.

When Java was new, some developers thought and said nonsense such as, "Oh, great! Java will manage my memory for me!" Therefore, more than a few programs with an unfortunate tendency to use large amounts of memory were created as a result. Having a garbage collector doesn't allow us to be lazy. We still have to manage memory, but we don't do it explicitly.

Another common complaint with Java (and other languages that use garbage collection) used to be that everything stopped while garbage collection ran. The addition of incremental and concurrent garbage collection has reduced that complaint somewhat, and further refinements in Java's garbage collection algorithms have improved the situation greatly. It used to be common for Java programs to have long pauses when the garbage collector ran. With the modern Java virtual machines available now, those pauses are now very rare (and are a symptom of poor programming rather than the JVM).

Understanding Generations

The Java garbage collector uses the concept of generations. In most applications, nearly all objects exist for a very short time. If you look at the Target objects created by an instance of the TargetClickPanel class (listed in the previous chapter), you'll see that they exist for just a few seconds each. In fact, if a player clicks on one, an instance of the Target class might exist for only a fraction of a second. Conversely, the TargetClickPanel instance and the TargetClick instance both exist for the duration of the game, but there's only instance of each class for the entire time.

Suppose a game of TargetClick involves the creation of 100 Target objects. In that scenario, two objects (one instance of the TargetClick class and one instance of the TargetClickPanel class) exist for the entire life of the program, while 100 other objects (all the instances of the Target class) exist for no more than a few seconds each. So, at least in this case, we have a great example where nearly all objects are not present in the system for long.

All of these short-lived objects end up in the "young generation." The young generation has three spaces: "eden," "from," and "to." The eden space is where objects go first. So, when your program creates a new object (such as an instance of the Target class in the TargetClick game), the object goes into the eden space. The from and to spaces are called "survivor spaces," and objects that survive at least one garbage collection pass move to these spaces until they've survived sufficiently long to move to the tenured generation. At any given moment, one survivor space is empty. When the garbage collector runs, it moves the survivors from the eden space and the currently occupied survivor space into the currently empty survivor space.

Objects that last a while (either a certain amount of time or a certain number of collections) end up in the "tenured generation" (also called the "old generation" – the older I get, the more I prefer to talk about the "tenured generation"). Finally, the "permanent generation" isn't really a generation but is instead the area where the JVM stores the class definitions. The permanent generation isn't necessarily static, as Java programs can load and unload classes as they run.

Java's garbage collector sweeps the young generation more often than the tenured generations and uses different collection algorithms for the two generations. Further detail is beyond the scope of this book. If you're interested in greater detail about Java collection algorithms, you can find a number of books and web sites devoted to the subject. Efficient garbage collection is one of those problems that draws the best minds in the field of computer science, because it is both practical (every Java programmer needs a good one) and highly theoretical.

One of the very difficult issues facing the designers of garbage collection algorithms (including those used in Java) is how to deal with references that cross the generational boundaries. Before the garbage collector can remove an object from memory, it has to ensure that no references exist. That means checking references across the generations, which is a difficult task to do quickly.

Scavenges and Full Collections

The Java garbage collector can do partial garbage collection by collecting just the young generation. This type of operation is called a "scavenge." When the garbage collector collects both the young and the tenured generations, this is called a "full collection," or (often) just a "collection." A number of command-line switches modify the garbage collector's behavior with regard to the young and tenured generations. We'll encounter these and other switches later in the chapter, in the section entitled "Understanding Garbage Collection Settings."

Garbage Collection is Event-Driven

Garbage collection doesn't happen every time an object happens to no longer have any references. If it did, every Java program would spend more time removing unused objects than it would spend doing anything else, and the performance of all Java programs would be so poor that no one would use Java for anything.

Instead, the Java garbage collector works on an event-driven model. When certain conditions are met, the garbage collector runs. These conditions involve the ratio of heap space (the amount of memory) in use to the amount of free memory and the amount of total memory. In simple terms, when the JVM determines that it's running out of memory, it runs the garbage collector. So, when the amount of heap space relative to the amount of total memory gets to a certain percentage, the garbage collector removes any objects that have no references. Doing so readjusts the percentage of memory in use downward, so that the program can keep on running.

Understanding Garbage Collection Settings

The Java garbage collector uses another group of switches (similar to the memory switches we saw earlier) that you set when you start your program. Here's a summary of the most common switches:

Table 13-2. Garbage Collection Settings

Switch	Effect
`-XX:NewRatio=3`	Sets the ratio of objects in the young generation to objects in the tenured generation. This is a key setting for optimization, which we'll explore later in this chapter.
`-XX:NewSize=32M`	Sets the minimum size of the new generation area. This is a key setting for optimization, which we'll explore later in this chapter.
`-XX:MaxNewSize=32M`	Sets the maximum size of the new generation area. This is a key setting for optimization, which we'll explore later in this chapter.
`-XX:MaxHeapFreeRatio=70`	If the free memory after a scavenge or collection is less than the indicated percentage of total available memory, set total available memory to that value. This setting lets memory grow into the free space again. Its default value is 70. Remember that the JVM grows or shrinks the heap at each collection in order to preserve this ratio (within certain bounds).
`-XX:MinHeapFreeRatio=40`	If the free memory after a scavenge or collection is less than the indicated percentage of total available memory, this sets the total available memory to the value given in the argument. This setting keeps some memory immediately available in situations where the garbage collector has recovered a lot of memory. Its default value is 40.
`-XX:MaxPermSize=64m`	Sets the size of the permanent generation. If your program has a lot of classes, you may gain better performance by increasing this value. Its default is 64M (that is, 64 megabytes).
`-XX:+ScavengeBeforeFullGC`	Before trying to do a full collection, this scavenges first. If the result of the scavenge puts free memory in the desired range, a full collection isn't done.
`-XX:-UseParallelGC`	Uses parallel garbage collection for scavenges. Specifically, it uses one thread per processor on the machine. As a rule, for a single processor machine, this results in a loss of performance. On a two-processor machine, it's roughly equivalent. On machines with more than two processors, it's faster. The opposite setting is -XX:-UseSerialGC
`-XX:-UseParallelOldGC`	Uses parallel garbage collection for both scavenges and full collections. The same rules for efficiency on multiple processors applies.
`-XX:-UseSerialGC`	Uses serial garbage collection for both scavenges and full collections. This setting is more efficient on machines with only one processor (or machines with multiple processors that are running your Java program on just one processor).

Optimizing Garbage Collection

Now that you understand the basics of how to configure memory and garbage collection for Java programs, we can talk about how to gather the information you need in order to make intelligent decisions about the various switches and settings. Again, the JVM offers a number of switches you can set to create output related to memory usage and garbage collection. The following table describes these switches.

Table 13-3. Garbage Collection Output Switches

Switch	Effect
-verbose:gc	Enables the logging of garbage collection information. The other garbage collection logging switches require this one.
-XX:+PrintGCTimeStamps	Prints time stamps for the scavenges and full collections. The time is measured as seconds since the program started.
-XX:+PrintGCDetails	Adds various details to the log, including at least the following information:

1. Size of the young and old generation before and after scavenges and full collections

2. Size of the heap (that is, all the memory in use)

3. Time taken by a scavenge or full collection to happen in the young and tenured generations

4. Total size of all objects promoted from one generation to the next by the garbage collector

Here's a bit of sample output from running the TargetClick game from the command line with the -verbose:gc, -XX:+PrintGCTimeStamps -XX:+PrintGCDetails switches:

Listing 13-3. Garbage Collection Output Sample

```
C:\temp>java -verbose:gc -XX:+PrintGCTimeStamps -XX:+PrintGCDetails TargetClick
Heap
 PSYoungGen      total 17920K, used 8077K [0x00000000ec000000,
   0x00000000ed3f0000, 0x0000000100000000)
  eden space 15424K, 52% used [0x00000000ec000000,0x00000000ec7e3538,0x00000000ecf10000)
  from space 2496K, 0% used [0x00000000ed180000,0x00000000ed180000,0x00000000ed3f0000)
  to   space 2496K, 0% used [0x00000000ecf10000,0x00000000ecf10000,0x00000000ed180000)
 PSOldGen        total 40960K, used 0K [0x00000000c4000000,
0x00000000c6800000,0x00000000ec000000)
  object space 40960K, 0% used [0x00000000c4000000,0x00000000c4000000,0x00000000c6800000)
 PSPermGen       total 21248K, used 9423K [0x00000000bee00000, 0x00000000c02c0000,
0x00000000c4000000)
  object space 21248K, 44% used [0x00000000bee00000,0x00000000bf733cc0,0x00000000c02c0000)
```

Let's examine these results a bit. First, we can see that the young generation has 17920K allocated and is using 8077K of it. All of the objects in the young generation are in the eden space. Given how briefly instances of the `Target` class last, there should never be one in the from and to spaces. In the tenured generation (called PSOldGen here), we find nothing, although 40960K has been allocated to it. The instances of the `TargetClick` and `TargetClickPanel` class are not in the tenured generation because I took this snapshot shortly after starting the TargetClick game, so those objects are still in the eden space. Finally, the permanent generation contains the three class files, which use 9423K of 21248K allocated.

To really make this information useful, we'd have to let the program run for a while, find a number of these blocks of information, and compare them to one another, watching for changes over time. As you can imagine, analyzing this kind of information for a large and complex program can take quite a while. For one thing, developers working on those kinds of applications often have to let their applications run for days at a time to get a sufficiently broad window of input. Also, if the number of users or number of network connections or other load factors change (and they nearly always do – very few programs exist in constantly stable environments), those factors need to be captured and then identified in the log. Then there's the difficulty of reading this kind of information (which is why many programmers write additional utilities to "scrape" this data and put it into some handy application, such as a spread sheet). All of this together makes analyzing garbage-collection data a non-trivial task. However, the task pays off with better performance, happier users, happier programmers, and so on. Therefore, the investment in time and effort often pays off nicely.

■ **Tip**   You can get a good optimization by monitoring the size of the tenured generation over the lifetime of your program and setting its size to closely match (with perhaps a 10% increase) the tenured generation size to the largest size you observe over a few runs of your program. You can control the size of the tenured generation by controlling the size of the new generation, which you can do with the -XXNewRatio, -XX:NewSize, - XX:MaxNewSize switches. Suppose your testing reveals that your program needs 256MB of memory and that the tenured generation should be 4 times the size of the new generation (meaning you have a lot of long-lived objects). You could set the following switches: -XXNewRatio=4 -XXNewSize=52MB -XXMaxNewSize=52MB

Collection Hints

Java developers can give hints to the garbage collector. The following line asks the JVM to do garbage collection for your program:

Listing 13-4. Garbage Collection Hint

```
System.gc();
```

However, most of the Java programming community frowns on using garbage collection hints. Instead, you should try to organize your code so that the garbage collector doesn't need a hint. Most of that organization comes down to arranging your classes such that each class has a clear, well-defined job to do. For example, `TargetClickPanel` maintains a collection of five `Target` objects. When it needs a new instance of the `Target` class, it sets a member of that collection to the new instance. Thus, old instances become free for collection. If I had tried to do more with that collection of `Target` objects, I might easily have gotten into a situation where garbage collection wouldn't work correctly, as I'd still be hanging onto the Target objects.

■ **Note** Using a garbage collection hint will not prevent your program from running out of memory if it is about to run out anyway. That's yet another reason to not use garbage collection hints. As a rule, they don't help.

Blocking Garbage Collection

Sometimes, you need an object to exist for as long as your program runs. To make sure it continues to exist, you need to ensure that a reference to that object always exists. Java offers a couple of handy ways to ensure a reference always exists: singletons and reference lists.

A singleton is a class that can never have more than one instance. Java developers have a number of techniques for creating a singleton, but Listing 13-5 shows one common way to do it.

Listing 13-5. Making a Singleton

```
public class Singleton {

  private static Singleton instance = new Singleton();

  private Singleton() {
    // initialization stuff goes here
  }

  public synchronized static Singleton instance() {
    return instance;
  }
}
```

Because there's always a static instance of the class held within the class itself, there's always a reference to this kind of singleton. We make the instance method synchronized so that, if two objects call the method at the same time, they take turns. Otherwise, they might get the object in the wrong state (in cases where some other method updates the data in the singleton class). As a rule, synchronize any method that returns a static object (not including constants).

Of course, if you need more than one instance of a class, that's not going to work. In those cases, you can use a reference list. Consider the program class shown in Listing 13-6.

Listing 13-6. Program Class with a Reference List

```
package com.bryantcs.examples.referenceList;

import java.util.ArrayList;

public class ReferenceProgram {

  // This list lasts as long as the program runs
```

```java
    public static ArrayList<Object> referenceList;

    public static void main(String[] args) {
        referenceList = new ArrayList<Object>();
    }

}
```

As the comment within the class says, the referenceList object will have a reference for as long as the program runs. So far, so good, but how do we add to it? The trick to that is to have any class we need to keep around to add itself to the list, as shown in the next code listing:

Listing 13-7. Class that Adds Itself to a Reference List

```java
package com.bryantcs.examples.referenceList;

public class ClassToList {

    public ClassToList() {
        ReferenceProgram.referenceList.add(this);
    }
}
```

Since `ReferenceProgram.referenceList` is static, it is a class variable, which means there's only one of them, regardless of the number of instances we may make of the `ReferenceProgram` class. (Of course, in this very simple example, we wouldn't make more than one instance of the `ReferenceProgram` class anyway.) As a result, we can add to that single list from anywhere within the program. Thus, we have a handy mechanism for ensuring that a reference to any given class always exists and, consequently, that any instance of this class will never be garbage collected.

While these techniques work, you should avoid overusing both the singleton pattern and the reference list pattern. If you prevent the garbage collector from removing many objects, your program performs that much more slowly.

A New Garbage Collector

As we saw earlier in the chapter, Java 7 includes a new garbage collector, called G1. G1 is a concurrent garbage collector, meaning that it uses multiple processors (if available) at the same time. Also, as we read earlier in the chapter, the G1 collector's "garbage first" algorithm offers better performance than other collectors, regardless of the number of processors. For a computer with just one processor (or a shared computer that makes only one processor available to the JVM), G1 should offer some improvement over any other garbage collector (though the nature of the application may limit the improvement). If G1 can get access to at least two processors, the improvement in performance should be even better. Given that most modern computers have multiple processors and modern server-class computers often have numerous processors, G1 may provide a sizable performance boost for some applications. That's going to result in games that play more smoothly, web applications that return web pages more quickly, and all the other good things that come with higher-performance applications.

Summary

In this chapter, we've touched on one of Java's more advanced concepts: garbage collection. We've just skimmed the surface of this advanced topic, with an eye toward providing you with the basic information for optimizing your own applications. If you really get into optimization, you can find whole books written about the subject.

In this brief overview, we covered:

- Memory allocation

- The garbage-collection algorithm used by Java

- The variations on the algorithm (naïve, incremental, and concurrent)

- How the G1 collector improves on the overall algorithm

- The difference between a scavenge and a full collection

- That garbage collection is event-driven

- That garbage collection is beyond our direct control, but can be controlled indirectly

- The most common settings that control garbage collection

- How to see what the garbage collector does in each of its runs

- How to use that information to optimize our garbage collection settings (and thus the performance of our programs)

- How to prevent an object from ever being garbage collected.

- That Java 7 offers an improved garbage collector named G1 (for "garbage first")

For all that we've learned, I'd like to point out that you can do a lot of programming without ever thinking about garbage collection. Other than to collect sample data for this chapter, I haven't changed a single garbage collection setting for the programs in this book. However, if you stick with programming in Java, your programs will eventually run into the bottleneck that arises from not controlling your garbage collection settings. At that point, I want you to come back to this chapter and cover the basics. Eventually, you may need more advanced information, but this set of basic information will let you solve a lot of garbage collection problems.

CHAPTER 14

Recursion

Recursion has an undeserved reputation for being hard to do and hard to control. For various reasons, many developers have trouble using recursion as one of their programming tools. I suspect the difficulty stems from two predicaments: having to give up control so that the recursive classes or methods can do their work and not being able to "see" the recursion work (though the debugger can solve the latter problem). Also, the first try at recursion usually ends poorly, resulting in an infinite loop (that is, a process that never stops), and software developers are trained to be very wary of infinite loops. All of these problems can be overcome with surprisingly easy-to-use and easy-to-understand techniques, which I'll address later in the chapter.

Before I dive into how to work with recursions, though, let's take a close look at what recursion is.

Recursion is Natural

The main reason I am surprised that so many developers distrust recursion is that recursion is a feature of human language. We all use it every day when we talk to one another. English utilizes recursion in a number of situations. One of the rules (from the field within Linguistics called Transformational Grammar, which I studied in college) of the English language is that one sentence can be embedded into another sentence. I won't dive into the sentence diagrams to prove it, but I'll give you an example in the form of a children's rhyme from long ago:

This is the house that Jack built.
This is the malt that lay in the house that Jack built.
This is the rat that ate the malt that lay in the house that Jack built.

As you can see, kids can keep going for as long as they can think of things to add (or until their parents yell at them to stop). English supports recursion in other situations as well. For instance, another rule in English is that we can stack up prepositional phrases as deep as we like, thus:

The princess lives in the castle.
The princess lives in the castle on the hill.
The princess lives in the castle on the hill by the road.
The princess lives in the castle on the hill by the road in the swamp.

Again, we can keep doing this for as long as it amuses us to do so.

Recursion is Common

You encounter instances of recursion every day and never think twice about them. The only notable feature about the following sentence is that it involves a princess and a castle: "The princess lives in the castle on the hill." How many times have you said something similar to "I live in a red house on Mulberry Street"?

Recursion is common in the field of computer science, too. A number of languages use recursion as their main idiom for processing data. The most famous recursive programming language is probably Lisp. Lisp stands for "List processing" and treats everything as a list. The usual method of processing in Lisp is to read the first item of a list (reducing the original list), process it, read the first value of the remaining list, process it, and so on until the list is empty. XSLT (a grandchild of Lisp through another language called DSSSL) works in a similar way, processing XML nodes until it runs out of nodes.

All the programming languages with which I am familiar also have one mechanism or another for supporting recursion. Recursion may be easier or harder to achieve depending on the language, but in my experience, it's always possible.

Know Your Stop Condition

Now that you know what recursion is and have discovered that recursion is actually all around us, let's look at how to make it work. We'll start with a problem that many software developers fear: the infinite loop.

Recursion usually generates an infinite loop because the developer fails to check for a stop condition or for the correct stop condition. The trouble is that the stop condition always depends on what you're doing. If you're processing a factorial, your stop condition is the argument to the factorial symbol. Therefore, if you're calculating 10! (10 factorial), you stop when you get to 10. Similarly, if you're processing an XML file, the stop condition is the last child node.

The other problem is that those conditions are not similar enough for many developers. People like to be sure of things: they don't want to have to figure out the stop condition every time. This issue often persuades developers to avoid recursion, even when recursion is the best way to solve a problem.

Let's look at one of the examples I just mentioned, calculating a factorial:

Listing 14-1. Calculating a Factorial

```
package com.bryantcs.examples.factorial;

public class Factorial {

  int calculate(int number) {
    if (number < 0) {
      throw new IllegalArgumentException("integer must be 0+");
    }
    if( number == 0) {       return 1;
    } else {
      return number * calculate (number - 1);
    }
  }
}
```

```
    public static void main(String[] args) {
    Factorial factorial = new Factorial();
    System.out.println(factorial.calculate(4));
  }

}
```

In the calculate method, after checking for valid input, check for the stop condition, which is the argument "1". (Note the recursion in the preceding sentence: "In . . . after . . . ." It really is common.)

When to Avoid Recursion

The biggest problem with recursion is that each pass through the method puts another object in the call stack. If you have a lot of recursion to do, you can overflow the stack. As the following image shows, there are four instances of the **calculate** method on the stack when the factorial of four (4!) is calculated.

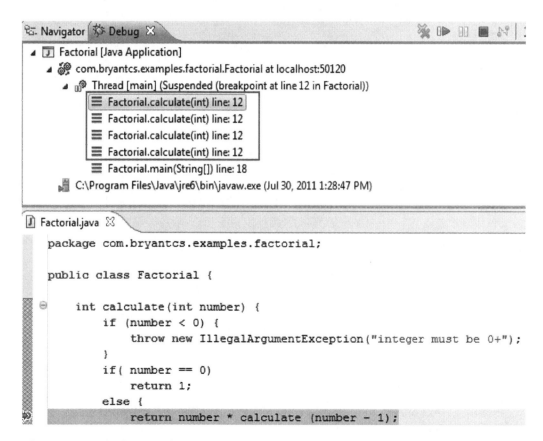

Figure 14-1. *calculate Methods on the Call Stack*

If I had calculated the factorial of ten (10!), I would have had ten instances of the `calculate` method on the stack. To avoid this problem, I can rewrite the method to use a loop instead, thus:

Listing 14-2. *Converting Recursion to a Loop*

```
package com.bryantcs.examples.factorial;

public class Factorial {

  int calculate(int number) {
    if (number < 0) {
      throw new IllegalArgumentException("integer must be 0+");
    }
    if( number == 0 || number == 1)
      return 1;
    else {
      int total = 1;
      for (int i = 1; i < number + 1; i++) {
        total *= i;
      }
      return total;
    }
  }
    public static void main(String[] args) {
    Factorial factorial = new Factorial();
    System.out.println(factorial.calculate(4));
  }

}
```

Since it contains no calls to itself, the calculate method appears on the stack only once. Therefore, the lesson here is that any time you can easily replace recursion with a loop, you should do so.

When to Use Recursion

If you should replace recursion with loops whenever you can easily do so, when should you use recursion? The simple (but not helpful) answer is: when it's useful to do so. But when is that? Essentially, you should use recursion when you can't know (or can't be sure of) the number of times you need to process something. Processing an XML file is a good illustration of this problem. When you write a program to process an XML file, you can't be sure how many nodes will be in the given XML file. It is possible to solve these kinds of problems with while loops, but in this case, recursion is easier both to code and to understand.

In addition to parsing, other problems are simply easier to code with recursion. If you can significantly reduce the size of your code or gain an algorithm that is easier to understand, you should consider recursion, even in cases where the problem can be solved with loops. What sorts of things are solved with recursive algorithms? Let's look at some common problems that utilize recursion (and I'll code some of the more interesting ones later in the chapter):

- Repetitive mathematical functions, such as a factorial, a sum of digits, the Fibonacci sequence, and many others

- Any problem in which the depth of processing is hard to predict (e.g., processing files and other data streams)

- Certain kinds of searches (such as finding all the instances of a substring within a string and finding all the instances of a particular data element in a tree structure)

- Fractal images (which I'll focus on later in the chapter).

Without further ado, I'll get to the fun stuff: coding solutions to problems that are a good fit for recursion.

Calculating the Fibonacci Sequence

The Fibonacci sequence (named after Italian mathematician Leonardo Bigollo, also known as Fibonacci) is a sequence of numbers consisting of 0, 1, and numbers that are each the sum of the previous two. Thus, the Fibonacci sequence is 0, 1, 1, 2, 3, 5, 8, 13, 21, 34, 55, 89, 144, and so on for as long as one cares to do the math.

While the Fibonacci sequence can be calculated with a loop, it's commonly used as an example when folks discuss recursion. I'll stir up my own code for it:

Listing 14-3. Recursively Calculating the Fibonacci Sequence

```
package com.bryantcs.examples.fibonacci;

public class Fibonacci {

  private int calculate(int length) {
    if (length < 0) {
      throw new IllegalArgumentException("Input must be 0 or greater");
    }
    if (length <= 1) {
      return length;
    } else {
      return calculate(length - 1) + calculate(length - 2);
    }
  }
    public static void main(String[] args) {
    Fibonacci fibonacci = new Fibonacci();
    for (int i = 0; i < 10; i++){
      System.out.println(fibonacci.calculate(i));
    }
  }
}
```

■ **Note** Fibonacci numbers turn up in all kinds of interesting places. They are closely linked to the golden ratio (important in the history of art and architecture), appear in the ratios of a number of objects in nature, and have been used to determine when to buy stocks. While they are well beyond the scope of this book, the origin and uses of the Fibonacci sequence are interesting subjects in their own right.

Calculating Fractals

Fractal images involve using the output of one calculation as the input to a subsequent calculation—a perfect task for recursion. I'll start with my personal favorite.

Drawing a Sierpinski Triangle

A Sierpinski triangle (named after Polish mathematician Waclaw Sierpinski) is a triangle consisting of other triangles. Each smaller triangle can itself consist of other triangles. Thus, you can have triangles within triangles within triangles to any depth you like. (Note the recursion within the preceding sentence; just talking about recursion requires recursion.)

Here's a pair of classes that draw a Sierpinski triangle to a depth of 7 (a number I picked because I liked the resulting output). As usual, I've created a program class that uses another class to do the drawing.

Here's the program class:

Listing 14-4. SierpinskiTriangle.java

```
package com.bryantcs.examples.fractals;

import java.awt.Color;
import java.awt.Dimension;
import java.awt.event.ActionEvent;
import java.awt.event.ActionListener;

import javax.swing.JFrame;
import javax.swing.JMenu;
import javax.swing.JMenuBar;
import javax.swing.JMenuItem;

public class SierpinskiTriangle implements ActionListener {

  private SierpinskiTrianglePanel
    sierpinskiTrianglePanel = new SierpinskiTrianglePanel();
  private JFrame frame = new JFrame("Sierpinski Triangle");

  private void addMenu(JFrame frame) {
    JMenu file = new JMenu("File");
    file.setMnemonic('F');
    JMenuItem exitItem = new JMenuItem("Exit");
```

```
        exitItem.setMnemonic('x');
        exitItem.addActionListener(this);
        file.add(exitItem);
        JMenuItem redrawItem = new JMenuItem("Repaint");
        redrawItem.setMnemonic('r');
        redrawItem.addActionListener(this);
        file.add(redrawItem);
        JMenuBar menuBar = new JMenuBar();
        menuBar.add(file);
        frame.setJMenuBar(menuBar);
    }

    private void createAndShowGUI() {
        addMenu(frame);
        frame.setDefaultCloseOperation(JFrame.EXIT_ON_CLOSE);
        sierpinskiTrianglePanel.setPreferredSize(new Dimension(400, 400));
        sierpinskiTrianglePanel.setBackground(Color.WHITE);
        frame.getContentPane().add(sierpinskiTrianglePanel);
        frame.pack();
        frame.setVisible(true);
    }
    public static void main(String[] args) {
        SierpinskiTriangle sierpinskiTriangle = new SierpinskiTriangle();
        sierpinskiTriangle.createAndShowGUI();
    }

    public void actionPerformed(ActionEvent e) {
        if (e.getActionCommand() != null) {
            if (e.getActionCommand().equals("Exit")) {
                System.exit(0);
            }
            if (e.getActionCommand().equals("Repaint")) {
                sierpinskiTrianglePanel.repaint();
            }
        }
    }
}
```

By now, you're accustomed to how this kind of program class works: it handles the input from the user, sets up the window that holds your content, and manages the class that does the more interesting work.

Here's the class that does the drawing:

Listing 14-5. *SierpinskiTrianglePanel.java*

```
package com.bryantcs.examples.fractals;

import java.awt.Color;
import java.awt.Graphics;
import java.awt.geom.Point2D;
```

```java
import javax.swing.JPanel;

public class SierpinskiTrianglePanel extends JPanel {

    private static final long serialVersionUID = 1L;

    int maxLevel = 7;

    private void drawTriangle(int level, Graphics g, Point2D.Double point1,
            Point2D.Double point2, Point2D.Double point3) {
        if (level < maxLevel) {
            // Work our way down through the levels
            Point2D.Double midPoint1 = getMiddlePoint(point1, point2);
            Point2D.Double midPoint2 = getMiddlePoint(point2, point3);
            Point2D.Double midPoint3 = getMiddlePoint(point1, point3);

            g.setColor(new Color((int)(Math.random() * 0xFFFFFF)));

            drawTriangle(level + 1, g, point1, midPoint1, midPoint3);
            drawTriangle(level + 1, g, midPoint1, point2, midPoint2);
            drawTriangle(level + 1, g, midPoint3, midPoint2, point3);
        } else {
            // At the bottom level, draw the actual triangles
            // (which are parts of the larger triangles)
            int[] xPoints = {
                new Double(point1.getX()).intValue(),
                new Double(point2.getX()).intValue(),
                new Double(point3.getX()).intValue()
            };
            int[] yPoints = {
                new Double(point1.getY()).intValue(),
                new Double(point2.getY()).intValue(),
                new Double(point3.getY()).intValue()
            };
            g.fillPolygon(xPoints, yPoints, 3);
        }
    }

    private Point2D.Double getMiddlePoint(Point2D.Double point1,
            Point2D.Double point2) {
        double newX = (point1.getX() + point2.getX()) / 2;
        double newY = (point1.getY() + point2.getY()) / 2;
        return new Point2D.Double(newX, newY);
    }

    public void paint (Graphics g) {
        super.paintComponent(g);
        int height = this.getHeight();
        int width = this.getWidth();
        // Here's one way to get the height of an equilateral triangle    Double doubleHeight
        = Math.sqrt(height * height - (width / 2) * (width / 2));    // 0 on the Y axis is at
the bottom, so this seems upside-down
```

```
      Point2D.Double lowerLeft = new Point2D.Double(0, doubleHeight);
      Point2D.Double lowerRight = new Point2D.Double(width, doubleHeight);
      Point2D.Double top = new Point2D.Double(width / 2, 0);
      drawTriangle(1, g, lowerLeft, lowerRight, top);
   }
}
```

The SierpinskiTriangleJava class really starts in the paint method, where it calculates the corners of the outer triangle and passes those values to the drawTriangle method. Then the drawTriangle method calculates a series of triangles within triangles, down to the depth specified in the maxLevel variable that is stated at the top of the class. You can change the depth by changing that value, and a good exercise is to add setting that value to the user interface.

The actual drawing happens only after the class reaches the maximum level. At that point, there are 729 (3 to the 6th power) triangles that draw themselves and 364 triangles that contain other triangles. Three hundred and sixty-four is not a power of 3, so how was that number obtained by calculating six levels of depth? The following table shows the progression:

Table 14-1. drawTriangle *Methods on the Stack, by Level of Recursion.*

Step	Number of Triangles
1	1
2	4
3	13
4	40
5	121
6	364
7	1093

As you can see, the inclusion of the outer triangle throws off the numbers a bit so that the total is never a power of three. However, the difference between any two steps is a power of three. This kind of pattern appears whenever a single item contains other items that scale in a regular fashion.

Within the drawTriangle method, I calculated the midpoints of the current triangle and created three new triangles based on those points. That's the essence of the Sierpinski algorithm. The remaining code in the method does the work of drawing and of making sure I don't miss the stop condition.

■ **Note** The code for `drawTriangle` could be made simpler by starting at the outermost layer and counting backwards. However, I wanted to have a `maxLevel` value to make setting the depth as easy as possible. I also used Point2D rather than Point to obtain a greater level of accuracy (and thus prevent small mismatches in the positions of the triangles within the window).

Finally, here's the result of my SierpinskiTriangle program:

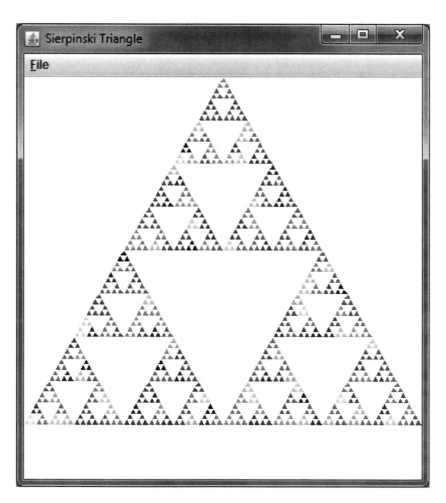

Figure 14-2. Output from the SierpinskiTriangle Program

Drawing a Fractal Tree

One of my other favorite fractals is the fractal tree because it really does resemble a tree (at first glance, anyway). Here's the program class:

Listing 14-6. FractalTree.java

```java
package com.bryantcs.examples.fractals;

import java.awt.Color;
import java.awt.Dimension;
import java.awt.event.ActionEvent;
import java.awt.event.ActionListener;

import javax.swing.JFrame;
import javax.swing.JMenu;
import javax.swing.JMenuBar;
import javax.swing.JMenuItem;

public class FractalTree implements ActionListener {

  private FractalTreePanel
  fractalTreePanel = new FractalTreePanel();

  private JFrame frame = new JFrame("Fractal Tree");

  private void addMenu(JFrame frame) {
    JMenu file = new JMenu("File");
    file.setMnemonic('F');
    JMenuItem exitItem = new JMenuItem("Exit");
    exitItem.setMnemonic('x');
    exitItem.addActionListener(this);
    file.add(exitItem);
    JMenuItem redrawItem = new JMenuItem("Repaint");
    redrawItem.setMnemonic('r');
    redrawItem.addActionListener(this);
    file.add(redrawItem);
    JMenuBar menuBar = new JMenuBar();
    menuBar.add(file);
    frame.setJMenuBar(menuBar);
  }

  private void createAndShowGUI() {
    addMenu(frame);
    frame.setDefaultCloseOperation(JFrame.EXIT_ON_CLOSE);
    fractalTreePanel.setPreferredSize(new Dimension(600, 450));
    fractalTreePanel.setBackground(Color.WHITE);
    frame.getContentPane().add(fractalTreePanel);
    frame.pack();
    frame.setVisible(true);
  }
```

273

```
    public static void main(String[] args) {
        FractalTree fractalTree = new FractalTree();
        fractalTree.createAndShowGUI();
    }

    public void actionPerformed(ActionEvent e) {
        if (e.getActionCommand() != null) {
            if (e.getActionCommand().equals("Exit")) {
                System.exit(0);
            }
            if (e.getActionCommand().equals("Repaint")) {
                fractalTreePanel.repaint();
            }
        }
    }
}
```

As I'm sure you know by now, the FractalTree class merely manages the user interface and provides a place for another class to do the drawing. So let's move on to the class that does the fun stuff: drawing our fractal trees.

Listing 14-7. *FractalTreePanel.java*

```
package com.bryantcs.examples.fractals;

import java.awt.Color;
import java.awt.Graphics;
import java.util.Random;

import javax.swing.JPanel;

public class FractalTreePanel extends JPanel {

    private static final long serialVersionUID = 1L;

    private final static double RADIANS = Math.PI / 180.0;
    Random rand;

    public FractalTreePanel() {
        rand = new Random();
    }
        private void drawSegment(Graphics g, int x1, int y1, double angle, int depth) {
        if (depth == 0) return; // the stop condition
        int xAngleOffset =       new Double(Math.cos(angle * RADIANS) * depth * 10.0).intValue();
        int yAngleOffset =
            new Double(Math.sin(angle * RADIANS) * depth * 10.0).intValue();
        int x2 = x1 + xAngleOffset;
        int y2 = y1 + yAngleOffset;
        int colorValue = 256 - ((depth - 1) * 32) - 1;
```

```
    if (colorValue < 0) {
      colorValue = 0;
    }
    g.setColor(new Color(0, colorValue, 0));
    g.drawLine(x1, y1, x2, y2);
    int randFactor = rand.nextInt(20) + 10; // a value between 10 and 30
    drawSegment(g, x2, y2, angle - randFactor, depth - 1);
    randFactor = rand.nextInt(20) + 10; // a value between 10 and 30
    drawSegment(g, x2, y2, angle + randFactor, depth - 1);
  }

  public void paint(Graphics g) {
    super.paintComponent(g);
    drawSegment(g, getWidth() / 2, getHeight(), -90, 9);
  }
}
```

The algorithm for a fractal tree is quite simple: draw a line; from the end point of that line, draw two more lines; and so on. I can do that by using fixed values, but I will generate trees that are more realistic by adding some randomness. To that end, I also changed the color for each part of the tree, using lighter shades of green towards the top.

In my case, I configured the algorithm from the maximum depth down to 0. For this kind of algorithm, doing so results in less code (and so should be easier to understand). Since I liked the look of the tree with a depth of 9, I didn't set the depth value out separately like I did in the SierpinskiTrianglePanel class. Another interesting feature of this class is that the initial angle is -90. If it were 0, the tree would grow sideways to the right. This would happen because an angle of 0 draws a line that lies on the X-axis. Thus, to make the lines go up the Y-axis, I had to rotate 90 degrees to the left (i.e., -90). An angle of 90 would produce a tree that grew downward (which could be a handy way to model roots).

The next page shows one result (each result is a bit different) of the FractalTree program.

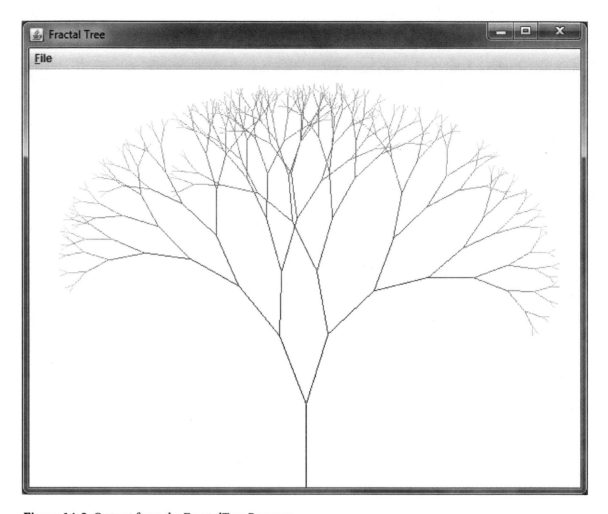

Figure 14-3. Output from the FractalTree Program

Summary

In this chapter, I explained the unusual but sometimes useful idea of working with items that refer to themselves, known as recursion. In particular, you learned that:

- Recursion occurs in human languages.
- Recursion happens all the time (but we often don't notice it).
- Recursive algorithms need stop conditions.
- It's sometimes a good idea to avoid recursion.

- Conversely, recursion is sometimes the best answer to a problem.

- Recursion can be an elegant solution to some problems, such as that of generating the Fibonacci sequence.

- Recursion is the underlying algorithm in making fractals.

I hope you enjoyed this chapter. It was one of my favorites to write, and I enjoyed creating sample code for it. In fact, I played with many variations of the code, just for fun. You should do the same. In particular, regarding the Sierpinski triangle program, try changing colors at every other depth or every third depth value rather than at every depth value (hint: use the modulus operator). Then, play with the values that control the appearance of the fractal tree. In particular, play with different numbers as inputs to the `randInt` method. Also, rotate the tree and fiddle with the colors to create roots instead of the branches of a tree.

I leave you with two challenges that will help you grow as a programmer. First, create a Sierpinski gasket (a square of squares rather than a triangle of triangles). Second, create a Mandelbrot or Julia fractal. I nearly included sample code for a Julia fractal (one of my favorites), but I thought it would be a great exercise for you, now that you know the basics of recursion in Java. You'll need to do a bit of research to find the algorithms and math behind the Sierpinski gasket and the Mandelbrot and Julia fractals, but discovering algorithms and formulae is part of the job when you develop software. I'm sure you'll get used to performing this kind of research.

CHAPTER 15

Generics and Regular Expressions

Readers who already know Java may very well ask why these two topics are together in the same chapter. The answer is that they both involve pattern matching. A generic specifier (also known as a parameter) is a pattern that code must match in order to use a particular block of code (which might be an interface, a class, a method, or other things). Regular Expressions, on the other hand, use patterns to select substrings within strings. In both cases, the pattern restricts the available selections. Both have additional benefits as well, which we'll get to next.

Generics

Generics offer a way to specify the kind of objects that a class, variable, or method can use. The most common use of generics is to specify what kind of object can go into a collection (such as a list or a tree or a hashmap). Another use is to allow a type that has yet to be specified to be used where the generic is specified. In that sense, the type is generic, which is where the name of this idea comes from. We'll see examples of both kinds of generics as proceed through this section.

Prior to Java 5, Java had no mechanism for specifying generics. That lack led to a number of problems, including being able to assign unexpected types of objects to a collection (leading to run-time errors), the necessity of casting objects from one type to another, and overly verbose and complex code. Fortunately, we now have a way to avoid those problems.

The syntax of generic specifiers relies on the angle bracket characters (< and >). To create a collection with a generic specifier, add the generic expression at the end of the type specifier for the collection, as shown in Listing 15-1.

Listing 15-1. A Simple Generic

```
LinkedList<JPanel> panelList = new LinkedList<JPanel>();
```

That line of code declares a LinkedList that can only contain JPanel objects. Java 7 introduces a nice shorthand that slightly reduces the amount of code. In particular, you can leave out the type declaration when creating an instance of a parameterized object, provided the compiler can infer the type from elsewhere in the line. Thus, the code in Listing 15-1 could be replaced with the code in Listing 15-2.

Listing 15-2. *A Simplified Generic*

```
LinkedList<JPanel> panelList = new LinkedList<>();
```

Notice that the constructor for our LinkedList object indicates that it's a generic but doesn't provide the type of the objects that can go in the list. We can leave that out because the compiler can infer a type of JPanel from the type declaration portion of this variable declaration. By the way, the <> expression is often called "the diamond."

An object can have multiple parameters, provided a matching class exists to define that object. Listing 15-3 shows an example.

Listing 15-3. *A Generic with Multiple Parameters*

```
package com.bryantcs.examples;

public class GenericRole<Actor, Role> {

        private Actor actor;
        private Role role;

        public GenericRole(Actor p, Role a) {
                actor = p;
                role = a;
        }

        public Actor getActor() {
                return actor;
        }

        public Role getRole() {
                return role;
        }
}
```

A significant feature of this class is that you do not have to create an Actor class or a Role class. Because it uses generics, the declarations that create instances of the GenericRole object must specify the types of the Actor and Role objects.

As I mentioned at the beginning of this section, this arrangement is where the word "generic" comes from. These objects can be undeclared at this point, so they are, in a sense, generic.

So let's look at a class that does something with our GenericRole class. Consider Listing 15-4.

Listing 15-4. *Using a Multiple-Parameter Generic*

```
package com.bryantcs.examples;

import java.util.LinkedList;

public class GenericRoleProgram {
```

```
    public static void main(String[] args) {
            LinkedList<GenericRole<String, String>> roleMap =
                    new LinkedList<GenericRole<>>();

            roleMap.add(new GenericRole<String, String>("Humphrey Bogart",
                        "Sam Spade"));
            System.out.println(roleMap.getFirst().getActor() +
                        " appeared on screen as " + roleMap.getFirst().getRole());
    }
}
```

Notice that we now have parameters nested within parameters (in `LinkedList<GenericRole<String, String>> roleMap`). When a parameterized (that is, generic) collection consists of a type of object that itself has parameters, you get nested generic specifiers. It may seem odd, but it's common practice once you start using generics.

You can also specify that a collection can contain multiple kinds of objects, provided that the objects all extend the same class or implement the same interface. To do so, Java includes a wildcard (in the form of the question mark character) that you can use with generic specifiers. For an example, consider Listing 15-5.

Listing 15-5. *Using the Generic Wildcard*

```
LinkedList<? extends JPanel> panels = new LinkedList<>();
```

That declaration says any class that extends `JPanel` can be a member of this list. Remember all the times I extended `JPanel` in the chapters about animation, video games, and recursion? If I ever need a single list to hold those different panels, the list above would do the job nicely.

The `extends` keyword works with interfaces, too. So, if I wanted a list of classes that implement the `MouseListener` interface, I could use the declaration shown in Listing 15-6.

Listing 15-6. *A Generic for an Interface*

```
LinkedList<? extends MouseListener> mouseListeners = new LinkedList<>();
```

Listing 15-7. *A Generic with the Super Keyword*

```
LinkedList<? super JPanel> panelAncestors = new LinkedList<>();
```

The super keyword specifies that any object extended by the JPanel class can be a member of this list. For this list, that would be objects of type `javax.swing.JComponent`. The super keyword is probably most useful when you want to ensure that the objects that satisfy a parameter are comparable (so that they can be sorted). In my experience, it's not often used, so I won't dive into it any further.

Now that we've seen the syntax for generics, let's talk about why you want to use them. The biggest benefit is earlier error detection. It's a truism in software development (and many other professions) that the earlier you catch an error, the less expensive it is to fix. If we can catch an error at coding time, fixing it is just a matter of re-writing code we're already working on; the cost is trivial. If an error makes it to the testers (assuming we have testers—not all software companies have test teams), it's more expensive. The test team has to find it and tell the developer about it, the developer (who has moved on to some other task) has to re-open and modify that code, and then the test team has to verify that the fixed code works correctly. The worst result is when an error gets all the way to the customer; we get all the added expense of communicating with the test team and the customer, with the added (and usually more important) cost that the customer now thinks less of our software and our company. So let's adopt techniques, including generics, that catch errors early.

Listing 15-9 and Listing 15-10 demonstrate why generics promote early error detection.

Listing 15-8. An Ordinary List

```
List integerList = new LinkedList();
integerList.add(new Integer(0));
integerList.add("here's a problem"); // perfectly legal and very wrong
```

In listing 15-9, `integerList` can contain any object. I can pass objects of type `String` into that list. A name is just a name and, while it reveals the intent (which is good practice), it doesn't offer any protection against someone passing things other than objects of type `Integer` into the list. Consequently, when someone does pass something other than an Integer object, we get a run-time error when we try to get `Integer` objects out of this list.

So let's see how generics prevent the testers or, worse, the customer from ever seeing our error.

Listing 15-9. A Generic List

```
List<Integer> integerList = new LinkedList<Integer>();
integerList.add(new Integer(0));
integerList.add("here's a problem");
```

The generic expression (or parameter) on the `List` declaration in the second example specifies that this list can contain only `Integer` objects. The `Integer` parameter prevents anyone from passing a `String` object (or anything but an `Integer` object) to `integerList`. When some other programmer tries to add an object that isn't of type Integer to `integerList`, they get a compiler error. Their code can't be compiled, and there's no chance the customer will ever see an error because some sloppy coder confuses a `String` with an `Integer`. Figure 15-1 shows the error that Eclipse produces when I try it.

```
List<Integer> integerList = new LinkedList<Integer>();
integerList.add(new Integer(0));
integerList.add("here's a problem");      }
}
```
The method add(Integer) in the type List<Integer> is not applicable for the arguments (String)

Figure 15-1. Type match error from trying to misuse a generic list

Notice how it says the proper argument for the add method is an Integer object. The `List` interface has no such method, in fact. However, the Eclipse compiler creates an instance of the `LinkedList` class that has such a method. Consequently, no one can compile code that violates the intention of our generic list. That prevents all the problems that might occur at run-time and prevents our fellow programmers, the testers, and ultimately our customers from thinking we must be idiots.

Personally, I also find this kind of code to be easier to read and to write. Casting always feels like clutter to me. Purist that I am, I also much prefer to have the proper type in the first place and not need to cast.

Finally, ensuring that your collections contain only the types you expect is one aspect of defensive programming (another good practice every programmer should adopt). If you ensure that no other programmer (including yourself at a later date) can pass bad values to your code, you ensure less trouble for your users. It's a thankless task, as no one (except possibly your co-workers) will ever realize you did it, but it's a good idea all the same. If you wish to think of it in more positive terms, think of it as ensuring that the developers who use your code are more likely to write error-free code. One of my co-workers (Matt Hinze, who also writes books about MVC when not coding) calls it "pushing our customers into a pit of success." However you phrase it, limiting the possibilities for errors to creep into the system is the epitome of good software development practice.

Regular Expressions

If you've ever worked with files from the command line on your computer, you may very well have used a regular expression without realizing it. For example, I recently wanted a list of all the HTML files in a directory (on a Windows 7 system). In a command window, I typed **dir *.htm** and got the list I wanted. ***.htm** is in fact a regular expression that means all the files with an extension of **htm**. Suppose I had wanted all the HTML files with names that start with "s". The command would have been **dir s*.htm**. Regular expressions in Java work in much the same way, except that you can specify much more complex patterns.

The Java regular expression package is **java.util.regex**. It contains the **MatchResult** interface, the **Matcher** class (which implements the **MatchResult** interface), the **Pattern** class, and the **PatternSyntaxException** class. You can't directly instantiate the **Matcher** and **Pattern** classes, as they have no public constructors. In other words, **new Matcher** and **new Pattern** don't work. Instead, the pattern for using them is to get a **Pattern** object by calling one of the **compile** methods within the **Pattern** class. Then you get a **Matcher** object by calling the **matcher** method within the **Pattern** class. Finally, to find the substrings that match your pattern, you call the **find** method within the **Matcher** class. Let's create a class that will let us experiment with the Pattern and Matcher classes. Listing 15-11 shows one possible implementation of such a class.

Listing 15-10. *RegexTester Class*

```
package com.bryantcs.examples;

import java.util.regex.Matcher;
import java.util.regex.Pattern;

public class RegexTester {

  public static void main(String[] args) {
    Pattern pattern = Pattern.compile(args[0]);
    Matcher matcher = pattern.matcher(args[1]);
    while(matcher.find()) {
      String groupText = matcher.group();
      int matchBegin = matcher.start();
      int matchEnd  = matcher.end();
      StringBuilder sb = new StringBuilder("Found a match for ");
      sb.append(groupText);
      sb.append(" beginning at ");
      sb.append(matchBegin);
```

```
        sb.append(" and ending at ");
        sb.append(matchEnd);
        System.out.println(sb);
    }
  }
}
```

`matcher.group` gives us the text being matched (that's essentially the result of the pattern we specify in the second argument). `matcher.start` gives us the starting position of the matched string within the input string (the first argument). `matcher.end` gives us the ending position of the matched string. I used a **StringBuilder** object to avoid a really long line, which is awkward to read in a book. I often use **StringBuilder** objects within my production code, too, for the sake of performance (the concatenation operator is the worst way to create a **String** object).

Before we plunge into the syntax of regular expressions, let's cover how to pass values to the RegexTester program. In doing so, we'll also run it for the first time. To set up arguments for RegexTester, follow these steps.

1. From the **Run** menu, choose **Run Configurations**. The Run Configurations window appears, as shown in Figure 15-2.

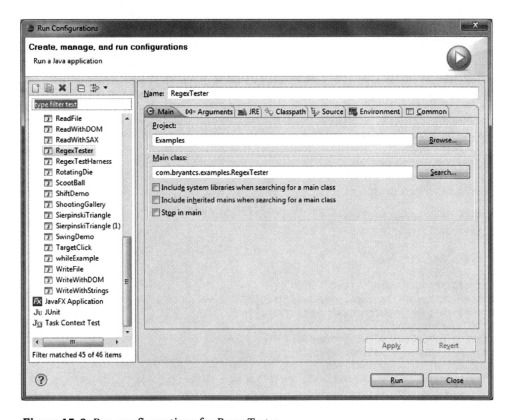

Figure 15-2. *Run configurations for RegexTester*

2. In the right pane, click the **Arguments** tab. The Arguments tab appears, as shown in Figure 15-3.

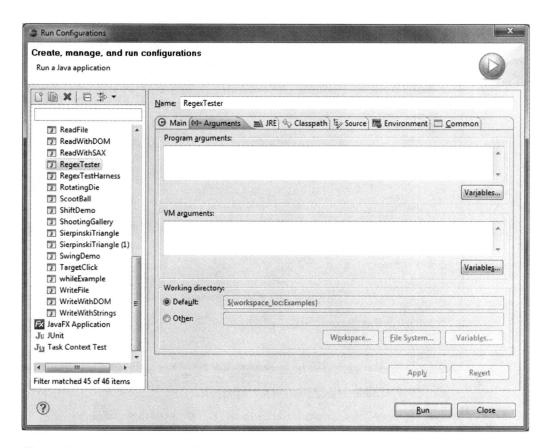

Figure 15-3. *Empty parameters for RegexTester*

3. To set up our first test data, type the following text (including the quotation marks) into the **Program arguments:** field:

    ```
    "Sam" "Sam Spade;Yosemite Sam;Sam Merlotte;Samwise Gamgee;"
    ```

    When you're done typing, the window should look like the window shown in Figure 15-4.

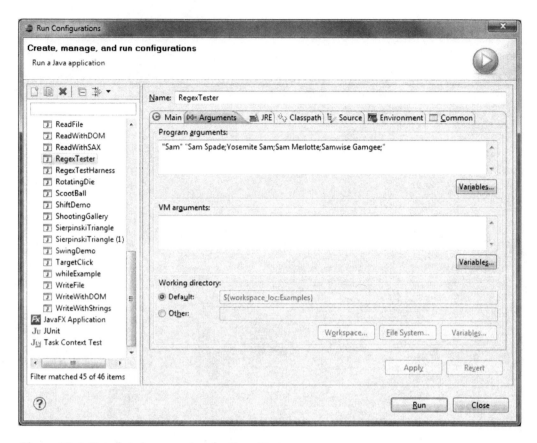

Figure 15-4. *Populated parameters for RegexTester*

4. To run the RegexTester program, click **Run**. The output of the program
   appears in the Eclipse console, as shown in Figure 15-5.

Figure 15-5. *Output of RegexTester in the Eclipse console*

I won't show all those steps for each test, but I thought it might help you to see them for the first
test. For the subsequent tests, I'll just show what to type in the **Arguments** tab and what appears in the
console.

Now that we have a testing program and know how to use it, we need to focus on the regular expression syntax that Java supports. Regular expression syntax is almost a language unto itself, so we'll focus on the basics and some of the more commonly used advanced bits. The whole thing is worthy of a book (and such books exist).

Our simple test case uses a string literal. A string literal is just a piece of text. In the example we just ran, "Sam" is a string literal. "Spade" is another string literal. If we replace "Sam" with "Spade," we get the following output in the console:

```
Found a match for Spade beginning at 4 and ending at 9
```

We won't be able to accomplish much with just string literals. We can find all the instances of a particular string, but we can't find anything that matches a pattern. To create a pattern, we have to dive into the key component of regular expressions—metacharacters.

Metacharacters are characters that create patterns. Rather than represent a single literal character, a metacharacter represents a set of characters. Some metacharacters work by themselves, while other metacharacters are meaningless in the absence of other metacharacters. Table 15-1 describes the metacharacters supported by the Java regular expression syntax.

Table 15-1. *Java Regular Expression Metacharacters*

Metacharacter	Description
(	Starts a subpattern (a pattern within the larger pattern). For example compan(y|ies) lets you match either "company" or "companies".
	Also starts the definition of a group. (Dog) treats those three characters as a single unit for other regular expression operators.
[	Starts a set of characters. For example, [A-Z] would match any upper-case character. A[A-Z]Z would match "AAZ", "ABZ", and so on to "AZZ".
{	Starts a match count specifier. For example, s{3} would match three s characters in a row: sss. Pas{3} would match "Passs".
\	Starts an escape sequence, so that you can match a literal instance of a metacharacter. For example, if you needed to match the periods in a paragraph, you'd use \. (that is, a backslash and a period). The period character (.) is itself a regular expression metacharacter, so you must escape it to find the actual periods. Similarly, to find an actual backslash character, you must escape the escape character, thus: \\
^	Matches the start of the string. ^A finds any line that begins with "A". ^[0-9] finds any line that begins with a digit. ^[0-9]{2} finds any line that begins with two digits. ^[0-9]+ matches any line that begins with a number of any size.
	Inside of a range, ^ is the negation character. [^abc] matches any character other than a, b, or c. [^abc]at matches "rat" and "sat" and "eat" (and many others) but not "bat" or "cat" (or "aat").
-	Used within range expressions, such as [0-9], which would match any digit.

Continued

Metacharacter	Description
$	Matches the end of the string. Z$ matches a Z character at the end of the string.
|	Matches the expression on either side of itself. (This character is sometimes called the pipe character.) For example, this|that would match either "this" or "that". The expressions need not be string literals. [a-s]|[u-z] finds any lower-case character other than t.
]	Closes a set of characters. For example, [a-z] would match any lower-case character.
}	Closes a match count specifier. For example, n{2} would match two n characters in a row: nn. ban{2} matches "bann", and [a-z]{2}n matches any lower-case three-letter string that ends with n, such as "sun", "fun", "ban", "wan", and so on. Of course, it also matches nonsense strings, such as "dcn".
)	Closes a subpattern (a pattern within the larger pattern). For example identit(y|ies) lets you match either "identity" or "identities". Also ends the definition of a group. (Cat) treats those three characters as a single unit for other regular expression operators.
?	Matches the preceding character 0 or 1 times. For example, ban? matches "ba" and "ban".
*	Matches the preceding character any number (including 0) of times. For example, ban* matches "ba", "ban", "bann", "bannn", and so on.
+	Matches the character one or more times. For example ban+ matches "ban", "bann", bannn", and so on. It does not match "ba" because the n character has to appear at least once.
.	Matches any single character. For example, bar. matches "bark", "bard", "bar9", and so on. .* matches any number of any character. It is probably the most used regular expression, because it lets you skip over any text you don't want to match to find the bits you do want to match. We'll see some examples later in this chapter.

From all those examples, I bet you're beginning to get an idea of how powerful regular expressions can be. In truth, though, describing the metacharacters is just scratching the surface of regular expressions. There's lots more to it than what I've shown here. Let's learn a little more by looking at examples.

Returning to our example involving fictional characters named Sam, suppose we want to get the whole name (including the separator, which is a semicolon). We might try something like the following:

```
(Sam).*;
```

The output of that is:

```
Found a match for Sam Spade;Yosemite Sam;Sam Merlotte;Samwise Gamgee; beginning at 0 and
ending at 51
```

That's not going to work. The trouble is that the `.*` pattern matches everything it can (that's called a greedy match). In this case, it matches the whole line. Fortunately, the Java regular expression syntax includes a way to make a pattern not be greedy (regular expression programmers would say it's reluctant). To make a match be reluctant, we can append the question mark character (?) to the pattern, as follows:

```
(Sam).*?;
```

The output of that regular expression is:

```
Found a match for Sam Spade; beginning at 0 and ending at 10
Found a match for Sam; beginning at 19 and ending at 23
Found a match for Sam Merlotte; beginning at 23 and ending at 36
Found a match for Samwise Gamgee; beginning at 36 and ending at 51
```

We're getting closer, but what happened to the "Yosemite" in "Yosemite Sam"? Well, the expression starts with (Sam), so it will match only bits that start with "Sam", which doesn't include "Yosemite Sam". The solution is to use the `.*?` pattern at the beginning as well as at the end, as follows:

```
.*?(Sam).*?;
```

Notice that the leading pattern must be reluctant, too, or we get the whole line again. Now the output is:

```
Found a match for Sam Spade; beginning at 0 and ending at 10
Found a match for Yosemite Sam; beginning at 10 and ending at 23
Found a match for Sam Merlotte; beginning at 23 and ending at 36
Found a match for Samwise Gamgee; beginning at 36 and ending at 51
```

In this fashion, we've parsed a line containing multiple records. We could then add code to write each match to a separate line in a file or otherwise manipulate each of the matching values. This kind of parsing is a common task in software development, and regular expressions offer one good way to do it.

As I have indicated, regular expressions can get a lot more complicated. The following regular expression removes "Sam" from each entry that starts with "Sam":

```
S(?!am)|(?<!S)a|a(?!m)|(?<!Sa)m|[^Sam](.*?;)
```

Its output is:

```
Found a match for  Spade; beginning at 3 and ending at 10
Found a match for Yosemite Sam; beginning at 10 and ending at 23
Found a match for  Merlotte; beginning at 26 and ending at 36
Found a match for wise Gamgee; beginning at 39 and ending at 51
```

The code to also remove the "Sam" in "Yosemite Sam" would be even more complex. As it happens, negating a group is one thing that regular expressions don't make easy. In those cases, it's often best to mix regular expressions with other **String** operations and to pass the result of one expression to another regular expression (a process known as chaining). Those techniques let you manage the complexity of your regular expressions and may offer better performance than a single complex regular expression.

If you want to know more about regular expressions, start with the official Regular Expression Tutorial at http://download.oracle.com/javase/tutorial/essential/regex/index.html

Summary

This chapter covered the things that benefit from pattern matching: generics and regular expressions. About generics, we learned that:

- We can specify the kind of content that goes into a collection.

- Thanks to an improvement introduced in Java 7, we can use the diamond specifier (<>) to shorten our code a bit, so long as the compiler can determine the type from earlier in the line.

- Generics can have multiple parameters.

- We can nest generic parameters to ensure we get the proper kinds of objects at any depth.

- We can use wildcards within generic parameters, to accommodate similar objects (any object that extends a particular class or implements a particular set of interfaces or both).

- Generics let us catch problems at coding time rather than at run time, saving time and embarrassment.

About regular expressions, we learned:

- How to instantiate the member classes (`Matcher` and `Pattern`) of the `java.util.regex` package.

- What each of the metacharacters does.

- How to combine the metacharacters in a number of useful ways.

- How to make a pattern be reluctant (match the fewest possible characters) rather than greedy (match the most possible characters).

- That regular expressions can become very complex and a bit about how to manage that complexity.

This chapter covered two language features that I hope you will find useful as you develop your own programs. I especially hope that you'll use generics any time you use a collection, as you should embrace best practices whenever you can. As for regular expressions, remember that they are supposed to make things simpler. If you find that a regular expression is too hard to figure out, break it up with other `String` operations and use multiple regular expressions rather than one big one.

Index

F

■ W, X, Y, Z